THE PIRATES' CODE

THE
PIRATES'
CODE

Laws and Life Aboard Ship

Rebecca Simon

REAKTION BOOKS

*To Adelaide Ever Egbert, as an introduction to her
auntie's passion for piracy*

Published by
REAKTION BOOKS LTD
Unit 32, Waterside
44–48 Wharf Road
London N1 7UX, UK
www.reaktionbooks.co.uk

First published 2023
Copyright © Rebecca Simon 2023

Printed and bound in Great Britain
by TJ Books Ltd, Padstow, Cornwall

A catalogue record for this book is available from the British Library
ISBN 978 1 78914 711 7

CONTENTS

A GENERAL
HISTORY
OF THE
PYRATES,
FROM

Their firſt RISE and SETTLEMENT in the Iſland of
Providence, to the preſent Time.

With the remarkable Actions and Adventures of the two Female Pyrates

MARY READ and ANNE BONNY;

Contain'd in the following Chapters,

To which is added.

A ſhort ABSTRACT of the Statute and Civil
Law, in Relation to Pyracy.

The ſecond EDITION, with conſiderable ADDITIONS

By Captain CHARLES JOHNSON.

LONDON:

Printed for, and ſold by *T. Warner*, at the *Black-Boy* in *Pater-Noſter-Row*, 1724.

Title page of Captain Charles Johnson, *A General History of the Pyrates* (1724).

INTRODUCTION:

The Pirates' Code of Honour

The 2003 film *Pirates of the Caribbean: The Curse of the Black Pearl*, the first instalment of the wildly successful film franchise, brought forth a new wave of popular interest in piracy. Since the film's release, its namesake ride at Disneyland has received a makeover to incorporate the movie's plotline. Countless podcasts have devoted episodes or entire series to the history of piracy, online forums on the subject have increased and the television shows *Black Sails* (2014–17) and *Our Flag Means Death* (2022) created an entirely new venue for the genre.

The history of piracy from the ancient period to the modern has always been a subject of fascination. Interest in it may ebb and flow, but it has proved to be a pop-culture mainstay and there is a large, active community of pirate historians across the globe. In popular culture, the lives of pirates are the most intriguing part of this history. Who were these sailors? Why did they choose a life of piracy? And what are the truths behind this life?

The Curse of the Black Pearl weaves historical context into mythology to bring pirate life to the forefront. One of the primary themes that remains is 'keeping to the code'. The code is first mentioned when the female protagonist, Elizabeth Swann (the daughter of the governor of Port Royal), is captured and invokes the right of parley. 'According to the Code of the Brethren set down by the pirates Morgan and Bartholomew, you have to take me to your captain,' she says. 'If an adversary demands parley, you can do them no harm until the parley is complete.' The pirates have no choice but to comply and thus her pirating adventure begins. The other code consistently referred to throughout the film is to leave any person who falls behind. In this case they are simply told to 'keep to the code'.[1]

While these codes were fictional, real eighteenth-century pirates did in fact have their own set of rules. Elizabeth Swann was likely referring to the seventeenth-century pirates Henry Morgan and Bartholomeu Português, and the former of whom did maintain his own set of rules and regulations, more commonly known as 'articles'. In the 1720s, four pirates emerged with sets of codes that set the standards for piratical conduct on ships: Edward Low, George Lowther, Bartholomew Roberts and John Phillips. Low's articles are the most significant because his was the only set to be published for general consumption, in the 1 August 1723 edition of the *Boston News-Letter* and in *The Tryals of Thirty-Six Persons for Piracy, Twenty-Eight of them upon Full Evidence were Found Guilty and the Rest Acquitted*, published in the same year. The only other source to publish pirate codes in full is Captain Charles Johnson's *A General History of the Pyrates* (1724), which belonged to the other three captains. All of the pirates' articles were similar but each had a specific emphasis on keeping their crews in line and guaranteeing loyalty. The primary purpose of pirate codes was to prevent conflict and allow for a peaceful and orderly ship. The most significant codes that guaranteed a successful pirate crew were the ones that outlined punishments for theft and violence, the two main causes of social disorder.[2] Edward Low's articles were the most tolerant in terms of punishments – ironically, however, because he was known to be one of the most violent and cruel pirates to have existed during the Golden Age of Piracy (at least to his victims). Low's list of codes was, in full:

The Articles of Capt. Edward Low the Pirate, with his Company

I. The Captain shall have Two full Shares, the Master a Share and a half, the Doctor, Mate, Gunner, Carpenter, and Boatswain a Share and a quarter.

II. He that shall be found Guilty of Striking or taking up any unlawful Weapon either aboard a Prize, or aboard the Privateer, shall suffer what Punishment the Captain and majority of the Company shall think fit.

III. He that shall be found Guilty of Cowardice in the Time of Engagement, shall suffer what Punishment the Captain and the Majority of the Company shall think fit.

IV. If any Jewels, Gold or Silver is found on board of a Prize to the Value of a Piece of Eight, and the finder do not deliver it to the Quarter-Master in Twenty-four Hours Time, shall suffer what Punishment the Captain and majority of Company shall think fit.

V. He that shall be found Guilty of Gaming, or playing at Cards, or Defrauding or Cheating one another to the Value of a Royal of Plate, shall suffer what Punishment the Captain and majority of Company shall think fit.

VI. He that shall be Guilty of Drunkenness in the Time of an Engagement, shall suffer what Punishment the Captain and majority of the Company shall think fit.

VII. He that hath the Misfortune to loose any of his Limbs in the Time of an Engagement in the Companies Service, shall have the Sum of Six Hundred Pieces of Eight, and kept in the Company as long as he pleases.

VIII. Good Quarters [mercy] to be given when Craved.

IX. He that sees a Sail first shall have the best Pistol, or Small Arm aboard of her.

X. And lastly, No Snapping of Arms in the Hold.[3]

George Lowther's articles are significant because, of these four pirates, he is the only one to demonstrate the democratic nature of his ship. The punishments of nearly every violation of the listed articles were decided upon by both the captain and crew. Not only that, he emphasizes rewards for jobs well done:

The Articles of Captain George Lowther, and his Company

I. The Captain is to have two full Shares; the Master is to have one Share and a half; the Doctor, Mate, Gunner, and Boatswain, one Share and quarter.

II. He that shall be found guilty of taking up any unlawful Weapon on board the Privateer, or any Prize, but us taken, so as to strike or abuse one another, in any regard, shall suffer what Punishment the Captain and Majority of the Company shall think fit.

III. He that shall be found Guilty of Cowardice, in the Time of Engagement, shall suffer what Punishment the Captain and Majority shall think fit.

IV. If any Gold, Jewels, Silver, &c. be found on board of any Prize or Prizes, to the Value of a Piece of Eight, and the Finder do not deliver it to the Quarter-Master, in the

'The Articles of Captain George Lowther, and his Company', from Captain Charles Johnson, *A General History of the Pyrates* (1724).

352 *Of Capt. WORLEY.*

The Articles of Captain *George Lowther*, and his Company.

1. **T**HE *Captain is to have two full Shares; the Master is to have one Share and a half; the Doctor, Mate, Gunner, and Boatswain, one Share and a quarter.*

2. *He that shall be found Guilty of taking up any unlawful Weapon on Board the Privateer, or any Prize, by us taken, so as to strike or abuse one another, in any regard, shall suffer what Punishment the Captain and Majority of the Company shall think fit.*

3. *He that shall be found Guilty of Cowardize, in the Time of Engagement, shall suffer what Punishment the Captain and Majority shall think fit.*

4. *If any Gold, Jewels, Silver, &c. be found on Board of any Prize or Prizes, to the Value of a Piece of Eight, and the Finder do not deliver it to the Quarter-Master, in the Space of 24 Hours, shall suffer what Punishment the Captain and Majority shall think fit.*

5. *He that is found Guilty of Gaming, or Defrauding another to the Value of a Shilling, shall suffer what Punishment the Captain and Majority of the Company shall think fit.*

6. *He that shall have the Misfortune to lose a Limb, in Time of Engagement, shall have the Sum of one hundred and fifty Pounds Sterling, and remain with the Company as long as he shall think fit.*

7. *Good Quarters to be given when call'd for.*

8. *He that sees a Sail first, shall have the best Pistol, or Small-Arm, on Board her.*

It was the 13th of *June*, that *Lowther* left the Settlement, and on the 20th, being then within twenty Leagues of *Barbadoes*, he came up with a Brigantine, belonging to *Boston*, called the *Charles, James Douglass* Master, which they plundered in a pyra-

Space of 24 Hours, [he] shall suffer what Punishment the Captain and Majority think fit.

v. He that is found Guilty of Gaming, or Defrauding another to the Value of a Shilling, shall suffer what Punishment the Captain and Majority of the Company shall think fit.

vi. He that shall have the Misfortune to lose a Limb, in Time of Engagement, shall have the Sum of one hundred and fifty Pounds Sterling, and remain with the Company as long as he shall think fit.

VII. Good Quarters [mercy] to be given when call'd for.

VIII. He that sees a Sail first, shall have the best Pistol, or Small-Arm aboard her.[4]

Captains Roberts's and Phillips's articles were similar to Low's and Lowther's in that these men included promises of equal shares among the crew and compensation for injuries, rules against drinking and gambling, and regulations about weaponry care. However, there was a stark contrast between the latter two men and the former. The latter emphasized the cruel punishments that would befall any pirate who disobeyed them. Captain Roberts's articles were as follows:

The Articles of Bartholomew Roberts

I. Every Man has a Vote in the Affairs of the Moment; has equal Title to the fresh Provisions, or strong Liquors, at any Time seized, and may use them at Pleasure, unless a Scarcity make it necessary, for the Good of all, to vote a Retrenchment.

II. Every Man to be called fairly in Turn, by List, on board of Prizes, because, (over and above their proper Share) they were on this Occasions allowed a Shift of Cloaths: But if they defrauded the Company to the Value of a Dollar, in Plate, Jewels, or Money, Marooning was their Punishment. If the Robbery was only betwixt one another, they contented themselves with slitting the Ears and Nose of him that was Guilty, and set him on Shore, not in an uninhabited Place, but somewhere, where he was sure to encounter Hardships.

III. No Person to Game at Cards or Dice for Money.

IV. The Lights and Candles to be put out at eight a-Clock at Night: If any of the Crew, after that Hour, still remained enclined for Drinking, they were to do it on the open Deck.[5]

V. To keep their Piece, Pistols, and Cutlash clean, and fit for Service.

VI. No Boy or Woman to be allowed among them. If any Man were found seducing any of the latter Sex, and carry'd her to Sea, disguised, he was to suffer Death.

VII. To Desert the Ship, or their Quarters in Battle, was punished with Death or Marooning.

VIII. No striking one another on board, but every Man's Quarrels to be ended on Shore, at Sword and Pistol thus: The Quarter-Master of the Ship, when the Parties will not come to any Reconciliation, accompanies them on Shore with what Assistance he thinks proper, and turns the Disputants Back to Back, at so many Paces Distance: At the Word of Command, they turn and fire immediately (or else the Piece is knock'd out of their Hands). If both miss, they come to their Cutlashes, and then he is declared a Victor who draws the first Blood.

IX. No Man to talk of breaking up their Way of Living, till each had shared a 1000 *l*. If in order to do this, any Man should lose a Limb, or become a Cripple in their Service, he was to have 800 Dollars, out of the publick Stock, and for lesser Hurts, proportionably.

X. The Captain and Quarter-Master to receive two Shares of a Prize; the Master, Boatswain, and Gunner, one Share and a half, and other Officers one and a Quarter.

XI. The Musicians to have Rest on the Sabbath Day, but the other six Days and Nights, none without special Favour.[6]

And Captain John Phillips's articles were listed thus:

The Articles on Board the *Revenge*

I. Every Man shall obey civil Command; the Captain shall have one full Share and a half in all Prizes; the Master, Carpenter, Boatswain and Gunner shall have one Share and [a] quarter.

II. If any Man shall offer to run away, or keep any Secret from the Company, he shall be maroon'd, with one Bottle of Powder, one Bottle of Water, one small Arm and Shot.

III. If any Man shall steal any Thing in the Company, or game to the Value of a Piece of Eight, he shall be maroon'd or shot.

IV. If at any Time we should meet another Marooner (that is, Pyrate) that Man that shall sign his Articles without the Consent of our Company, shall suffer such Punishment as the Captain and Company shall think fit.

V. That Man that shall stroke another whilst these Articles are in force, shall receive Moses's Law (that is, 40 Stripes [lashes] lacking one) on the bare Back.

VI. That Man that shall snap his Arms, or smoak Tobacco in the Hold, without a Cap to his Pipe, or Carry a Candle lighted without a Lanthorn, shall suffer the same Punishment as the former Article.

VII. That Man that shall not keep his Arms clean, fit for an Engagement, or neglect his Business, shall be cut off from his Share, and suffer such other Punishment as the Captain and the Company shall think fit.

VIII. If any Man shall lose a Joint in Time of an Engagement, he shall have 400 Pieces of Eight, if a Limb, 800.

IX. If at any Time we meet with a prudent Woman, that Man that efforts to meddle with her, without her Consent shall suffer present Death.[7]

Jacob Bucquoy, a former prisoner on a pirate ship who witnessed the process of signing the articles, described them thus:

Each band or association has its laws and statutes, which are agreed by consensus and signed by the interested parties who intend to uphold them by placing, in English fashion, two fingers on a bible . . .

The first article of their code declares as enemies all those who are not part of their association, permits the use of force or guile to take their goods, commands each man to give no consideration or mercy to anyone and to put to death any who resist or defend themselves, even his own father.

The following article obliges each man, under pain of death, to keep faith and to give assistance to any in danger.

A further article allows the looting of prizes, but everything taken must be delivered up to the quarter-master, under pain of flogging and confiscation into the common pool of all the possessions of the guilty party.

The code is very severe against violence committed on women travelling on prizes, who must be taken to land as soon as possible and, if no land is in view, must be left to the hazards of the sea . . .

Such are the main provisions of the code which aims to maintain peace on each vessel and to promote courage and vigour against the enemy. The pirates were utterly committed to these obligations, even though they had accepted them voluntarily.[8]

However, numerous primary sources mention pirate 'articles' and that newly recruited and forced pirates were required to sign these articles upon entry to the ship. Forced pirates were innocent sailors who were pressed into piracy for several reasons: to replace pirate crew members who were killed in battle, to be held for ransom, or to be brought on as skilled workers such as surgeons or physicians, carpenters, coopers, navigators, musicians and others.[9] If they were lucky enough to survive their tenure as pirates, they could provide excellent testimony at pirate trials either as the accused or as witnesses. The forced pirate had to be very careful about what he said, especially if he himself was on trial for piracy. Any man who was conscripted onto a pirate ship had to sign the articles, and this alone would implicate him. Therefore, he had to describe his situation in as much detail as he could, including as many accounts of barbarities against him as possible. His life depended on his words.

One of the most common defences was simple: that he had been threatened with death unless he signed the pirate articles. This was the case for several men from different ships who were captured by the pirate captain Bartholomew Roberts.[10] Roberts and his men attacked a man-o'-war called the *Swallow*, captained by a man named Joseph Trahern. Trahern attempted to appeal to Roberts for his release, to no avail; instead, he 'was dragged along to the Signing of their Articles; that he was the last among his Men that did sign them, and shew'd himself the most unwilling to go'. Trahern's first mate, George Fenn, faced a similar predicament but he had one advantage on his side: he was a Dutchman, not an Englishman, and 'he had heard the Pyrates would accept of no Foreigners.' As a result he was not forced to sign any articles. One of his fellow prisoners, Stephen Thomas, who had already been acquitted, verified this under oath. Both Trahern and the first mate, Fenn, were acquitted thanks to eyewitness testimony.[11]

Another member of Trahern's crew, William Philips, was also put on trial but his situation proved to be very different. He gave a graphic account of the various cruelties and violence committed against him. Fenn gave an eyewitness account that Philips 'had been obliged to Sign the Pyrate Articles that Night'

Captain Bartholomew Roberts with two ships, engraving from Captain Charles Johnson, *A General History of the Robberies and Murders of the Most Notorious Pyrates* (1724).

under threat of being shot. However, Fenn proved to be Philips's downfall. According to Fenn, Philips had been a problem on Trahern's ship, frequently disobeying orders to the point that Trahern had threatened to cut off his ears as punishment. Once Philips signed the pirate articles, Fenn said that he believed 'from his Heart, [Philips] entered Volunteer', meaning that he happily became an active pirate. Philips was found guilty and subsequently executed.[12]

Roberts continued to capture more and more men who managed to survive but were forced to turn pirate. Henry Glasby, chief mate of Captain Cary who commanded the *Samuel* of London, was thrown overboard several times and maimed by pirates when he repeatedly refused to sign their articles. The pirates tried to make him one of the crew by forcing some of their prize shares on him, but Glasby refused to keep them. He managed to make his escape when they landed in the West Indies, because he had developed a friendship with one of the pirates, who gave him the opportunity to leave. Since Glasby did not actually sign the articles or keep his given share, he was found innocent of piracy.[13]

A similar situation happened to a man named William Guineys, second mate on a ship called the *Porcupine*, which was burned by pirates. He survived by trying to keep in favour with the pirates, going so far as to share a meal with the pirate captain, and eventually did sign the articles. However, Guineys did not take any shares. When he tried to escape onto another ship, the pirates threatened to shoot him. Guineys only found his freedom when he managed to desert the pirate ship unnoticed during a time of conflict. Richard Wood, a crewmate of Guineys's on the *Porcupine*, was also taken prisoner and was so brutally beaten that he became lame for life. The *Porcupine* was transporting enslaved people and Wood was forced to unshackle the prisoners and turn them over to the pirates. Like Guineys, Wood had to sign the articles, but he received no shares. Both men were acquitted of piracy.[14]

Captain Edward Low, despite having the most neutral pirate code, was one of the most violent pirates to sail during the eighteenth century. He forced men to swear by the articles and then act as willing pirates. At least, this is what a man named John Brown claimed when he was put on trial for piracy. Brown stated that Low 'beat him black and blue to make him sign the Articles' and that is why he became an active member of Low's crew. Since he was on board the ship and participated in one of Low's many pirate attacks, he was found guilty of piracy and executed.[15]

Nearly every account of men forced to sign the pirate articles has one thing in common: they signed out of fear for their lives or to avoid dreadful punishments, which was their main defence when captured by maritime authorities. This was the case for a man named Bridstock Weaver, who was forced onto a pirate ship captained by a man named John Smith. Initially, the pirates promised Weaver that he would be set free so long as he surrendered goods such as 'four Hogsheads of Cyder', but ultimately he was manhandled onto the pirate ship, the *Good Fortune*. He was dragged to a table and told to sign the articles and swear loyalty with his hand on a Bible. He stood 'before a large Looking-glass', and two men were stood behind him 'with loaded Pistols to shoot me if refused, so that I was terrified into compliance'.[16]

Some pirates released prisoners who did not want to sign the articles and join the pirate crew, but this came at a grave cost. A man named Richard Hawkins, captured by the pirate Francis

Spriggs, described his fellow crew member's refusal to sign. The man showed no fear and 'kept himself sober and grave'. When the pirate crew asked him if he would sign the articles, he kept his cool and lied that he could not sign because he had a family and an estate to care for. Surprisingly, the pirates agreed, but told him, 'we will give you your Discharge on your Back,' and he received ten lashes from each person on the pirate ship. Hawkins did not say whether his fellow crewman survived the ordeal.[17]

These popular pirate articles were unique to what is often referred to as the Golden Age of Piracy. This is a time period in which piracy ebbed and flowed in an organized manner during three different pirate 'rounds' in the seventeenth and eighteenth centuries. The first round took place between approximately 1650 and 1680, known as the buccaneering period, when French, English and Dutch pirates terrorized the West Indies and South American coasts. They were referred to as buccaneers (from the French word *boucanier*, which refers to smoking meat) because these pirates, especially the French, were known to roast meat on land and on their ships – quite an unusual practice for mariners. The second round was British piracy in the Indian Ocean during the 1690s, which includes the activities of the notorious pirate captains Henry Avery and William Kidd, both of whom nearly destroyed British trade with India. The third and most infamous pirate round, and the one that most people are familiar with, took place between 1713 and approximately 1730. This is the period in which famous pirate captains such as Benjamin Hornigold, Edward Teach (commonly known as Blackbeard), Jack Rackham, Anne Bonny, Mary Read, Stede Bonnet, Charles Vane and the above-mentioned Edward Low (among others) led organized bands of pirates. This period became known for the War on Pirates, an extermination campaign run by the British government. They faced 'a clique of 20–30 pirate commodores and a few thousand crewmen' who all knew each other. Many of them were veteran privateers of the War of the Spanish Succession (1701–13) who had decided to embark on lives of piracy. During this third round it is said that there were anywhere between 1,800 and 2,400 pirates sailing in and around the Atlantic Ocean between 1716 and 1718 and 1,500–2,000 between 1719 and 1722. Anywhere between 4,500 and 5,000 sailors went 'on the account', that is, became pirates. The majority of pirates were in their mid- to late twenties, with some as young as fourteen years old and some as old as fifty. It was a dangerous life; most pirates lasted for only a year or two before their eventual death or capture.[18]

The majority of pirates were concentrated within the West Indies. In his book *The History of the Buccaneers of America*, Alexandre Exquemelin gave three reasons as to why pirates preferred this area. First, the large area of uninhabited islands and cays was an ideal place for pirates to take shelter and hide their loot if necessary. The second reason is because the maritime trade in the Caribbean was extremely active thanks to its extensive trade routes for Spanish, French, Dutch and English ships, which gave pirates ample opportunities for robbery. Finally, the West Indies meant that it was difficult for authorized ships to pursue them: 'the many small inlets, lagoons, and harbours, on these solitary islands and keys, [was] a natural security', which meant pirates could avoid harassment from the British Admiralty officials and the Royal Navy.[19]

Tortuga and Jamaica became infamous pirate havens despite the fact that English law was formally declared in Jamaica in 1664 and again in 1674.[20] These islands discouraged sailors who were unfamiliar with their geography because of their dangerous

Title page of A. O. Exquemelin, *De Americaensche zee-roovers*
(1678; in English as *The Buccaneers of America*).

coastlines. The isolated region and difficult terrain made the islands attractive to drifters, escaped enslaved people (who fled into the mountains and formed 'maroon' communities), indentured servants, transported criminals, prostitutes, religious dissenters or minorities, criminals, religious radicals and political prisoners, who gained newfound freedom in these areas.

But while pirates sailed throughout the Caribbean with impunity, the area was a site of conflict between major European powers during the seventeenth century. Constant wars and rivalries led to multiple treaties and truces, causing several major islands to frequently change ownership. Jamaica was often the subject of these conflicts. Its ports and proximity to other islands made it desirable to the English. The Crown insisted that the island come under British control because its loss 'would mean the loss of all English interest in the West Indies'.[21] The Caribbean waters, as a result, were politically unstable and the authorities were too distracted to persecute pirates, even while pirates were able to attack frazzled English ships with relative ease.

The English faced additional challenges in maintaining control because Caribbean plantation leaders were not innocent bystanders or even victims of piracy. Nicholas Trott, governor of the Bahamas, was known to frequently make deals with Henry Avery and his crew in 1695. The following governor, Read Elding, was actually charged with piracy.[22] Making deals with pirates allowed unprecedented wealth to pass through the islands into the governors' pockets. Pirates brought in restricted goods that colonists could not get because of the Navigation Acts, which had choked off trade with non-British nations since 1651 in an attempt to cripple Spain's economy. However, the Navigation Acts did the exact opposite: they strangled colonial commerce and drove many colonists to pursue illegal avenues to procure desired goods and currency, such as turning toward pirates.[23] Colonists were happy to work with pirates to get the goods they wanted. Governors therefore knew that punishing pirates would hurt their colonies.

The Navigation Acts were described as so severe that they discouraged 'all people' due to the trading restrictions they placed upon the North American and Caribbean colonies and plantations. Colonists were only allowed to trade with England but officials claimed that England did not efficiently supply the colonies with the goods they could have received from 'our neighbours the French and Dutch at easy rates'.[24]

Plantation Island governors, many of whom had long enjoyed their own autonomy with little British interference, were happy to collude with pirates. In one instance, a French pirate landed at St Thomas 'and asked if the Governor would permit him peaceably to come in to the port at his voyage's end. The Governor replied that he might freely come in and sent refreshments to the pirate, who, in return, sent him silks and satins and arranged with him a private signal.'[25] After Henry Avery's disappearance, many members of his crew scattered and found safe haven in North American colonies such as Pennsylvania and Rhode Island.[26] Rhode Island in particular became known as 'a receptacle for pirates, who are encouraged and harboured by its Government', and its inhabitants aided pirates 'at all times'.[27] Pirates were also 'entertained and settled in New Jersey, Pennsylvania, Maryland and Virginia'.[28] South Carolina had a long history of congenial relationships with pirates to the point where some referred to the colony as a 'second Jamaica'. During the mid-seventeenth-century wars against Spain, pirates often obtained provisions in South Carolina ports, where they paid in cash and developed friendly commercial relationships as a result.[29] But no matter; these arrangements continued to thrive, much to the frustration of merchants who suffered from the harsh trade restrictions that encouraged piracy.[30] It is no surprise that many merchants decided to ignore British proclamations and trading restrictions and openly colluded with pirates throughout British America and the West Indies.[31]

The most popular locations for pirates in the West Indies were Port Royal, Jamaica and Nassau on the Island of Providence in the Bahamas. The last was consistently undefended and ungoverned by the British Crown, which made it a perfect place for pirates to congregate. This region was full of uninhabited islands with craggy cliff faces and intricate coastlines that provided ideal security from larger naval ships. By 1716, pirates sailed into Nassau by the hundreds.

The West Indies were ideal for plunder thanks to conflicts between the British and Spanish. Political issues distracted the royal governments, which allowed pirates to sail in and out without much risk. The British and Spanish engaged in wars over control of major plantation islands such as Jamaica, which caused them to change rule several times over. Treaties and truces were written, passed, signed, rescinded and rewritten. Finally, in 1670, the Treaty of Madrid was officially signed, which granted Britain control of Jamaica if they promised to protect Spanish trade.[32] While it technically solved their disputes, Spain considered it to be a humiliation and would put consistent pressure on the British to eradicate piracy.

Jamaica, specifically Port Royal, was the largest pirate hub during the seventeenth century because it was the most contested space between the British and Spanish in the West Indies. Its proximity to other plantation islands, and to routes to Central, South and North America, allowed access to many active sea lanes. Its shores were difficult to manage because of tricky terrain and it had many hiding spots ideal for pirate ships.[33]

Piracy continued to flourish as Britain and Spain continued to fight over Jamaica. However, on 7 June 1692 a devastating earthquake hit the island and a portion of Port Royal slid into

the sea, causing most of the pirates to scatter. A survivor described the earthquake:

> Betwixt eleven and twelve at noon, I being at a tavern, we felt the house shake and saw the bricks begin to rise in the floor, and at the same instant heard one in the street cry, 'An earthquake'! Immediately we ran out of the house, where we saw all people with lifted up hands begging God's assistance. We continued running up, others thrown on heaps; the sand in the streets rise like

Map of the island of New Providence, *c.* 1751.

the waves of the sea, lifting up all persons that stood upon it and immediately dropping down into pits; and at the same instant a flood of water breaking in and rolling those poor souls over and over; some catching hold of beams and rafters of houses, others were found in the sand that appeared when the water was drained away, with their arms and legs out. The small piece of ground where sixteen or eighteen of us stood (thanks be to God) did not sink.[34]

The Royal Navy finally had the opportunity to take full control of the island and establish order. By 1679, the island had an influx of 5,396 white immigrants and 11,816 enslaved people to produce sugar.[35] Atlantic piracy expanded after the earthquake, which forced pirates from the island as the Royal Navy swooped in and took over. They set about searching for new havens.

The timing was fortunate, because just nine years later, the War of Spanish Succession broke out, which created a need for skilled mariners. The war concerned the succession of the Spanish throne after the Habsburg king Charles II died childless; he had promised the crown to Philip, Duke of Anjou, the grandson of France's King Louis XIV. The alliance between Spain and France rocked Europe, so England, Holland, Prussia and Austria formed the Grand Alliance and began a campaign to put the Habsburg archduke Charles of Austria onto the Spanish throne. This large conflict took place on both land and sea. The British government, in particular, promised a pardon to any pirate who agreed to

Map of the harbours of Port Royal and Kingston, 1756.

fight for the Grand Alliance as a privateer. Hundreds of pirates and thousands of sailors jumped at the chance, including future infamous pirates such as Benjamin Hornigold, Edward Teach, Charles Vane and Samuel Bellamy. The war finally ended in 1714 with the Treaty of Utrecht, in which Philip of Anjou would ascend the throne on the condition that Spain and France would never unite. Peace seemed to finally rest on Europe, but conflicts at sea would increase as thousands of privateers found themselves unemployed overnight.

These ex-privateers turned to piracy and began to settle in the port city of Nassau on the Island of Providence in the Bahamas. This set of islands was ideal for piracy thanks to its proximity to North America, being just off the coast of Florida and the West Indies. Nassau, however, did not have efficient governance, so the city was violent, dirty, full of disease and mostly populated by pirates, sex workers and other people who were considered to be degenerates.[36] However, the former privateering captain

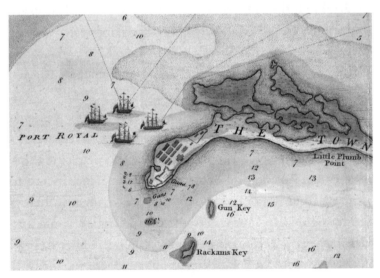

Port Royal harbour, 1756.

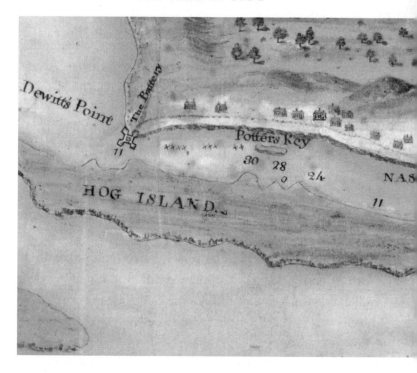

Benjamin Hornigold recognized the city as an excellent place to create a home base for pirates. He stepped in, created law and order and soon became known as the 'Pirate King of the Pirate Kingdom'. Over the next several years, the Bahamas attracted hundreds or even thousands of pirates.[37]

The Island of Providence, in general, was fully sheltered and had an abundance of food, water and natural resources to replenish and restock supplies to build and/or repair ships. Planters and plantation owners retreated further inland to escape or recuse themselves from the pirate community. Thanks to Hornigold, the city was transformed. Traders came into Nassau to sell goods to pirates and buy plundered items cheap in return. By 1715, there were so many pirates there that the British officials began to refer to it as a 'nest of pirates'. One person

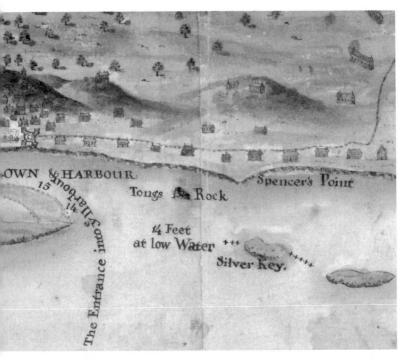

Nassau town and harbour, c. 1751.

who left Nassau described them as committing 'great disorders on the island, plundering inhabitants, burning their houses, and ravishing their wives'. Residents left 'for fear of being murdered'.[38]

In the meantime, local British officials struggled to maintain control of the Bahamas. As of 1716, the Commissions of the Board of Trade and Plantations made eight reports to the British Crown that detailed the miserable conditions of the Bahamas and 'the consequences it wou'd be of, shou'd they fall into the hands of the French, Spaniards, or pirates'.[39] They begged for support and forces to protect the Bahamas, arguing that control of these islands would help secure the rest of the Caribbean: 'whoever is master of them, may if they please be master of all the Spanish and most of the French trade in those parts.'[40] However, this would prove to be nearly impossible because of the fastest-growing piratical network: taverns.

The drinking community of the tavern was essential for pirates to recruit new crew members. Waterfronts at every port city had numerous taverns where all kinds of sailors and travellers congregated. These establishments were usually family-owned, but it was the landlady and her daughter who were in charge and set the tone for the locals, sometimes offering maternal care for the men who wandered in. Pirates came into these taverns and showered women with their earnings, buying them drinks and paying for their company. This was so lucrative that women were often hired as tavern prostitutes to increase revenue and patronage.[41]

However, the increase in taverns meant a surge in public drunkenness and disorderly behaviour. Even after Hornigold established an organized 'pirate kingdom' in Nassau, there was no strict legal system to enforce rules against these behaviours. Hornigold, too, enjoyed getting drunk in Nassau and Port Royal at the end of his voyages.[42] Although the plantation islands had many churches, economic security was a higher priority for patrons, workers and governors. Tavern keepers even extended credit to their return customers, who were often pirates.[43] Commercial and social ties were essential to keep their morale high.[44]

Taverns were informal places of knowledge exchange, politics and networking. They were spaces where people engaged, conversed and socialized with each other without the social stress of class and hierarchy. This was especially true for sailors and pirates looking for maritime news.[45] Pirates had to know which ships were arriving at and from various ports, which indicated the places that were ripe for plunder and where they could recruit new crew if needed.[46] This was not a simple business, however. Taverns also served as spaces where merchants and members of the Royal Navy could coerce people into their own crews. Merchants sometimes hired 'spirits', or recruiters, who travelled to various taverns to offer downtrodden men a place on their ships. If a man was resistant, the spirits got him drunk until he could be manipulated into signing a contract. The poor man would wake up on a ship the next day with no idea how he got there.[47]

Pirates, however, depended on loyal crews, so they did not go to taverns to force anyone to join.[48] Many pirate commanders recruited non-mariner volunteers or volunteer officers, known as 'reformados', along with a crew of experienced seamen. The non-mariners were recruited for speciality positions such as musketeers, boarders and soldiers. Inexperienced seamen were hired if they had previous employment as cooks, owners' agents, translators or surgeons, all of whom were essential for a successful voyage.[49] Once a person joined a pirate ship, or was coerced onto one, they had to sign the articles, but they were not officially considered to be a pirate until they had seen action in battle.[50]

Age had to be taken into consideration when entering a pirate life. A pirate needed to be old enough to have extensive maritime and fighting experience, but they also had to be young enough to be in top physical shape in order to withstand the rigours of this lifestyle. The ages of pirates varied from as young as fourteen years old to as old as fifty; the average age was mid-twenties.[51] This does not mean young boys were exempt from piracy. Pirate ships were full of young volunteers eager to rebel against society. They were usually from port towns where they had lifelong exposure to sailors and their stories. Residents of port towns, especially men and boys, were often employed in the shipping industry and boys as young as seven years old were sometimes sent to sea as cabin boys. An example is John King, one of Samuel Bellamy's recruits. Bellamy welcomed new crew members and was especially kind to ready volunteers. King proved to be the most unusual recruit of all, being only ten years old. He was travelling as a passenger with his mother on a British sloop called the *Bonetta* from Jamaica to Antigua. When Bellamy asked if any of the *Bonetta*'s crew wanted to join his, King immediately volunteered. His mother begged him not to and implored Bellamy to refuse due to King's youth. However, the boy said he would kill himself if he were not allowed to become a pirate and even threatened to attack his mother if she stopped him. She had no choice but to relent, and Bellamy welcomed King into his crew.[52]

Diversity was common on a pirate ship, whether it was intentional or not. Many pirate ships had Black crew members, who could be former enslaved people, escaped enslaved people or freedmen. They were often just as valued as the rest of the crew members and received their fair share of plunder as payment. Between 1715 and 1726, between 25 and 30 per cent of pirates were Black. Of Captain Bartholomew Roberts's crew of 152 men, at least 25 were Black, according to the trial transcripts.[53] Edward Teach was known to have many Black crew members – up to sixty at one point during his piratical career.[54] How they were treated, however, is unknown and likely varied. Edward Low, known for his brutality, was said to 'once strike a Negro but never a White Man'.[55] There are few historical records to indicate whether they were treated well and equally or whether they were the lowest members of the crew with the worst positions. Many of them became pirates after being captured in pirate raids. These recruits either worked as lowly labourers – doing 'drudgery',[56] as on Bartholomew Sharpe's ship – or were resold as human chattel.

People on the outside viewed Black pirates differently. When pirates were captured, Black crew members were sometimes treated as property and sold into slavery rather than being put on trial, leaving their accounts mostly absent from pirate history.[57] However, there is evidence that some Black pirates were treated the same way as white pirates. Some took the stand in major pirate trials. John Quelch and his men stood trial for piracy in 1704; one of them was 'a young Negro Boy' baptized Joachim. It was said that he was kidnapped by Quelch, but since Joachim did not speak English, French or Spanish, the court was unable to proceed and there is no record of his fate.[58] Joachim was not the only Black pirate in Quelch's crew: Caesar-Pompey, Charles and Mingo, who were also Black, all pleaded 'not guilty'. According to the trial transcript, they all had specific roles as crew members. Caesar-Pompey and Charles were cooks and sounded the alarm when attacks were near, but Mingo's job was not listed. They claimed that Quelch had forced them into piracy. Surprisingly, none were found guilty.[59]

There are numerous examples of enslaved people entering pirate ships as cargo rather than crew. Quelch included a 'Negro boy, value Forty Pounds', as part of his cargo.[60] The pirate captain Stede Bonnet captured a ship and kept 'fourteen Negroes' as part of his loot rather than as new recruits. Throughout his piracies he captured at least a dozen other enslaved people as cargo.[61] So while pirate ships could be interpreted as havens for diverse marginalized groups, the reality was much more sobering and complicated.

With all of these factors, what exactly made someone a pirate? In order to properly capture and try these sailors for the appropriate crimes, their category had to be defined. The laws established among the plantation colonies in the West Indies had a section specifically for the definition of piracy. The power that decided who was a pirate was the Admiralty Court, the legal head of maritime affairs. According to these laws, anyone who committed murder and robbery upon any body of water, be it an ocean, sea, lake, river or stream, was a pirate. The Admiralty Court had the jurisdiction to try and judge anyone accused of 'all Treasons, Felonies, Piracies, Roberies, Murthers or Confederacies committed upon the Sea, or in any Haven, or Bay, where the Admiral hath Jurisdiction'. Not only that, anyone who was discovered to aid or abet a pirate or 'knowingly entertain, conceal, trade, or correspond with any Person that shall be deemed Privateer, Pirate, or other Offender within this act' would also be tried as such.[62]

With all these dangers facing pirates on a daily basis, why would someone want to enter into this life? Many pirates had a history of working on merchant ships or in the Royal Navy. These lines of work had harsh conditions. They lived in cramped quarters that were claustrophobic and suffocated. Food and water were scarce and of low quality. Punishments were cruel and often included beatings that left permanent scars. Wages could be withheld indefinitely, particularly on naval ships. All the while they suffered from illness and injury and received poor, or even no, treatment.[63] An eighteenth-century publication about piracy provided a detailed description of the conditions that caused people to turn to piracy:

> The real Cause [of piracy] (to name only one) is undoubtedly the general depravation of Semens manners, and their little or no sense of Religion. The Pretended

one, what the Pyrats usually alledge themselves, and are such as follow.

1. The hard usage they met with at home during the War, by being press'd, and haled from their Families like Dogs on board the Men of War, and then for little or no faults cruelly beat and abus'd by their Officer, which usage from Countrymen was more unsufferable, than the most severe hardships they could endure from barbarous Foreigners.
2. They were often deprived of a considerable part of their provisions, or oblig'd to eat such stinking meat, as was more like to kill than nourish Mens Bodies.
3. They complained much of the severe confinement they endur'd many Months after they were press'd, tho' both necessary business, and their health required their being on shore.
4. They said it was an irresistible provocation, to see their Wives and Families reduc'd to the extremities of pinching Want and Beggary, because they were not duly paid yearly.

Such as Sail'd in Merchants Ships, complain'd of the barbarity of their Commanders, especially in depriving them of their sustenance, not allowing them half of what was necessary to preserve their Bodies in health, they frequently suffering extream thirst by the denying them of Water, notwithstanding many Tuns left when they came into Port. Some blam'd their Captains, that had made them believe, they had lawful Commissions against the Enemies of the Nation, but when at Sea, they met not with their desir'd success, their Commanders by their Authority and Example engag'd them to do those things, they formerly never thought to be done.

Others said, They would never have engag'd, and been guilty of such Crimes, had they not been destitute of an Opportunity of getting out that Country by the real seizure or shipwreck of the Vessels they came in.

But some of the old hardened Pirats said they lookt on it as little or no sin to take what they could from such Heathens as the Moors and other Indians were.

These are the chief Causes of Piracy, at least the chief Reasons commonly given by Pirats, why they betake themselves to that horrid way of Living.[64]

On a pirate ship, however, men were guaranteed an equal portion of the prize based on their ranks. Robbing ships meant that food and water were replenished often, so pirates were generally healthier and stronger than their maritime counterparts. Pirates were also seen as agents of social mobility during a time in which it was nearly impossible to change one's social status. If a man was born poor, he would stay poor, and so would subsequent generations. Pirates, however, were able to transcend this situation and become quite wealthy in a short amount of time. They could go home to their families and retire on a comfortable income for the rest of their lives. Pirate ships were often egalitarian communities in which the crew could vote a captain in or out depending on conditions and successes. These communities were not beholden to anyone else, or to specific laws or governments. They considered themselves to be their own nations rather than obligate to a mother country. Not only that, they were not tied to social norms. Pirates were known to frequently blaspheme, swear, curse, drink excessively and enter violent encounters without any fear of death. This type of life was both appealing and fascinating, especially to people who desperately wanted to leave socially and professionally constricted lives.[65]

These communities were very diverse. Approximately 50 per cent of a pirate ship's crew were generally English white men. The rest of the crew were a medley of seamen from Spain, France, the Netherlands, Germany, Scotland, Wales, Ireland, India, Africa and sometimes even as far away as China. They were extremely close in that they were all connected to a rigorous regime of authority and discipline. They had limited space, opportunity for movement and sensory stimulation, and little choice of leisure activities and play. 'There was too little space aboard the ship and too much space outside.' Cooperation, friendship and strict regulations were essential to the pirates' survival.[66]

Religious folk, particularly those who were marginalized, also found their place on a pirate ship. Even though these spaces were not particularly religious, various Christians, Catholics, Jews, Muslims and those without religion were welcome on board. This was a time in which Jews and Muslims did not have a place in the British world and Catholics often faced discrimination. Jews were rarely welcome in any part of Europe, save the Netherlands for a time. Muslims, or Moors (a slur attributed to them), had also been cast out of their Spanish homeland. Pirate ships only had two requirements: to be a brave sailor and a courageous fighter. Religion and race did not matter here.[67]

The British government did everything it could to curb piracy. At the turn of the eighteenth century, the Act for the More Effectual Suppression of Piracy was passed, offering pardons to any pirate that would turn himself in and name members of his crew. This law was reissued several times until the late 1720s. In 1719, Nicholas Lawes, governor of Jamaica, was given strict orders to offer pardons to pirates who surrendered to him and offered their services for the defence of the island, to no avail.[68] While there were some pirates who took advantage of the pardon, such as Vane and Teach, most re-entered piracy.

THE PURPOSE OF THIS BOOK is to break down the life of the pirate based on the outline of this introduction. The pirate code is essential to understanding how pirates kept their vessels in order. The main purpose of these articles was to make the ship a safe environment to ensure pirates' survival. They defined the pirate life, but were also the pirates' downfall.

The chapters of this book follow the general set of pirate articles. Although they had their minor differences, each code followed the same basic rules listed earlier in this chapter. The first chapter discusses how goods and payment were distributed among pirates to make sure everyone got their fair share and explores how these allowances also led to pirates' doom when they were captured. The second chapter discusses appropriate punishments for pirates who violated the laws of the ships and for their prisoners who refused to participate in the pirate life. This chapter will also demonstrate the ranking members of the pirate crew and discuss how these decisions were made in a largely democratic fashion. The third chapter discusses health and safety on the ship, in terms of how to treat illnesses and injuries and the compensation each victim was entitled to. The fourth chapter covers the debated ideas of sex, sexuality and relationships on and off pirate ships. It goes into theories about whether there were romantic sexual relationships between men on the ships, how they engaged with women onshore and what life was like for their families left behind on land. The fifth chapter discusses safe handling of weapons before, during and after battle to ensure success. The sixth goes into food and drink, in terms of what made a realistic but healthy diet on the ship and whether drinking was acceptable and why. The seventh chapter discusses vices that could cause discord among the crew, such as gambling, and therefore examines why certain activities were banned. The final chapter continues this discussion by looking at the lively culture of the pirate ship, including merrymaking and keeping morale high. Finally, the book concludes with an account of the end of piracy.

All these chapters are intended to illustrate how each one of these codes was essential to pirates' survival. It is time to dive deep into these articles to understand the intricate and ordered life on the pirate ship.

1

WORK, LIFE AND WAGES
ON THE PIRATE SHIP

'The Captain shall have Two full Shares, the Master
a Share and a half, the Doctor, Mate, Gunner, Carpenter,
and Boatswain and Share and a quarter.'
The Articles of Capt. Edward Low the Pirate, with his Company

One of the things that made pirates truly unique was the
way they distributed goods. Unlike on most naval or merchant ships, pirates got a guaranteed equal share based on rank,
partly because the pirate brotherhood was entirely voluntary.[1]
All each pirate had to do was bring 'what he needs in the way
of weapons, powder and shot'.[2] During the eighteenth century,
there was no formal rank or hierarchy among the crew. All
pirates were equal in status, and they voted on where they would
cruise for plunder: after the pirate captain Edward England
and his men successfully went out to sea, for example, 'they put
it to a Vote what Voyage to take, and the Majority carrying it
for the East-Indies, they shap'd their Course accordingly, and
arrived at Madagascar, the Beginning of the Year 1720'.[3] Pirates
came up with a system for how they would 'deliver the hunt', a
chasse partie. Typical chasse parties called for equal wages after
the needs of the ship, carpenters, provisioners and the wounded

had been met. After that, the rest of the goods were equally distributed.[4] According to Alexandre Exquemelin, 'Everything taken – money, jewels, precious stones and goods – must be shared among them all without any man enjoying a penny more than his equal fair share.'[5]

To maintain order in regard to the distribution of goods, there had to be a strict hierarchy, but at the same time pirates needed agency to make sure they had a say in how wages were handed out. Indeed, there were several captains who faced discord and challenges to their authority from the crew when items were not evenly doled out or were withheld altogether. This was a form of control and could be their downfall. Pirates' captives were required to participate in looting or else they would face severe punishment. But if they participated and took their share, regardless of whether they did so willingly or not, the Admiralty would find them guilty of piracy, if they were caught.

Handing out equal shares was not just a way to keep crews happy and loyal. This was also a method to coerce hostages and force men into becoming official pirates. Sometimes pirate captains promised their would-be victims mercy and equal shares if they joined their crew, as was the case with Captain George Cusack. After he robbed a ship, he stole all that ship's captain's chests, 'and there divided betwixt [the pirates] all the Goods and Money in equal proportion'. The pirates declared that they would take the ship and sink it unless the sailors joined their crew, 'promising to all persons aboard that joined with them, their proportion and shares of the Ship and Cargo'.[6] Cusack was so successful and ruthless in his captures that he sometimes had to force victims to join his crew simply to help manage the amount of goods he and his crew plundered. He captured a ship called the *Saint Joseph*, captained by David Godfrey out of Lisbon, which contained 'Campeach Wood, Varenus Tobacco, Coco, and other Merchandize to the value of 25,000 pieces of Eight, whereof 20,000 were in ready money'. After storing the cargo and money, Cusack 'thought it convenient for the better security of the Ship to strengthen her with as many men as they could conveniently get'.[7] Those who refused to sign the articles would not receive a share, but many had to swear an oath of loyalty for survival.

Ironically, their survival could also be their downfall. When captured pirates went on trial, evidence of receiving an equal share was used against them and helped determine their guilt regardless of their true circumstances. Several members of Henry Avery's crew were cross-examined about their shares, demonstrated in this excerpt from their trial transcript:

J. DAN [PIRATE] We expected a [Moorish] fleet to come down.

MR. CONIERS [LAWYER] What fleet?

J. DAN The Moorish Fleet, that came from Mocha. They past us on Saturday night unseen, and then we took a Vessel which gave us an account that they were gone. And then we followed them, and about 3 days after we made Land, we came up with one of them about 2 or 300 tuns, and we fired a Broadside at her, and small shot, and took her, which, after we had taken her, we plundered, and took out some Gold and Silver.

MR. CONIERS And what did you do with it?

J. DAN We brought it aboard our Ship.

MR. CONIERS Did you share it?

J. DAN Not then, but after we took the other Ship.

MR. CONIERS What was that other Ship?

J. DAN After we had taken her, we put some Men aboard to keep her with us; and about two days after, we were lying at Anchor at St. Johns, and there was a great Ship called the Gunsway, and weigh'd Anchor, and fought her about two hours, and took her, and put some Men aboard her, and plunder'd her. And after we had done as much as we though convenient, we sent her to the Surat with the People in her. And then we stood further to the Indian Coast, and shared our Money about a week after.

L.C. J. HOLT That was a brave Prize, was it not, the best you had all the Voyage?

J. DAN Yes, my Lord.

L.C. J. HOLT Did you all share?

J. DAN Yes, all that were in the Ship.

L.C. J. HOLT You have given a good account of this matter. Was Ed. Foreseth there?

J. DAN Yes, my Lord.

L.C. J. HOLT What did he do? Was he active?

J. DAN I did not see him act.

L.C. J. HOLT Had he a share?

J. DAN Yes my Lord, he had.

L.C.J. HOLT Was W. May there?

J. DAN Yes my Lord.

L.C. J. HOLT What did he do there?

J. DAN He could do but little then; he had his share.

L.C. J. HOLT And when you took him in again, what did he do? Did he do his business as a Seaman?

J. DAN Yes my Lord, 'till he was sick.

L.C. J. HOLT Was W. Bishop there?

J. DAN Yes my Lord, he was among the rest.

L.C. J. HOLT What did he do? Did he consent and agree to what was done?

J. DAN He had a share of the money.

L.C. J. HOLT Did Ja. Lewis share too?

J. DAN He had a share, as far as was allowed by the Company.

L.C. J. HOLT Did J. Sparks share with you too?

J. DAN Yes my Lord, as far as the Company thought fit to give him.

MR. COUPER [LAWYER] When you said, as the Company thought fit, what do you mean? How did they share it?

J. DAN Some had 1000 *l.* some 500, others 300.

MR. COUPER Had all the Prisoners some share?

J. DAN Yes Sir, they all had some share.[8]

One of the most infamous pirate trials was that of Captain Kidd, who was accused of the murder of William Moore and of robbing the *Quedah Merchant* in the East Indies. Even though the trial was really about his own actions, his crew was not exempt from blame. This event focused on how shares from the pirated ship were distributed. One of the crew members who spoke out against Kidd, Robert Brandingham, listed out the different shares. His testimony is a great example that shows just how goods were distributed. The following is an excerpt that is basically a list of who received which number of shares:

MR. JUSTICE POWELL They are indicted for the Quedagh-Merchant; Were al the Prisoners in that Action? You have given an Historical Account from the beginning, that he was a meer Plunderer; but now you are come to the Quedagh, for which they are Indicted; Go not beyond it.

MR. CONIERS Look on the several Prisoners at the Bar, and tell whether any of the Prisoners were at the Taking of the QM.

CL. OF ARR Was William Kidd there, at the time the Ship was Taken?

ROB BRANDINGHAM Yes.

CL. OF ARR Was Nicholas Churchill there?

RB Yes.

CL. OF ARR Do you know James Howe? Was he there?

RB Yes.

CL. OF ARR Had he a share?

RB Yes.

CL. OF ARR Had Robert Lamley a Share?

RB Yes. He was a Servant, and had but Half a Share of the Money, and a Whole Share of the Goods.

CL. OF ARR William Jenkins, was he there, and had a share?

RB Yes.

CL. OF ARR Gabriel Loffe, did you know what he had?

RB He had Half a Share of the Money, and a Whole Share of the Goods.

CL. OF ARR Hugh Parrot, what had he?

RB Half a Share.

CL. OF ARR Had Richard Balicorn a Share?

RB He had Half a Share of Money, and a Whole Share of Goods.

CL. OF ARR Had Abel Owens any?

RB He had Half a Share.[9]

Thanks to their willingness to take their shares, no matter the context or consequences, the pirates were found guilty.

LIFE AT SEA WAS HARD and, for the average seaman, maintaining a fair or desirable lifestyle was even harder. As on any fishing, merchant or naval ships, pirates had ranked officer positions to keep things in order. By the turn of the eighteenth century, a hierarchy had begun to form on pirate ships, but compared to naval and merchant vessels, the distribution was much more egalitarian. The captain and quartermaster received the highest shares of plundered booty (about a share and a half), followed by those who held specific skilled positions on ships, such as the surgeon, boatswain and gunner (about one and a quarter shares). The rest of the crew received the lowest amount (one share). This was to prevent disputes between sailors. The simple action of handing out payments of stolen goods was enough to condemn people as pirates, as was the case with Henry Avery's crew, especially Joseph Dawson, who served in a high-ranking position on the pirate's ship. Avery had escaped but Dawson and other members of the crew were found guilty of 'Feloniously and Piratically taking and

Spanish dollar, 1739, also known as pieces of eight (8 reales).

carrying away, from persons unknown, a certain ship called the *Gunsway*, with her Tackle, Apparel and Furniture, to the Value of 1000*l*. and Goods to the value of 110*l*. together with 100000 Pieces of Eight, and 100000 Chequins, upon the High Seas, ten Leagues from the Cape St Johns near Surat in the East-Indies'.[10]

Their trial listed every ship they attacked and the goods they stole. No item was safe. From the *Charles the Second*, they stole 'Forty Pieces of Ordinance . . . her tackle, apparel and Furniture, of the Value of One Thousand Pounds: Fifteen Tun of Bread, of the Value of One Hundred and Fifty Pounds; and Two Hundred pair of Woolen Stockings, of the Value of Ten Pounds . . .'.[11] Captain Edward England captured a ship called the *Cassandra*, on which the pirates found a cache of diamonds. They 'divided their plunder, sharing 42 small Diamonds a man, or in less Proportion according to their Magnitude'.[12]

The main officers were the captain, lieutenant and the quartermaster, followed by lesser officers and mates. Different pirate ships, of course, had different ways of making up the crew. Jacob Bucquoy's account of his adventures, published in the eighteenth century, described the ship ranks. According to Bucquoy, the captain and quartermaster were

> the first estate . . . under whose orders are a boatswain and petty officers. The captain is responsible for the running of a ship and above all for command in battle. The quartermaster, who is the principal agent on board, leads the crew, whose spokesman he is with the captain. He maintains discipline, allocates rations, is the custodian and distributor of booty, convokes general meetings, controls the captain's decisions and very often dictates instructions to him in the name of the men.[13]

Edward England, engraving from Captain Charles Johnson, *The History and Lives of All the Most Notorious Pirates, and Their Crews* (1725).

This was consistent among pirate ships. John Phillip's ship's officers were a captain, master, carpenter, boatswain and gunner. George Lowther had a captain, quartermaster, doctor, mate, gunner and boatswain. The quartermaster held one of the most important positions, if not the most important position, on the ship. He was the one who assisted the master or mate with the watch and assisted with connecting the helm of their ship with their victim's. The quartermaster represented the pirates and always held the highest authority except in battle, which was the captain's domain. If the captain met his death, the quartermaster stepped into his role. Not only that, but the quartermaster was also the one who selected and organized plundered goods from other ships.[14] He dispensed food and provisions among the crew along with other allowances. However, the quartermaster's most important role was to counterbalance the captain's power to prevent any misuse of authority.[15]

The only higher authority than the captain or quartermaster was the common council. Pirates turned to an ancient custom that had died out on all other kinds of ship: consulting the entire crew in making crucial decisions on anything from distribution of goods to punishments. The common council was made up of every member of the crew, and met regularly to make decisions that affected their welfare. It was an opportunity to civilly address any outstanding issues and might feature lively debates. The council of pirates determined matters such as where the best prizes could be taken and how any arguments over the goods could be resolved. Some crews turned to their council frequently to settle disputes by voting on various matters, even setting up a court.

The decisions made among the council were so sacred that not even the captain could override them.[16] Although captains oversaw the ships, this did not mean that they made all the final decisions. They were in charge at the pleasure of the crew, and needed to command their respect, show bravery in battle and be a skilled mariner.[17] Not even the toughest or boldest captain dared go against the council's rulings.[18] If he did, he could be voted out, which is what happened to Captain Bartholomew Sharp. He had promised his crew that they would be able to go home after one last prize. Sharp had a share of 3,000 pieces of eight, but more than two-thirds of his company were left without parts of their prizes. Not only that, Sharp had lied to his crew: they would not be returning home. 'This Fewd was carried on so fiercely, that it was very near coming to a civil War, had not some prudent men moderated the thing.' They ended up electing the quartermaster, John Watling, as their commander until Sharp agreed to honour his original promise, which he eventually did.[19]

However, some pirate captains did have caveats to this rule. The pirate captain Samuel Bellamy captured numerous men and forced them into piracy. At the height of his captaincy, he had a crew of over two hundred men, working on two ships. Of those, only eighty were there voluntarily. He required all forced men to sign his pirate articles if they wanted to be granted full privileges. If they refused, they were not given any of their share of plunder. One of two survivors of Bellamy's wrecked ship, the *Whydah*, Thomas Davis, was a forced pirate who had refused to sign Bellamy's articles. He later testified,

> When the company was called together for Consuls, and each Man to give his Vote, they would not allow the forced Men to have a Vote. There were one hundred and thirty forced Men in all, and Eighty of the Old company [Bellamy's original crew before he gathered a fleet]; and this Examinate being a forced Man had no opportunity to discover his mind.

Davis was tried separately from the rest of the pirates and was one of only two men to be acquitted.[20]

Many pirates were former merchantmen who had suffered a great amount of abuse from their superiors, so they made sure to create a more egalitarian society. Pirate captains were not necessarily secure in their roles. The way to prevent a captain from abusing his power was to create a system of checks and balances as well as divide responsibilities among the crew. This also allowed pirates to elect and depose captains and quartermasters.

All pirates, therefore, had a chance of becoming a leader and it was in their best interest to conduct themselves in the best way possible at all times.[21] If the crew felt their leader was doing a poor job, not taking advantage of good prizes or cruel, they could vote him out. Captain Kidd faced such a challenge on his 1696 voyage in the East Indies as a privateer on the *Adventure Galley*. Everyone had high hopes for plunder, but they were soon dashed. Not only did the ship sustain damage and leaks on the journey, but cholera broke out during the first half of his voyage, killing a third of his crew. By the time they landed on Grande Comore in the Indian Ocean, the surviving crew were ready to leave.

Even worse, they had not won any prizes. The men were angry, and Kidd knew his investors would not be pleased. After Kidd was able to convince his crew to continue once they restocked and recuperated, they came across some ships that appeared to be excellent prizes. However, the attacks were poorly planned, and they failed to take any of the vessels. The sailors began threatening mutiny because they felt that Kidd was too timid a leader who was costing them great opportunities. The next time they docked, several men abandoned ship altogether.

The problems came to a head in 1697. The crew had not been paid for some time. Then, on 30 October 1697, one of the crewmen, William Moore, spotted a Dutch ship in the distance and insisted that they attack it. Kidd refused because they could not identify whether it was a pirate ship or another privateer. Moore insisted that the men would mutiny because of their withheld payment. Kidd called him a 'lousy dog', to which Moore replied, 'If I am a lousy dog, you have made me so.' This escalated into a fight. Kidd hit Moore over the head with a

Blackbeard the pirate, engraving from Captain Charles Johnson, *A General History of the Robberies and Murders of the Most Notorious Pyrates* (1724).

metal bucket and the man died of his injuries the next morning. Kidd insisted it was an accident and the surgeon did not question it. After that, Kidd appeared to have a change of heart and commanded his crew to chase any ship they came across.[22] No one was happy, but he managed to prevent a mutiny.

Stede Bonnet, on the other hand, was completely usurped in his leadership when he joined forces with Edward Teach, commonly known as Blackbeard. Bonnet was an inexperienced sailor who abandoned his family and his successful Barbados plantation, commissioned a ship called *Revenge* and hired a pirate crew. After suffering a severe injury in an attack against a Spanish man-o'-war, they headed to Nassau. Blackbeard took advantage of Bonnet's inexperience and agreed to join forces.

Blackbeard and the crew had little respect for Bonnet and soon enough, even though Bonnet kept control of the *Revenge*, Blackbeard took on the main authority and the men deferred to him. In March 1718, Bonnet came upon a merchant ship called the *Protestant Caesar* off the coast of Honduras but failed to capture it. By this point, his crew had had enough of his poor leadership. Many of his crew moved onto Blackbeard's ship, the *Queen Anne's Revenge*. Blackbeard put one of his own men in charge of the *Revenge* and demoted Bonnet to a mere guest on the ship.[23] Bonnet would not be a captain again until he and Blackbeard unceremoniously parted ways permanently in North Carolina. If Bonnet ever wanted to succeed, he would need to learn proper battle tactics. But how does one manage to gain the requisite respect to become known as a fearsome pirate?

Sailors were tied to their service via a contract that required them to stay on board and continue in service until the ships had been completely 'unladen', as 'such Voyage is not ended til that time'.[24] The wage system was necessary to incentivize new recruits while also preventing desertion. Edward England was able to recruit new pirates thanks to a wage dispute. Some of his crew came from a ship called the *Skinner* on which a group of the men had killed the captain because he refused to give them their wages.[25] There were three types of wage system employed between the seventeenth and eighteenth centuries. The first was the share system, which had been around among ancient mariners and was the standard form of payment during the medieval period. The shift from 'share' to 'wage' did not happen until the sixteenth century and by the eighteenth century the former system was used exclusively by fishermen, whalemen, privateersmen and pirates. The second wage agreement was a fixed amount of money for labour on various voyages, paid out in a lump sum. The third, final and most common form of wage system was the monthly wage, in which seamen were paid on average between 22 and 35 shillings per month during peacetime and between 35 and 55 shillings during wartime. The money was paid in three parts: at the second port of delivery, every second port thereafter and at the completion of the voyage.[26]

Wages for high-ranking officers were substantially higher. Captains received on average between £5 and £6 per month, although wartime wages were only 10 per cent higher than in peacetime. The first mate of a merchant ship received between £3 and £4 a month but, unlike those of captains, their wartime wages were more than a third higher than their average peacetime pay. The captain also received special privileges that included his own private and spacious cabin. On the other hand, since egalitarianism in various forms was expected on board a pirate ship, any crew member had the right to eat or drink with their captain, enter his cabin at any point and even swear at him.[27]

Stede Bonnet,
engraving from
Captain Charles
Johnson, *The History
and Lives of All
the Most Notorious
Pirates, and Their
Crews* (1725).

As on other ships, the pirates' quartermaster was second in command and served as a trustee and civil magistrate for the crew. The quartermaster, not the captain, was the first to board a prize, conduct negotiations and decide which goods to take and what to leave behind. He managed the storage and distribution of goods among the crew, determined the fair allocation of food and drink, resolved minor issues among the men and decided on fair punishments. If a captain was killed or voted out, the quartermaster was often promoted to the role.[28]

The highest-ranking member of the non-officer crew was the carpenter, who received the same share as the first mate. If the carpenter trained an apprentice, he would receive an extra

£2 or £3 per month. If a ship was lucky enough to have a surgeon on board, he would make the same amount of money as the first mate and carpenter. Next in line was the boatswain, who was paid on average £2.60 per month during peacetime and £3.20 during wartime. By the eighteenth century, gunners were standard members of crews, especially as piracy expanded, and made about £2 or £3 per month. Less skilled, but just as important, was the cook, who made £2 per month. Finally, the largest category of maritime workers was the 'common tars', with average wages of £1.66 per month during the first half of the eighteenth century. Although they had the lowest pay, they had the largest increase during wartime, during which they earned 50 per cent more.[29]

Sometimes the guaranteed wage system was not enough to lure new employees onto ships. The maritime world was extremely dangerous and required a long-term commitment that could last years without any relief. Voyages with the East India Company, for example, could last up to two years. A solution was the advance system, in which deep-sea sailors could receive up to two months of wages in advance for particularly long voyages. Sailors could pay off debts, have a grand time before setting off and sustain their family before their long absence.[30]

However, despite all these solutions, the money was not always enough, so sailors turned to another method to add to their earnings: embezzlement, in which they took a cut of the products meant for market. The most pilfered item was alcohol, which was the subject of most embezzlement lawsuits. Sugar and tobacco were also lucrative. Embezzlement happened on nearly every merchant ship. Everyone, including captains, took a cut of the goods.[31] Anything that could add to a sailor's purse was up for grabs.

Sailors needed money when they were in port and sometimes there were challenges in accruing the wages owed to them. There were cases when they were not paid at the required second port; those seamen often retaliated by refusing to 'doe a Stroak of work, nor wash or Clean the Ship'. The captain's dilemma, however, was the risk that sailors would receive their payment and then desert, especially if they landed at one of the American colonies.[32]

Sailing was very expensive and captains looked to cut costs in all directions while at the same time keeping as many of their crew as possible. Expenditure on wages was kept lower by forcing seamen to buy their own ship goods, such as brandy, rum, wine, extra food, sugar, tobacco, caps, coats, shirts, trousers, breeches, stockings, shoes and thread. Surgeons sometimes charged fees for their services.[33] The sailors paid for these goods by having the price deducted from their pay and sometimes they were none the wiser about this system until payday.[34] If this became intolerable, the sailors would withdraw from their employment and the wage system entirely in one of three ways. First, they might move to land-based labour. Second, many chose a marooning life, which meant they deliberately withdrew from the 'imperial economy and culture to a non-accumulative life on the world's periphery'. Finally, they could turn to piracy.[35]

Pirates' equal shares were either cash or actual goods plundered from ships that the pirates could later sell. Itemized shares were given out based on their value. In the early seventeenth century, a pirate named Captain Downes practised this method. He and his crew plundered a ship called the *Royall of Leeth* off the coast of Portugal. They did not find any money, but they took 'fifty tunnes of salt, and above a hundred pound of Royalls of plate, being in six bags of pepper, one pack of Calecutes, two hundred weight of Tobacco, give hundredth weight of cordage, for the account of themselves and their partners'. Soon they captured another ship. When Downes took an inventory from his victim, he was not satisfied with what the other captain relayed, so Downes ordered his crew to do a full plunder. They came away with five rugs, two sets of clothes and a pair of coral bracelets. This was not a bad haul, but then they found the items that the victim captain was hiding: 'a whole chest of apparel, some diamonds, Tobacco and other things ... worth a hundred Marks'.[36] All of these items combined would make the pirates very rich indeed.

Most of the pirates' plunder was made up of items they could sell at a high price: textiles, wines and spices. They also stole items to replenish their ship, such as tackle, and as much food as they could carry. The idea that they stole treasure is mostly fiction blended with rumour. However, on rare occasions they might strike gold – literally. The most infamous example is the Spanish treasure fleet that was smashed by a hurricane off the coast of Florida on 31 July 1715. Seven million pesos worth of bullion and coin, dyestuffs, tobacco, hides and other raw materials sank. Spain immediately set to work to try to recover as much of their goods and cash as they could and by October Spanish divers had managed to recover 5 million pesos. Unfortunately for Spain, however, the English in the neighbouring Carolinas, Jamaica, the Bahamas and other parts of the British Americas learned about this tragedy, and all moved to snatch up as much loot as possible. Some even attacked incoming Spanish ships. The first outsiders to reach the wreckage were pirate hunters commissioned out of Port Royal. The pirate Henry Jennings and his partners stole 120,000 pesos from the Spanish ships that were attempting to recover more of their countrymen's lost goods. Despite outcry in Spain and the country's demand that Britain end the piracy, it could not be stopped. Between 1716 and 1718, hundreds if not thousands of pirates had leeched the whole area dry.[37]

After pirates won a ship, they had to make decisions in terms of what to plunder and how to sort the goods. Pirates worked with the stolen ship's quartermaster to search for loot. If the quartermaster refused to cooperate, the rest of the pirates might torture the crew and passengers until someone gave up the information. Pirates had no idea what items or cash the ship might carry so this was not only the most important part of their attack, but the most anticipated. Would the prize be worth their time and blood, or was it a waste of both?[38]

A pirate's goal was to become wealthy, and it did not matter how they accrued their wealth. This was extremely attractive to sailors. Seamen in general wanted ready money that would fund all the pleasure and sustenance they could imagine. Their priority was to find a tavern once they arrived on land to 'ease themselves of their Golden Luggage'.[39]

During wartime, many pirates went into the privateering business. They would receive a letter of marque charging them to rob specific enemy ships, and their payment was a proportion of the goods they stole. Even though governments took a percentage of their booty, the privateers walked away with quite a comfortable salary. In 1708, Britain's Prize Act even allowed privateering shipowners to keep the full value of what they had captured. This was a compelling reason why pirates continued their activities even after their privateering contracts ended.[40] The one negative was their lack of autonomy.

This is another reason why privateers turned back to piracy. Unlike privateers, non-shipowners did not have to turn over any of their profits to a governing body. They got to keep it all for themselves. Piracy gave many men the opportunity to become much wealthier than they would be in any other sailing career.[41] At the height of Henry Avery's career, the average sailor on a long voyage earned approximately £12 a year. Pirates, however, 'could realise a hundred or even a thousand times more'. Avery's pirate fleet captured a prize of £600,000 in precious metals and jewels, which meant each crew member received £1,000, the equivalent of a sailor's earnings over a forty-year career.[42] According to Captain Charles Johnson, author of *A General History of the Pyrates*, Bartholomew Roberts could not fathom why someone would turn away from piracy and its monetary opportunity:

> In an honest Service, there is thing Commons, low Wages, and hard Labour; in this, Plenty and Satiety, Pleasure and Ease, Liberty and Power; and who would not ballance Creditor on this Side, when all the Hazard that is run for it at worst, is only a lower Look or two at choaking. No, a merry Life and a short one, shall be my Motto.[43]

Pirates needed to find ways to protect their stolen goods, especially if they were either being chased or on a particularly long voyage. Henry Avery plundered several Mughal ships in the East Indies and made off

> with all their Slaves and Attendants, their rich Habits and Jewels, with Vessels of Gold and Silver, and great Sums of Money to defray the Charges of the Journey by Land ... Having taking all the Treasure on board their

Captain Avery and his crew taking one of the Great Mughal ships, engraving from
Captain Charles Johnson, *A General and True History of the Lives and Actions of the
Most Famous Highwaymen, Murderers, Street-Robbers . . .* (1742).

own ships, and plundered their Prize of every Thing else they either wanted or liked, they let her go.

After their success, the pirates agreed to sail to the closest pirate haven, Madagascar, 'intending to make that Place their Magazine or Repository for all their Treasure, and to build a small Fortification there, and leave a few Hands always ashore to look after it, and defend it from any Attempts of the Natives', but this was ultimately abandoned. Instead, they decided their best course would be to either lie low or retire and 'make the best of their Way towards America; and none of them being known in those Parts, they intended to divide the Treasure, to change their Names, to go ashore, some in one Place, some in other, to purchase some Settlements and live at Ease'.[44]

Pirates might have stashed their plunder in specific locations, but this does not mean that they buried treasure. The idea of hidden riches is a pop-culture invention inspired by Captain Kidd, who was said to have buried his plunder. The reality is that this never happened.[45] Rumours about his buried treasure circulated around the Atlantic world from the time of his arrest in 1699 well into the twenty-first century. This is thanks to a 1699 letter written by the Earl of Bellomont – the man who lured Kidd into capture under the pretence of safety – in which he wrote that he had learned from one of Kidd's acquaintances, a 'Mr Emot', who had sheltered Kidd for a time, that

Kidd has left the great Moorish ship he took in India ... in a creek on the coast of Hispaniola, with goods to the value of £30,000: that he had brought a sloop, in which he was come before to make his terms; that he had brought the sloop with him several bales of East

India goods, three score pound weight of gold in dust and in ingots, about a hundred weight in silver and several other things which he believed would sell for about £10,000.[46]

It is interesting to note that Emot stated that Kidd abandoned the ship and gave a simple list of pilfered items. Yet, this information soon devolved into an idea that Kidd deliberately stored the ship with other goods rather than simply abandoning it.

Other official sources from the *Calendar of State Papers* estimated Kidd's lost treasure to be worth approximately £300,000.[47] The *London Post*, on the other hand, reported that Kidd's ship and cargo were 'said to be worth 20000*l*'.[48] A couple of weeks later, the *London Post* published a second article; although it did not repeat the exact monetary value of Kidd's prizes, it reported that 'he presented [Lord Bellomont] with a Gift in Jewels valued at 10000*l*'.[49] This specific detail about Kidd's treasure was never mentioned again, but it was enough to spark rumours for two years before his execution in 1701. One letter from Philadelphia described some gossip about Kidd's treasure by members of his crew: 'Wee have 4 men for prison Taken up as pyrates suppos'd to be Kidds men ... we have various Reports about their Riches and some talk of much money hid between this and the Capes.'[50] Another letter written to the Lords Justices in England from the East India Company advised that Kidd had sailed into the Americas 'with a great Treasure of Gold, Silver, Jewells, and other Merchandize being the Produce of his Pyracies'.[51]

To add to the mystery, a year later the Earl of Bellomont retracted his former statement about the inventory of Kidd's treasure and claimed that Kidd had refused to tell anyone its contents:

Capt. Kidd sent the Gaoler to me a fortnight ago to acquaint me that I would let him go to the place where he left the Quedah Merchant and to St. Thomas' and Curacao, he would undertake to bring off 50 or three score thousand pounds which would otherwise be lost ... I bad the gaoler to try if he could prevail with Capt. Kidd to discover where his Treasure was hid by him. But he said nobody could find it but himself, and would not tell any further.[52]

Lord Bellomont was very detailed about his correspondence with Kidd but soon distanced himself from the pirate captain when he realized the possibility that he might be associated with piracy.[53] In September 1699, the *Post Boy* published an article that claimed that 'Kidd sent a Present of Jewels to the Countess of Bellomont, to the value of some Thousands of Pounds,' and that Bellomont's wife refused the above-mentioned jewels, but the governor ordered her to accept it.[54]

The most convincing piece of supposed evidence comes from John Gardiner of Gardiner's Island off the coast of New York, which is the place where Kidd is said to have officially buried his treasure. Gardiner claimed that Kidd left gold, silver, jewels and other goods valued at a total of £6,500 there.[55] Despite numerous searches over the centuries, Kidd's supposed hidden wealth has never been recovered.

Blackbeard was another infamous pirate rumoured to have buried treasure. However, while the existence of Kidd's treasure is highly disputed, Blackbeard's hidden hoard is entirely fictional. This did not stop newspaper reports from claiming that newly discovered wealth must have had piratical origins. For example, a 'considerable treasure' attributed to Blackbeard was discovered off the island of Blanco in the West Indies.[56] This story had no follow-up or official evidence to suggest it was legitimate. The lack of evidence did not stop the emergence of more claims about Blackbeard's alleged lost treasure. In the nineteenth century, upwards of £14,000 worth of gold and silver coins was found on a farm in Virginia near Tanner Creek. This was claimed to be 'one of the numerous deposits made on our coast by Blackbeard the pirate'.[57] Reports such as this were likely exaggerated to generate media attention, because Blackbeard did not leave any treasure to find.

The reality was that pirates, while they wanted riches, also wanted valuable goods they could sell and use to replenish their own supplies. Pirates had difficulty coming into port, so there were fewer opportunities for them to buy new supplies and repair their ships. Useful items from their prizes were desired above all else. They raided ships for anything they could carry. These items ranged from 'cordage, sails, and tools to casks of dried fish, flour and water'. It was quite rare for pirates to amass a fortune, because their own needs were often more important than riches.[58]

THE DISTRIBUTION OF GOODS was the means of both the pirates' survival and their downfall. Equal pay was essential to keep the peace and guarantee further recruitment and willingness to participate in piracy. Pirates had power to oust their captain or challenge his authority if they felt they were not getting their fair share or had had their own agency taken away. However, taking their shares meant they could (and would) be implicated as pirates, so they had to work hard to make sure everything was protected. Such actions would eventually go as far as to create rumours of buried treasure that persist to the present time. Unfortunately, pirates' fair shares also meant their demise because their participation was said to prove their piracy. As a result, they had to find more ways to make sure order ran smoothly on ships, so a strict regime of regulations became necessary for survival.

2

PUNISHMENTS ON THE PIRATE SHIP, PIRATE OR NOT

'If at any Time we should meet another Marooner (That is, Pyrate) that Man shall sign his Articles without the Consent of our Company, shall suffer such Punishment as the Captain and Company shall think fit.'
Articles on Board the *Revenge*

Although pirate ships were egalitarian and fair societies compared to merchant and naval ships, this did not mean that they were lacking in cruelty. Just like any other ship, pirate ships had to maintain strict order and conduct for everything to run efficiently. Any amount of discord or outright fighting could be detrimental to the running of the ship. Bartholomew Roberts went as far as to outlaw quarrels on his ships. However, pirate ships were made up of a crew that included enslaved people, forced men and others who may have had dubious loyalties. Violence was inevitable. While it was a useful tool for plunder, it could also be necessary in maintaining stability and control aboard ships where conditions were regularly changing.[1]

In this egalitarian society, all of the crew had to be part of the decision-making process. If a punishment needed to be doled out, they all voted on it together. A ship's carpenter named Edward Evans had the bad luck to be captured by Bartholomew Roberts on his journey from 'Virginia to the Port of Bristol' just off the coast of Newfoundland. While Evans and his crew were in custody among Roberts's crew, Evans said that he and his shipmates were 'tried by [the pirates] for their lives by a Jury of Twelve men' led by a pirate named Thomas Lawrence. The pirate jury voted to shoot and kill two of Evans's mates and two others were 'ordered to receive five hundred Lashes each (with a Log line) or thereabouts which they received the same night as the other two persons were shott'.[2] Similar to Roberts, the pirate John Taylor also required a jury of twelve pirates to collectively decide on a pirate's punishment.[3]

Pirates had to develop their own system of punishments in order to maintain the appropriate decorum on board. Not only were strict rules and punishments necessary to keep crew members in line, but they had to be applied to any forced pirate or hostage to keep them from disobeying or causing trouble. Taylor issued rules to keep his pirates in line, such as:

Deserters are condemned to have the nose and ears cut off and to be cast away, naked, on desert isles.

It is forbidden on pain of death to kill or wound in cold blood anyone who has surrendered. It is also commanded to set ashore the crews of captured ships, which must be sent to the bottom if they cannot be used.[4]

However, pirates had to be prepared for such abuses to come back around. When Captain James Kelly attacked a naval vessel, he proved to be inadequately prepared to successfully subdue the officers. The naval officers fired their pistols at the pirates 'and killed them most in the water'. Once enough of the pirates had been killed, the officers seized Kelly's ship and 'abused [the pirates] inhumanely' to the point where they threatened to bite off the finger of anyone who wore a ring.[5]

One of the most frightening punishments one could receive was marooning. The main reasons for marooning were being generally disruptive, breaking various rules, taking more than one's proper share of plunder, deserting during battle, keeping secrets from the crew and stealing.[6] Most men who were taken captive and refused to join the pirate crew were threatened with this fate.[7] Joseph More, who claimed to have been forced into piracy onto Roberts's ship but was found guilty, asked one of the pirates to describe marooning. More said the pirate told him that 'it was a Punishment among them for something notoriously villainous, such they accounted Desertion; and whenever it was carry'd against an Offender, he was put on shore on some uninhabited Cape or Island, with a Gun, some Shot, a Bottle of Powder, and a Bottle of Water, to subsist or starve.'[8] Hostages who wished to escape often hesitated to do so because they knew that if they were caught, they would be either killed or marooned.[9]

If a prisoner knew that a fellow captive planned to escape, they could be punished. A man named Henry Watson was threatened with this while he was held in pirate captivity. In his account, he wrote that the mates and gunners of the captured ships, the *Calicut* and *Ruparrel*, managed to escape in a small boat. Since Watson knew these men, he was blamed for

Marooned pirate, illustration from Howard Pyle, 'Buccaneers and Marooners of the Spanish Main', *Harper's New Monthly Magazine*, LXXV/448 (November 1887).

their escape. He wrote, '[The pirates] called for me and threatened to make me fast and beat me, and afterwards turn me on shore naked on a bare rock, or maroon-key as they called it, without food, wood, or water,' meaning certain death, unless he was fortunate enough to find wood from trees or wrecked ships, find a water source, and have ample plants and animals at hand for food. Fortunately for Watson, he managed to convince the pirates that he had known nothing of the escapees' plans, and they relented.[10]

A man named Richard Hawkins, one of several men captured by the pirate Francis Spriggs, managed to survive his ordeal but described how his former captain, a man named Pike, was marooned. Pike refused to sign Spriggs's articles. Spriggs gave him the option of either signing and becoming a pirate or being cast out. Pike 'scratch'd his Head, and with a demure Look told them, that since he had a Family, and a small Estate . . . he would chuse rather to go than stay'. This was a ruse; he had neither wife, children nor estate. But Spriggs called his bluff and said, 'you shall go, and we will give you your Discharge on your Back; whereupon he was sentenced to receive ten Lashes with a Mannatie Strap from every Man and Boy in the Ship, which was rigorously executed.' Hawkins also refused to sign the articles, so he was given the same punishment. The two men were both 'marooned on an uninhabited island' for an undisclosed amount of time before they were mercifully rescued.[11]

Similar to marooning, keel-hauling was another extreme punishment for violating the rules on a pirate's ship, and was said to be a 'punishment . . . for something notoriously

Francis Spriggs, engraving from Captain Charles Johnson, *The History and Lives of All the Most Notorious Pirates, and Their Crews* (1725).

villainous'. The process was horrific. The insolent pirate was tied to a rope, tossed overboard and dragged underneath the ship. If he did not die from the fall or drown, his body would be mangled as it dragged against the barnacle-covered bottom of the ship. If the pirate did not die in the process, he would almost certainly die from his wounds and/or infection.[12] While this was not a common punishment, it was a terrifying prospect.

Another punishment that was quite rare, despite what popular culture suggests, was 'walking the plank'. According to Francis Grose, author of the 1788 book *A Classical Dictionary of the Vulgar Tongue*, this practice was defined as 'A mode of destroying devoted persons or officers in a mutiny on ship-board, by blindfolding them, and obliging them to walk on a plank laid over the ship's side; by this means, as the mutineers suppose, avoiding the penalty of murder'.[13] It stands to reason that this kind of punishment would be meted out by ruthless creatures such as pirates, but there is actually very little documentation that this happened. In his 1922 book *The Pirates' Who's Who*, Philip Gosse claims that the pirate Stede Bonnet was 'almost the only case known, otherwise than in books of romance, of a pirate making his prisoners walk the plank'.[14] However, he does not specify the event in question. Gosse also cites a Danish pirate named Captain John Derdrake, alias Jack of the Baltic, as being a man who enjoyed drowning his prisoners and was another 'one of the very few pirates, other than those found in works of fiction, who forced his victims to "walk the plank"'.[15] He is most likely referencing the 1883 novel *Treasure Island* by Robert Louis Stevenson, who immortalized this punishment in pirate lore. It is mentioned at the very start of the novel when the protagonist, Jim Hawkins, describes the 'old sea dog' Captain Flint's arrival at his mother's inn. Flint tells tales of his days as a pirate;

Walking the plank, illustration from Howard Pyle, 'Buccaneers and Marooners
of the Spanish Main', *Harper's New Monthly Magazine*, LXXV/448
(November 1887).

Howard Pyle, *Captain Kidd on the Deck of the 'Adventure Galley'*,
1902, crayon and watercolour on illustration board.

Jim states that the stories were 'dreadful ... about hanging, and walking the plank'. Much later in the novel, after Long John Silver arranges a mutiny and takes over the ship as a pirate, Hawkins describes the punishments men were forced to bear at pirates' hands and tells how they were forced to walk the plank blindfolded. Stevenson very likely took this description from Grose's *Dictionary of the Vulgar Tongue*. There is no reliable evidence pointing to any actual instance of a person being forced to walk the plank.

Bartholomew Roberts's article regarding violence stated, 'No striking another on board, but every Man's Quarrels to be ended on Shore at Sword and Pistol.'[16] The antagonists would fight with pistols but if they missed their shots they would turn to cutlasses and fight until the first person drew blood. Part of the reason Roberts ordered conflicts to be solved this way was to keep harmony below decks.[17] In rare cases, Roberts might order the execution of one of his pirates as the ultimate punishment. This was reserved for those who illegally brought women or boys onto ships, anyone who sexually assaulted a woman, or those who were caught deserting. Any of these actions could put an entire pirate ship in danger. On the rarest occasions, a captain might be sentenced to death if he severely abused his power.[18]

One example is Captain Kidd, who was nearly ousted by his disgruntled crew when he was given a privateering assignment in the East Indies between 1696 and 1699. He had been a privateer for the British government for over a decade and had a reputation as a troublesome sailor. He had experience in the Caribbean pursuing the French and had some success when he captured a French ship near Nevis worth £2,000. In 1696 he received his largest commission: to capture French ships in the

East Indies on the *Adventure Galley*. In September of that year he and his crew set out on their adventure towards the Cape of Good Hope.

As stated earlier, Kidd managed to come across a couple of ships but failed to capture either of them. At this point his crew began to outwardly threaten mutiny. By the time they docked in their next port, several of his men abandoned ship while those who stayed were still angry, especially after Kidd killed his gunner, William Moore, in an argument.

Thomas Grant had things to say about Bartholomew Roberts's crew's brutality. Roberts and his partner in crime, Walter Kennedy, plundered Grant's ship. Afterwards, Grant was forced onto their ship, where Kennedy led him into his cabin. Kennedy struck Grant across the face and said, "Damn You I know you and will sacrifice you" and then with his Fist struck the Informant with great Violence upon his Mouth which occasioned his Nose and Mouth to bleed.' It was only luck that spared him: at that moment, one of the other pirates came into the cabin and shouted at Kennedy to stand down. Grant testified that 'ye sd [Kennedy] would have muthered him if some of the crew had not ordered [Kennedy] out of the way'.[19] They knew Roberts would not tolerate such violence, at least not without his permission. However, Kennedy continued to beat the prisoners without Roberts's approval.

Edward Green was another one of Kennedy's unfortunate victims. After Green attempted to hide as many of his ship's goods as possible, Kennedy ordered his men to tie a rope around Green's neck. They 'drew him up under the main top and kept him hanging there about a Minute and let him down again and then put a Rope round his Head and tyed it cross his Ears and twisted it until he was almost blind and insensible'.[20]

Punishments were often reserved for hostages or people forced into piracy. Captain George Cusack was fond of using violence to subdue his victims. In one case after robbing a ship, he took 27 seamen captive and kept them locked for '17 months in close Imprisonment'.[21] Dismemberment was also a useful threat to quell any would-be escapees. Despite discouraging fighting on ships, Bartholomew Roberts was not averse to doling out severe punishments. When William Philips was captured by Roberts and his crew, he was forced to sign the articles and then took part in the pirates' brutality by threatening to cut off one of the other captives' ears. He claimed that he did not want to do this but had to for his own survival. The court did not care, however, and he was pronounced guilty of piracy.[22] Robert Lilburn also faced the threat of losing an ear. While the punishment was not carried out, his crewmate Edward Crispe testified that Lilburn 'seem'd always melancholy and disconsolate, lamenting the condition of Life he was in'. Lilburn was acquitted.[23] William May, another of Roberts's captives, managed to remain steadfast in his resolve. He valiantly refused to sign any articles or take part in piratical activities. Later, at their trial, the witness, John Taylor, who spoke in May's favour, said he saw 'Marks of the Blows upon his Body' after the latter was brutally punished. In this case, May was acquitted and let go.[24]

One of the most detailed eyewitness accounts of Roberts's brutality was from Henry Glasby, the chief mate on the ship *Samuel*. At his trial, he said that he tried to hide from the pirates as they boarded his ship but unfortunately they found him, beat him and threw him overboard. Glasby was then pulled from the water and forced onto the pirate ship. For the next seven days, Roberts's men tried to coerce him to sign the pirate articles. Glasby never wavered in his refusal, but the consequences were harsh. 'He was cut and abused very much.' Glasby attempted to escape his captivity when they landed at an undisclosed location in the West Indies. Unfortunately, 'he was sentenced with two more to be shot.' Luckily for Glasby, he was later acquitted.[25]

Pirates could be especially harsh to captains of conquered ships. As the pirate life was one of egalitarianism, attractive to those fleeing from tyranny, pirates were generally suspicious of the captains they came across. If they found out that a merchant captain on their prize was cruel, they would be so infuriated that their first action would be to perform the 'Distribution of Justice'. The process was to ask the crew whether their captain had treated them well. If the crew all stated that their captain was kind and fair, he was spared any torture or punishment and often allowed to keep his ship after the pirates finished looting it. However, if the captain was discovered to be a cruel leader, he was often beaten or even killed as a form of revenge against all harsh captains.[26]

The buccaneers of the seventeenth century had a reputation for using brutal violence to get what they wanted out of their victims. According to Alexandre Exquemelin, they used a method called 'woodling' in which the buccaneers twisted cords around their victims' foreheads and wrung them so hard that their 'eyes bulged out, big as eggs'. Dislocating their victims' legs via the rack was another popular punishment on their ships. If the rack was not available, the buccaneers would employ 'strappado', in which the victims' hands were tied around their back and then hung by the rope attached to their wrists, causing dislocation and immense pain. Prisoners were hanged, whipped and bludgeoned and had body parts such as noses and lips cut off, which became a favourite practice of Edward Low in the eighteenth

Edward Low shoots a man, engraving from the Dutch edition of
Captain Charles Johnson, *A General History of the Pyrates* (1725).

century. Hair was set on fire and captives were stoned until their bodies were bloodied and broken. If women were unfortunate enough to be held captive, they were abused, raped and held for ransom. The buccaneers starved children or forced them into extreme hard labour. If they were on land, the starving children were made to walk long distances and left to die from exposure to the elements. The captured men were hung by their genitals 'till the weight of their bodies tore them loose' and then the poor captives were stabbed to death. Some buccaneers bound prisoners' feet, smeared them with grease and roasted them over a fire.[27]

Despite pirates' viciousness, it did not serve them well to murder their victims. The above-mentioned brutalities were quite rare. Pirates were not as violent as one might assume and did not kill nearly as many people as one might imagine. Pirates depended on survivors to 'relay the consequences of resisting their demands and spread tales of their wickedness to others'. Sometimes it was best to sink a ship 'to prevent her returning to tell Tales at Home', but pirates still generally released some or all of the crew members who did not join them to return home so they could re-establish communication with others.[28]

Some pirates turned to torture to maximize profits, but it was often a last resort. Captives were loath to give up their goods and even took to hiding their profits or destroying them altogether, which meant lost revenue for the pirates. The most immediate solution was delivering threats of death if the captives resisted. The most severe punishments were restricted to the most uncooperative victims because the threat of torture followed by death was worth more than a simple death threat. However, torture itself was very costly for pirates. Proper torture took time, care, planning and execution and the pirates risked injury if their captive could fight back. The time it took to torture goods out of victims would delay the pirates' next voyage to gather booty and they could lose precious opportunities for grand prizes.[29]

This did not stop torture from happening. In 1721 the *British Gazetteer* published the account of a ship called the *Cassandra* that had been taken by pirates on 8 August 1720. They gave no quarter, with 'their black and bloody Flags being all the time display'd'. Three of the *Cassandra*'s crew were cut to pieces. The rest were held captive for 48 days.[30]

One of the most horrifying ways a pirate could torture a victim was through dismemberment and forced cannibalism. The pirate George Lowther was fond of this treatment. In 1724, the *London Journal* reported that Lowther and his crew 'murdered 45 Spaniards in cold Blood' and 'cut off the said Master's Lips and broiled them before his Face and afterwards murder'd him with the whole Crew being 32 persons'.[31] Another pirate, named John Upton, spent five years terrorizing merchant ships off the North American coast and throughout the West Indies. On 14 November 1725, Upton captured a merchant ship called the *Perry Galley*, captained by Story King. At Upton's trial, King stated that when the pirates took his ship, he was 'hauled up by the Neck till his Senses were gone' and did not regain consciousness until 'the Pirates ran Spikes into his Buttocks'. The man was wounded in 'above 20 places' and then '[the pirates] cut his ear in order to broil it, and thrust a Cartridge filled with Gun-Powder into his Mouth, [with] which they threatened to blow his Brains out'.[32]

To sidestep the need to torture their victims, pirates could fall back on a far less bloody tactic: the terror inspired by their reputations. Fear intimidated people and this allowed pirates to

George Lowther, engraving from Captain Charles Johnson, *The History and Lives of All the Most Notorious Pirates, and Their Crews* (1725).

win battles much more efficiently. The fewer people they killed, the fewer crew the pirates would lose. It was best to let people live. Edward Teach followed this philosophy throughout his career. As Blackbeard, he could subdue his victims without a single wound being inflicted. Teach seemed to have a special skill and knew exactly how to play his hand. Despite making sure that people far and wide believed him to be pure evil, he was not that violent. It is almost certain that he never killed anyone in his career until his final battle. His reputation was enough. He did not need to prove himself by acts of excessive violence.[33]

PIRATE SOCIETY WOULD CRACK without strict rules on a ship. Order had to be maintained or else everyone's safety could be at risk. Even more important, the pirates had to have an equal say in the punishment to make sure it fit the transgression. Pirates were allowed the power to keep their captain in check by voting him out if he was too cruel. Punishments served more than just maintaining order on a pirate ship. They were effective in allowing pirates to capture ships and subdue their enemies. This made them infamous and terrifying, prompting pirates' victims to surrender much faster than they might have done otherwise.

Extreme violence, such as torture and forced cannibalism, was very much the exception, not the rule, although one cannot deny its effectiveness. Most pirates did not demonstrate the brutality of men such as Low and Lowther. However, violence was inevitable on a pirate ship, whether it was because of malcontents, fighting, breaking the rules or a realistic consequence of battle. Therefore, it was necessary for pirates to know their articles and to swear by them. It kept everyone in check and all pirates knew where they stood. Strict regulations helped keep pirates safe so they could be successful when risks such as injury or illness became reality.

3

HEALTH AND SAFETY
ON THE PIRATE SHIP

'He that shall have the Misfortune to lose a Limb,
in the Time of Engagement, shall have the Sum of
one hundred and fifty Pounds Sterling, and remain
with the Company as long as he shall think fit.'
The Articles of Captain George Lowther, and his Company

Among pirates, injuries were so common that the Scottish writer Robert Louis Stevenson used them to create the look of the character Long John Silver in his novel *Treasure Island*: 'His left leg was cut off close by the hip, and under his left shoulder he carried a crutch, which he managed with wonderful dexterity, hopping about it like a bird. He was very tall and strong, with a face as big as a ham – plain and pale, but intelligent and smiling.'[1] Despite his disability, Long John Silver proves himself to be the most powerful pirate in the novel. Long John Silver's physical description is not wholly accurate of a typical pirate. Pirates' physical appearance took on the wear and tear of constant heat, sun and salt. They wore kerchiefs to prevent sunburn, but the long exposure darkened everyone's skin. They developed dark tans and their skin took on a weatherly and leathered look. Those with darker complexions would tan a deeper colour. Most had facial hair and the hair on the top of their head grew long and was often tied back. Pirates were slim and sinewy because of the hard work and limited quantities of food. Many had yellowed or missing teeth and they all had extreme body odour.[2]

Another character from *Treasure Island* is an apt image of pirates: Captain Flint, the 'old sea dog' who arrives at the beginning of the novel and ultimately leaves the famed treasure map behind. He is described as 'a tall, strong, heavy, nut-brown man, his tarry pigtail falling over the shoulders of his soiled blue coat, his hands ragged and scarred, with black, broken nails, and the saber cut across one cheek, a dirty, livid white'.[3] Life at sea was difficult and messy. Tar was commonly used in hair and on clothes because it protected pirates from wind, salt, rain and the sun.

We do not have pirates' records, such as logbooks or medical documents, either because they deliberately did not keep them or because they have been lost or destroyed. Therefore, in terms of how to ascertain how they treated illness and injury on ships, we must look at naval and merchant examples. Boiled down, pirates were sailors and all ships had their own methods for maintaining health and safety. Navy ships did take care in terms of medical practice. Ship's surgeons had to pass examinations and their chests and journals were inspected, while surviving logs show detailed daily attention to injuries and the various maladies that befell sailors, along with their treatments.[4] However, these ships were still reputed to be places of misery and suffering, which are major reasons why people left that career and entered piracy. Aside from cruel officers, navy ships were overpopulated, with sailors sharing cramped quarters. Illness swept through berths – one sick person could wipe out a whole ship. Bloodletting was still practised, which further weakened the patient. Injury was a constant risk and could be fatal if infection set in.[5]

The ship's surgeon oversaw keeping sailors fit and healthy. However, most surgeons only worked when illness or injury occurred and there was very little preventative care. Surgeons spent the majority of their time setting bones, treating wounds, pulling teeth, distributing medicine and administering treatments such as bloodletting. Typical illnesses included those that are diet-related – such as scurvy – malaria, yellow fever and sexually transmitted infections.

A pirate's career was fraught with danger due to the numerous battles they engaged in along with the hazards of sea life. Traumatic injury was common. Drowning was always a risk because few pirates knew how to swim. Sunburn, sunstroke, heat exhaustion, hypothermia, exposure and even frostbite could be risks as well.[6] However, a pirate's vocation was not necessarily ruined if he lost a limb or another part of the body. Missing arms, legs, hands, fingers and eyes were all relatively commonplace. Unlike on merchant or naval ships, however, pirates were adequately compensated for their injuries. Compensation was standard in every set of pirate articles. There was no guarantee that a pirate crew would be stable, so captains had to make sure they had good retention. One of the ways to guarantee this was to promise extra funds to those who were maimed in any manner on the ship. Evidence of this rule shows up as early as Alexandre Exquemelin's seventeenth-century book *The History of the Buccaneers of America*, in which he wrote that injured pirates received anywhere between two hundred and six hundred pieces of eight depending on the severity or location of their injury. The lowest amount of compensation was paid for the loss of an eye or finger, while the loss of a right arm guaranteed the most funds.[7] All pirates had to allocate some of their shares towards a common fund to provide for crew members who sustained one of these injuries. No disability was discriminated against. This rarely happened on a merchant or navy ship.[8]

Surgeons were not standard crewmates, and were a necessity, which is why pirates were always hoping to recruit or force one into their crew. In the seventeenth century, the Admiralty began regulating surgical practices at sea. Surgeons received higher pay, about twopence per head per treatment, along with a grant of £10 towards any instruments required. Not only that, by 1703 all surgeons were required to keep journals to record their cases, treatments and results.[9] As a result, a skilled surgeon had the necessary experience to treat and heal injuries and illness. It is no wonder that pirates were keen to force one of these professionals into their crew.

An experienced surgeon was expected to have a plethora of instruments to carry out their duties. The first known naval surgeon, John Woodall, author of *The Surgeon's Mate* (published in 1617), created an extensive list of the necessary items:

> Incision knives.
> Dismembering knives.
> Catlings [double-bladed surgery knife].
> Rasours [razors].
> Trepans [saws for perforating the skull].
> Trafine [cylindrical blade].
> Lavatories [bowls for washing].
> Head sawes.
> Dismembering sawes.
> Dismembering Nippers.

Mallet and chisel.

Speculum Oris.

Speculum Oris with a screw.

Speculum Linguae.

Speculum Ani.

Cauterizing irons.

Storks bills.

Crowes bills.

Terebellum [bullet extraction screw].

Incision sheers.

Probes or flamules.

Spatulaes great and small.

Spatulum Mondani.

For teeth.

    Paces.

    Pullicans.

    Forcers or punches.

    Crowes bills.

    Flegmes.

    Gravers.

    Small files.

One bundle of small German instruments.

Glister sirings.

Small sirings.

Catheter.

Wax Lights.[10]

The description of Long John Silver demonstrates the realities of the real dangers pirates faced. All types of sailing involved risks that were often destructive to the body. Injuries at sea were guaranteed. Wounds often led to infection, which might require amputation should they turn gangrenous.[11] Amputation was not taken lightly. This was an extremely risky surgery and the infection rate on a pirate ship was staggeringly high. If a pirate ship had a surgeon, this person would have to oversee the patient's progress for at least a month after the procedure. *The Surgeon's Mate* recommended a clean saw, a dismembering knife, an incision knife, two stitching needles and waxed thread. As soon as the limb was removed, topical treatments had to be applied, a combination of medicines and plasters. The first thing to do was to apply pressure to stop the bleeding and the medicines were used to close off the vessels to stem the flow. Astringents used included medicinal clays and powders and tinctures from various plants such as wild pomegranate trees.[12] Afterwards, it was necessary to make sure the patient kept the remaining limb elevated and ate 'a slender diet, namely, no flesh'.[13]

When justifying their turn to piracy, the pirates John Massey and George Lowther claimed that they had come upon men who were severely ill with diarrhoea and who had nothing to eat or drink but mouldy bread and contaminated water. They said the men were waiting for wages owed to them from their merchant ships but that 'there was no allowance granted from the Company that would either supply them with what was Necessary upon any Terms.' These men should have been allowed to go home after a six-month service, but had been told by the merchants that 'they should stay till they Rotted' because there were no doctors available. '[They] had no other prospect but to Dye there neither being due Care, Provision, nor Lodging suitable for any Christian.' The merchants would not even allow their men their daily ration of wine.[14] The terrible conditions Massey described were all too common. Illnesses such as typhus and dysentery killed many sailors during the seventeenth and

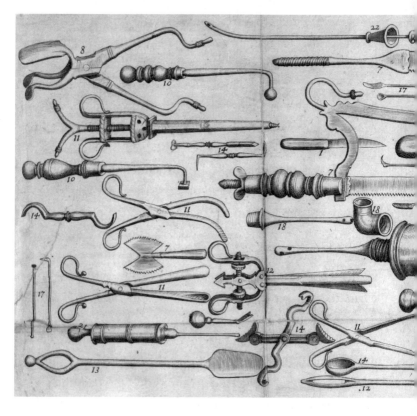

eighteenth centuries. These unsanitary conditions could become so dangerous that ships would have to be abandoned. Mass outbreaks of fever required fumigation by burning sulphur, applying lime or clearing out filth and human waste.[15]

There were several testimonies from either pirates or eyewitnesses about care they received while ill. Joseph Bradish, the pirate captain who was executed alongside Captain Kidd, was one such man who made sure his victims were treated against any illness. In 1698, cholera swept through Kidd's ship, so they had to make land in Madagascar. An account given by Robert Anby and Ralph Peck claimed that Bradish 'was as tender as a Mother to any that were sick, daily minding the Doctor of

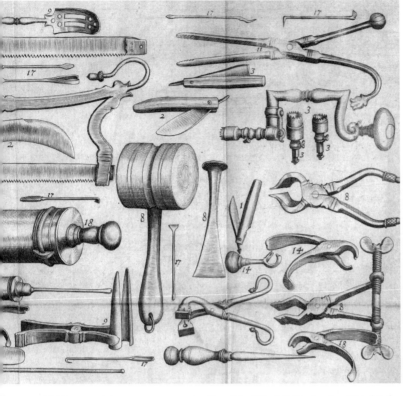

Ship's surgeon's instruments, engraving from John Woodall, *The Surgions Mate* (1617).

his charge'. He made sure to check in with the doctor daily to make sure that any sick person received 'fresh provisions'. Those who were in good health, '[Bradish] endeavoured to keep so, by refreshing twice or thrice a day in bad weather with Drams'. The witnesses swore that he was 'the most religious, sober, careful and kind Commander that we knew or heard of ever'.[16] The surgeon of the ship confirmed their statements:

> I do declare that I never saw in any of his Majesty's Ships, or any other where I have been, better Victuals or Victualling, nor never so much care taken, nor

kindness shewn, both toward Soul and Body, as was by the Commander, both to well and sick; for tho' it pleased God to bless us with so healthful a Passage, that we never had any Man lay down three days together, yet hath the Captain often circumvented me in sending Broth or other fresh Provisions to sick Men from his own Table ... Insomuch that I am ready to give Oath, I have heard them say sundry times, that they never saw so good Victualling, nor a Commander so kind and careful of his Men.[17]

Pirates knew they would receive the care they needed, which helped keep them loyal.

Battle was the number one cause of severe injury, including loss of limbs. Cannons and guns could rip arms or legs right off any of the fighters.[18] Splinters, chunks of wood and shot could tear through flesh and bone without mercy. Overturned guns crushed limbs while falling masts cracked skulls. Burns were common thanks to flames coming out of cannons' vents or cartridges that fired accidentally. These wounds were often subject to amputation, which could kill the injured person in such a chaotic and unsanitary environment. If pirates killed many of their foes, they would lay out the bodies on deck to demoralize their enemy. If the pirates lost crew members, they would be thrown overboard.[19]

Stede Bonnet infamously injured himself in a failed battle that practically ended his captaincy. He was an unusual pirate from the outset. Born in Bridgetown, Barbados, in 1688, he decided he had enough of marriage, fatherhood and a successful career as a plantation owner. Bonnet wanted to become a pirate, so in 1717 he left his family and hired a shipwright to build him a vessel, which he named *Revenge*. He hired a pirate crew but never had the respect of his men. For one thing, no legitimate pirate would ever purchase a ship. They would inherit or capture one. His biggest offence, however, was that he had no maritime experience whatsoever, so he made poor decisions, the most egregious of which was an attack on a large Spanish man-o'-war. The Spanish fired first and before the *Revenge* could counterattack, the Spaniards maneouvered round and unleashed a massive round of cannon fire. The battle killed or injured many of the crew, including Bonnet himself. He was knocked unconscious and had to be taken below deck. He would never fully recover from his injuries and was left with a painful limp for the final year of his life. This is likely one of the reasons why Edward Teach was able to assume command of his ship after the two joined up in Nassau.[20]

One of the ways pirates guaranteed their success – or at least forced their victims into total submission – was by maiming them. This was the favourite practice of the pirate Edward Low, who was known to brutally cut body parts off his victims. This was described in the trial against his pirates when his victim John Welland of the *Amsterdam Merchant* gave testimony about the torture he faced at the hands of Low. Welland 'deposed . . . that he was sent on board the Fortune [Low's ship] where Low was where he had his right Ear cut off, and was wounded very much with a Cutlass, and turn'd down the Hatches, where he lay bleeding for two or three Hours with a Centinel over him'. He said that if it were not for the kindness of a pirate named Patrick Cunningham, he would have died of his injuries. Cunningham brought Welland water and fetched a surgeon, who treated the wound before any infection could occur.[21]

Illness was a convenient excuse when pirates tried to claim their innocence at their trials. There were several cases when pirates happened to be down with the 'bloody flux', today known as dysentery, or something similar when a battle occurred, rendering them incapable of participating. Darby Mullins, a former member of Captain Kidd's crew who was a chief witness in his condemnation, provided testimony that he himself was taken ill when the crew landed at Madagascar. At the trial, Mullins said he was ready to take the Proclamation, meaning a pardon for confessing his crimes and naming his accomplices, that is, Kidd. At his cross-examination, he was asked, 'What have you to shew, to intitle you to the benefit of this Proclamation?' Mullins replied, 'I was ready to dye of the Bloody Flux, and not able to go in myself [to claim his pardon] but I sent my name in to the Governor [of Madagascar].' He then explained that he used this opportunity to leave Kidd's crew officially to escape further actions of piracy.[22] The bloody flux, which nearly killed him, ultimately saved his life: Mullins walked free with his pardon.

Mullins was an exception to the rule. This excuse was used so regularly that it was not often accepted. James Skyrm, one of Captain Roberts's forced pirates, said he was innocent of piracy because he was too ill to participate in any battles or raids. He said 'that he had been sick for several Months, unable for Duty, never on Deck at taking any Prize of late'. However, 'His being sick the Court thought was only an Aggravation of his Crime in coming out', and they could see he had been alert often enough to know about the piratical actions on board. The fact that he did nothing to stop any of it and therefore 'fought against the King's Colours' rendered him guilty.[23]

Diarrhoea, or the flux, was very common on ships. There was little knowledge about the inner workings of the body, but sailors believed food would be the cure and replenish the purging. William Dampier wrote that a starchy plant called sago mixed with 'Milk of Almonds' was a 'great Binder' and could alleviate symptoms.[24] That was a more exotic remedy, however, and sailors (including pirates) were inclined to use treatments and food more familiar to them. The physician William Cockburn said that 'the common People' preferred an egg boiled in brandy or vinegar. This treatment was also employed by the sea surgeon Thomas Aubrey.[25]

If the requisite foodstuffs were not available, the next solution was fumigation. For centuries, people believed that illness was caused by bad-smelling air, known as miasma. By that logic, the air needed to be cleansed and made to smell sweet again for the sick to recover. The bowels of the ship, however, provided no such relief. If a pirate ship was lucky enough to have a surgeon, they might try burning herbs and fanning the smoke in the direction of the sick seamen.[26]

Death at sea was all too common. Disposing of the dead was simple but still a ritual. Sea burials had to be done quickly because there was no place to store a dead body: the stench would become unbearable quicker than anyone could imagine, and seamen did not like carrying dead men on board. They were a superstitious lot and death was their greatest fear. Preparation of the body was simple. 'When he is dead [we] sew him up in an old blanket or piece of old canvas, and tie his feet two or three cannon bullets, and so to heave him overboard, wishing his poor soul at rest, not having a minister to read over his grave, nor any other ceremonies.'[27] The rituals included a prayer for the dead and firing the guns. Someone would usually offer some words or share a memory of the departed before the body was cast into the sea. The rest paid their respects, but they did not get emotional or allow grief to get in their way. The highest-ranking crew members had more elaborate sea burials and were often sent into the water in an actual coffin rather than a hammock or sack.

It stands to reason that most pirate burials would take place at sea. While some historians argue that at least half of mariners preferred to be buried on land, there are very few records from the Golden Age of Piracy to suggest this.[28] It is not implausible that many sailors might have preferred underground interment because of fear of drowning or even of the sea itself. *The General History of the Pyrates* mentions some land-based burials, all of whom were captains. The best description is of the grave of Captain John Halsey, which was 'made in a garden of water-melons, and fenced in with palisades to prevent being rooted up by wild hogs, of which there are plenty in those parts'.[29] The only other burials mentioned are of three more captains: Thomas White, John Cornelius and John Bowen, the latter of whom 'was buried in a highway [in Madagascar], for the priests would not allow him holy ground, as he was a heretic'.[30] *A General History of the Pyrates* suggests that pirate land burials were reserved for the highest-ranking crew members. However, it is not unlikely that other pirates were buried on land, because the majority of them sailed near coastlines to be ready for plunder and many took refuge inland.

If a pirate was to be buried on land, the body would have to be preserved. The best way to do this was through embalming the corpse. According to a sixteenth-century French surgeon, Ambroise Paré, one must remove the organs but separate the heart and embalm it on its own so the family can decide what to do with it. The blood was removed via arterial incisions 'along the arms, thighs, legs, back, loins and buttocks, especially where the greater veins and arteries run'. Once the blood ran out, the body had to be washed with a 'spunge dipped in aqua vitae, and strong vinegar, wherein shall bee boiled wormwood, aloes, coloquintida, common salt and alum'. After that, any open passage had to be stuffed with powdered spices such as mint, dill, lavender, rosemary, marjoram, thyme, wormwood, gentian root, cinnamon, benjamin, myrrh and aloes. Once the body was sufficiently stuffed and perfumed, it was to be 'annointed with Turpentine dissolved with oil of Roses and Camomil, adding, if you shall think fit some chemical oils of spices and then let it bee against strewed over with the forementioned powder: then wrap it in a linnen-cloth, and then in [waxed] cloth'.[31] This complex procedure allowed the body to stay whole for a certain amount of time without succumbing to putrefaction, which many captains feared led to disease. Unfortunately, these materials were not easy to come by and so receiving such treatment in death was often a pipe dream.

Without embalming, it was nearly impossible to keep a dead body until land was reached (unless, of course, the ship was already situated near a coastline), so burial at sea was the most necessary option. Therefore, a body had to be prepared quickly in the hot, humid climate. The body had to be washed and dressed and then weights were attached to the feet so it would sink. The feet were chosen deliberately, so the body would be dropped into the ocean feet first and sink in a standing position. However, it had to face away from the ship to ensure its ghost would not come back to haunt the crew.[32] Once the weights were attached, the body was sewn into a shroud. The material was usually the deceased's hammock, but sometimes it might be simply spare materials. Hammocks were generally preferred, however. According to David Stewart, this was because many sailors were suspicious of wearing a dead man's clothes, and it would be natural for this taboo to be applied to a deceased person's hammock as well. Also, the hammock would have been seen as an appropriate burial shroud because of its association with sleeping. Sleep was a popular metaphor for death.[33]

While documents do not officially state this superstition, the majority of sailors had numerous tales that symbolized death at sea. This would naturally transfer to real-life death practices.

One of the final practices is the debated last stitch through the nose. As the deceased's shroud was sewn up, the final stitch went through the nose, which was used as a confirmation that the person was actually dead. The idea that this was a standard maritime practice has become part of the pop-culture imagination. But the last stitch does not make a source appearance until an 1831 account of a sailmaker: 'I have heard it said that it was customary to run the needle in the last stitch through the nose of the corpse; some may do it, but I certainly never remarked it myself.' This suggests that it was always a mysterious topic.[34] There is no evidence of this practice being performed during the seventeenth and eighteenth centuries.

PIRATES' PHYSICAL HEALTH WAS instrumental in guaranteeing success on a pirate ship. They were generally healthier than many other maritime counterparts because they were able to plunder fresh food and medicines for their personal care. Frequent stops on land also allowed them access to more fresh water, citrus fruits to ward off scurvy and animals for protein and calories. With disease and injury major threats, a healthier diet was key to survival. Plunder allowed more surgical instruments, which meant that pirates could survive infections more often than sailors on merchant and naval ships. Pirates' health was instrumental in keeping a functioning ship and bonded crew.

4

SEX, SEXUALITY AND RELATIONSHIPS ON AND OFF THE PIRATE SHIP

'No Boy or Woman to be allowed among them.
If any Man found seducing any of the latter Sex,
and carry'd her to Sea, disguised,
he was to suffer Death.'
Articles of Captain Bartholomew Roberts

Did pirates have relationships? Did they have sex? Many pirates had families onshore that they would be with if they were lucky enough to be docked at home. Many were known to visit brothels, but it was not common practice to bring women onto the ship for sexual relations, and the penalty for those who did so was most often death. Many captains believed that bringing women or male companions onto the ship could cause conflict between pirates, competing allegiances and/or dangerous distractions. Often, misconduct onshore was forbidden, particularly rape, which was also punishable by death.

Some pirates developed romantic and sexual relationships with each other that were loving, or to relieve sexual frustration and/or to be legally bound to someone. Pirates could be married on ship and sometimes engaged in a social commitment known as *matelotage*. This meant that they could name their partner as their heir. However, some pirate captains banned sex and romantic relationships altogether. The goal was to discourage homosexuality and any potential form of dissent among the crew. This chapter will also discuss the reality of women on pirate ships, such as Anne Bonny and Mary Read, and dispel the myth that women were unlucky on board.

Sexual relationships on pirate ships are a subject that has led to much fascination in popular culture and social media. The television show *Black Sails* features several same-sex romantic plots between fictional characters and real-life figures such as Anne Bonny and a female sex worker named Max, intended to be a stand-in for her real-life crewmate, Mary Read. Similarly, Taika Waititi's TV show *Our Flag Means Death* features a fabricated romance between Stede Bonnet and Edward Teach. Popular fictions such as these have led to a widespread belief that homosexuality ran rampant on pirate ships. However, there is no written evidence of this, which has caused the subject to become fraught with debate among historians.

There is some evidence to suggest that pirates carried out sexual relationships with each other. Captain Bartholomew Roberts specifically stated in his articles that 'No boy or woman [was] to be allowed among them.' Boys often made up a portion of sailing crews, so it is notable that in this case they were banned alongside women. This implies that they were in the same category of possible sexual relationships, which could cause complications among the men such as jealousy and frustration.

Many pirates entered their career after leaving the Royal Navy, which was rife with same-sex relationships. Ships' officers were known to select those in the lowest tier as sexual partners. According to the historian B. R. Burg, surviving testimony stated that captains were

> almost never called to account for fondling, groping, kissing, or buggering other officers ... Captains did not have sex with lieutenants, lieutenants did not have sex with warrant officers, nor did warrant officers customarily have sex with other warrant officers, petty officers, or the 'ratings', as seamen were customarily called by those wielding power.

The preferred sexual partners were younger boys, who often made up anywhere between 6 and 10 per cent of the crew.[1] Higher-ranking pirates from this background may well have continued this practice.

Despite this sexual activity, the Articles of War under the Royal Navy had two laws specifically concerning sexual transgressions. Homosexuality was both silenced and taboo. At the time, homosexuality itself did not exist as a concept, and would not be established as such until the nineteenth century.[2] Instead, the laws came down to terminology. The 29th article read, 'If any person in the fleet shall commit the unnatural and detestable sin of buggery and sodomy with man or beast, he shall be punished with death by the sentence of a court martial.' 'Sodomy' and 'buggery' were interchangeable terms that meant acts of both penetration and ejaculation.[3] Roberts commanded a similar punishment for bringing a boy on board: death.

Part of this could be in reaction to the mistreatment sailors suffered on other ships. Sex could be used as a means of power and punishment. Admiralty law did not interfere with regulations on board ships, so captains decided appropriate punishments, which included targeted abuse. One captain named Samuel Norman ordered one of his ship boys to 'fetch a Pail of Water . . . to wash his Leggs, Thighs, & privy Parts'. When the boy refused, Norman forced him into submission, 'and whilst he was washing the same, he then said Samuel let down the [boy's] Trousers . . . & had the carnal use of him'. Captain Norman did this to the boy several times throughout the voyage. Some sailors believed that 'they had better be dead than live in Misery' under such a predatory captain.[4]

Homosexuality, though, was a reality in this environment. When male Europeans began colonizing the Caribbean during the seventeenth century, there was a shortage of women. Confined in tight quarters for long periods of time without any privacy for activities such as masturbation caused sexual frustration to build. This social situation, combined with close relationships between the men, allowed sexual relationships to begin. At some point, so many men were having sex with each other that the French governor of Tortuga, Jean Le Vasseur, sought to stop it at all costs. He believed that 'sodomy' was happening because of the lack of women in the Caribbean. To solve this problem, he imported 1,650 female prostitutes to the island to give the men a sexual outlet.[5]

Evidence of individual relationships is practically nonexistent. However, there is a possible case of two pirates who had a romantic relationship with each other: Robert Culliford and John Swann. Before meeting Swann, Culliford sailed with Captain Kidd in the 1680s, before the latter entered the East Indies. Culliford had a contentious relationship with Kidd and even instigated a mutiny against him. The two parted ways at

Madagascar and later some of Kidd's crew would abandon him to work with Culliford.

Culliford met John Swann while they were both in prison between 1692 and 1696. Over time they may have developed a romantic relationship. The evidence is sketchy, but records show that they lived together on Île Sainte-Marie just off the coast of Madagascar.[6] For reasons unknown, they parted ways in 1698 and Culliford took up with Kidd once again when the captain arrived in the East Indies and infamously robbed the *Quedah Merchant*. While Culliford went into pirating, Swann remained on Madagascar. Soon afterwards, they both independently decided to pursue a pardon, and received one together at the same time in Madagascar. However, they did not reunite. Swann decided to head to Barbados while Culliford broke his pardon, returned to piracy and was arrested and executed alongside Kidd on 23 May 1701.[7] While the sources are open to interpretation, it makes for good debate.

One of the most complex arguments between pirate historians concerns pirates' sexuality. Some forms of civil unions were performed on ships, but were they for love or logistical reasons? These unions were *matelotage* agreements, bonds between two men who would share everything in common with each other. This included food, drink, money and even women on occasion. The term comes from the French word *matelot*, which simply means 'sailor' but became associated with seventeenth-century sailors and pirates who created bonds with each other.[8] The purpose of a *matelotage* was to create a legal union so that one of the men could inherit the other's goods if they died. An example of this was an agreement signed between two pirates named Francis Reed and John Beavis:

Be it knowen to all men by this preasants that Francis
Reed and John Beavis are [entered] in Consortship
together, And in Caise that any sudden [Accident] should
happen to ye fords Francis Reed That what gold, Silver,
or any other thing whatsoever shall Lawfully become, or
fall to ye fords John Beavis. As also if that any sudden
[Accident] should happen to ye above written John Beavis,
That what gold, silver, or any thing [else] shall Lawfully
be Come or fall to the fords Francis Reed.

The agreement was written and signed in Fort Dauphin, Madagascar, by the two men and witnessed by Robert Arnott, making
the *matelotage* official.[9]

Very few pirates were able to help their families after arrest
and even fewer allowed any documents to survive, lest they be
their downfall. However, one pirate who escaped arrest despite
being part of Captain Kidd's crew, Robert Collover, managed to
contact a deceased crewmate's wife and provide her with her husband's share of loot. The fact that he had this share at the ready
suggests that the two may have been in a *matelotage*. He wrote:

Mrs Whalley
[Beknown] this is [Concerning] youer husbondes will
which is left wholly to you and yr Children ye same.
Beknown that he left thirty hundred Pcs of eight whereof
Capt. Shelley ships you ye Billes of Loading and Edward
Buckmaster [a former seaman turned New York tavern
keeper who signed on to Kidd's voyage, but left him at
St. Mary's to join Collover] Left in charge to be delivered
the [freight] to bee payed not mor.
     Madam, yours to com[mand]

Rob. Collover

April ye 6th 1699, from: St Maries[10]

One of the most detailed pirate relationships we know about is the marriage between 'Calico' Jack Rackham and the female pirate Anne Bonny. The latter became a pirate because she married this particular captain after leaving an unhappy marriage with a disaffected sailor named James Bonny. Bonny had married Anne, the daughter of a wealthy plantation owner in the Carolinas, for her dowry, but her father disowned her for eloping with a penniless sailor. Having lost the fortune he desired, Bonny no longer wanted Anne as a wife. The pair arrived in Nassau in either 1718 or 1719 and separated almost immediately. Alone and lonely, Anne began frequenting taverns and befriended sailors and pirates who passed through the city.[11] It was in one of these places that she met the freshly minted pirate captain Jack Rackham in the spring of 1720.

It was love at first sight for this couple. They wanted to marry, but there was the small inconvenience of Anne's marital status. They approached James Bonny to ask for an annulment and while he initially agreed upon the condition of receiving a sizeable sum of money, he later recanted. Rackham decided to see if Bonny would consent to sell Anne to him. Wife-selling was not an uncommon practice in the West Indies, where women were vastly outnumbered by men at a ratio of one woman to every nine men.[12] Women were seen as pieces of property for ownership, but in Anne's case, her sale was a divorce bargain. Anne volunteered to take place in this exchange because, oddly enough, it was one of the few ways she could claim agency. Women could put themselves up for sale to get out of a bad marriage, such as one with a violent or impotent husband.[13]

Jack Rackham, engraving from Captain Charles Johnson, *The History and Lives of All the Most Notorious Pirates, and Their Crews* (1725).

Unfortunately, Governor Woodes Rogers was against wife-selling. When he got word of Rackham's petition, he threatened to have Anne publicly whipped and thrown into prison for 'loose behaviour'.[14] Anne promised to stop the divorce proceedings and prove herself a good wife to her husband.[15] This, of course, was a lie. Once Woodes's threats went away, Anne and Rackham took matters into their own hands. On 21 August 1720, they sneaked away at night with a new crew headed to the high seas as pirates. The next day, they captured the fastest-known ship in the Bahamas, the *William*, which Rackham renamed *Revenge*. Anne's foray into piracy was complete, thanks to the love she had for her new husband.

Anne Bonny sailed with Mary Read (whose origins are unknown) under Rackham between August and October 1720.

During their two-month tenure as pirates, they were known to be two of the fiercest fighters their victims ever encountered at sea during the Golden Age of Piracy. They fought harder and cursed more than any of the men. Bonny and Read were also ruthless towards their would-be victims. One of the chief witnesses against them at their trial was a woman named Dorothy Thomas. Thomas provided one of the most detailed descriptions of their ferocity. They 'wore Mens Jackets, and long Trouzers, and Handkerchiefs tied about their Heads; and that each of them had a Machet and Pistol in their hands'. Dorothy said, despite their masculine behaviour, that she had immediately recognized they were women 'by the largeness of their Breasts'. Rackham was loath to take a woman prisoner, but both Bonny and Read 'cursed and swore at the Men, to murther [Dorothy Thomas]' lest she later identify and speak out against them. Rackham ignored their advice and ordered his crew to let Thomas go.[16] Unfortunately, the two women were correct. Thomas would be one of the chief eyewitnesses to give evidence against them at their trial in November 1720 at St Jago de la Vega, Jamaica.

Their male dress was not intended to disguise them, but was worn for practical reasons and to intimidate their victims. Male clothing allowed for more freedom of movement. Keeping their hair loose and shirts open startled their prey into submission. Who would expect such a feminine display?

The myths of sirens and mermaids influenced the view that female pirates might be seen as pagan goddesses while fulfilling matriarchal fantasies that had to be destroyed for men's safety. Pirate men were seen as virile. Women who invaded their space threatened their masculinity, especially if women assumed the men's virility by taking on their dress.[17] The feminist historian Jo Stanley argues that female pirates were depicted with

Anne Bonny and Mary Read convicted of piracy,
28 November 1720, engraving from Captain Charles Johnson,
A General History of the Robberies and Murders of the Most Notorious Pyrates (1724).

unsheathed swords while dressed in tight clothing to give them 'an erect, boyish appearance'. This provoked conflicting feelings in male pirates: arousal and alarm. The image of the magnificent female pirate reminded them of their own inferiority, as they were both attracted to and jealous of these female trespassers.[18] Early prints of Bonny and Read express this anxiety about gender. They were depicted with feminine hairstyles of long, curly hair that flowed behind them in the wind and large breasts openly displayed, while they also appear to have facial stubble.[19] This gave them a contradictory aggressiveness that threatened the natural order.

James Dobbin, one of Rackham's surviving victims, who testified at his trial, was shocked when two long-haired women emerged in battle. Bonny and Read cursed and swore with more ferocity than any of the other pirates. Their shirts were open, exposing their breasts for all to see. Their decision to fight topless was not meant to be sexual, but to use their femininity to defy their enemy's expectations of pirates. Not only that, this served as a way to shock their foes as a distraction tactic. This allowed the women to gain the upper hand in close combat. The two women had a choice: hide and submit to restrictive social norms or claim agency over their womanhood to show the world that they were not submissive to the female social order. Their fighting skills were equal to or even better than the men's. Their ferocity was unmatched. Their language was a signal that they had no fear of anyone or any consequence. Dobbin had never encountered these kinds of women and he and the other merchants in the attack were stunned into submission.[20]

Anne Bonny's and Mary Read's stories are also among the most debated subjects in regard to same-sex relationships on ships. There has been speculation that they were in a romantic relationship to the point where many accept it as fact rather than theory. Much of their history was recorded in Captain Charles Johnson's *A General History of the Pyrates*, but their biographies were heavily fictionalized for the sake of entertainment.

Johnson deliberately embellished their stories to give them 'a little Air of a Novel'.[21] One of the most famous parts of the story is when Anne attempts to seduce Mary, who is in disguise as a male pirate, only to be disappointed when she discovers the truth. Even so, they are said to have had such a close relationship that Jack Rackham, Anne's husband, is nearly driven to murderous jealousy until he learns that Mary is indeed female.

The idea of lesbianism did not exist during the eighteenth century because female sexuality was not a concept. Women were never criminalized for having sex with other women.[22] Sexual relations between women were generally seen as non-threatening because, in a man's view, sex between two women wasn't 'real' sex and would not result in a woman losing her virginity. Sexual acts that did not involve the penis and sperm were not perceived

Title page of the Dutch edition of Captain Charles Johnson,
A General History of the Pyrates (1725), showing Mary Read and Anne Bonny
with their pirate flag on the deck of a boat above a chained captive.

as threats to masculinity and manhood.[23] Not only that, women were economically dependent on men in all parts of society, so it was believed that a lesbian relationship could not be a long-term reality.[24]

The idea that Anne and Mary were a lesbian couple appears in a brief updated passage in the second edition of *A General History of the Pyrates*, known as *The History and Lives of all the Most Notorious Pirates and Their Crews*, published in 1725. According to the publisher of this edition, Mary entered into piracy because she fell in love with Anne while in Nassau.[25] According to Rictor Norton, a social historian of LGBTQ+ history, there is no historical evidence to support this idea, and the two women were 'at most' bisexual.[26] Even so, this idea became accepted as fact.

The idea about their possible lesbian relationship became solidified in 1974 when the feminist writer Susan Baker published an essay entitled 'Anne Bonny and Mary Read: They Killed Pricks', which described a sexual relationship between them. She used contemporary ideas from the women's movement about breaking the silence around lesbian identities, which have been lost or ignored in historical writings. She cited the infamous passage in *A General History of the Pyrates* that describes how Rackham flew into a jealous rage thinking that Mary was a man. Her essay circulated widely and her theory became so popular and accepted that some suggested that the pair's guilty sentences in November 1720 were actually a result of their sexuality.[27] As recently as early 2021, sculptor Amanda Cotton created statues in tribute to them to celebrate 'the pair who broke gender boundaries and, according to historians, became lovers after they pitched up on a pirate ship'.[28]

In reality, it is extremely unlikely that Anne Bonny and Mary Read were in a romantic and sexual relationship. Both of them were married to men on the ship and were pregnant at the time of their trial.[29] There is also historical proof that Mary did not enter the ship disguised a man. Woodes Rogers issued a proclamation for her and Anne's arrest on 5 September 1720, just two weeks after they set sail as pirates:

> WOODES ROGERS, Esq. GOVERNOR of New Providence, &c. A PROCLAMATION. Whereas John Rackum ... and two Women, by Name, Ann Fulford alias Bonny, & Mary Read, did on the 22d of August last combine together to enter on board, take, steal, and run-away ... Wherefore these are to Publish and make Known to all Persons Whatsoever that the said John Rackum and Company are hereby proclaimed as Pirates and Enemies to the Crown of Great-Britain, and are to be so treated and Deem'd by all His Majesty's Subjects.[30]

Violence towards women was an unfortunate reality if they came across pirates. There are several narratives about Henry Avery's exploits in the East Indies in 1695. The first account of his piracy is a pamphlet published under the pen name Adrian van Broeck in 1709. Avery operated in the Atlantic and Indian oceans between 1693 and 1695. His career as a pirate may have only been two years long, but he became notorious because of the havoc he created for English officials. Little is known about his early life but according to *A General History of the Pyrates*, he was born near Plymouth, England, and joined the Royal Navy around 1690. He entered into piracy when he worked on a ship called the *Dove* as a first mate. Avery mutinied against his captain, who had a widely known reputation for drunkenness, when a longboat called the *Duchess* hailed his ship. Sixteen sailors from the *Duchess* boarded the *Dove* knowing that the captain was likely inebriated. Avery took over in defence of the ship, declared himself captain and set sail towards Madagascar, a pirate haven in the East Indies, to begin his piratical career.

Avery and his crew's piratical career peaked when they attacked and robbed an Indian ship, *Ganj-i-Sawai*, of its vast wealth and treasure. Once the Mughal emperor realized that an Englishman had robbed him, 'he threatened loud, and talked of sending a mighty Army with Fire and Sword, to extirpate the English from all their Settlements on the Indian Coast'.[31] To protect their trade, the East India Company began a manhunt for Avery and his crew. When Avery discovered that the English were in hot pursuit, he and his men decided to sail for America, 'where no Person suspected them'. There he parted from his ship and upwards of 75 of his men scattered throughout North America. All were eventually arrested, but Avery himself was never captured and his whereabouts in his final days remain unknown.[32] His escape was a huge blow for the English because, owing to his actions, they nearly lost all of their trading opportunities with the Mughal empire.

There is another reason why the Mughals were so furious about Avery and England's inability to catch him. The 1709 narrative purports to be from a journal of someone who escaped Madagascar and had first-hand knowledge of Avery's activities. It claims that Avery married an Indian princess taken from the *Ganj-i-Sawai* and made a home for them both on Madagascar. The author writes that Avery gave the princess all the respect she and her status deserved and 'plunder'd her of something more pleasing than Jewels' after they were legitimately married by a local priest. His crew wanted to draw lots to take claim over each of the princess's ladies, but they were also told to marry the

Captain Avery, engraving from Captain Charles Johnson, *The History and Lives of All the Most Notorious Pirates, and Their Crews* (1725).

women they wanted to bed. This paints quite the romantic picture of the situation. In reality, Avery and his men committed mass rape of every woman on the *Ganj-i-Sawai* over a period of several days. After the pirates successfully plundered the ship, they let the male captives go but forced the women to stay.[33] Some of the women committed suicide rather than be subjected to further violence.

Daniel Defoe published his own take on these events in two letters written as if they were from Avery himself. He supports the 1709 publication and insists, as Avery, that he never assaulted the Mughal princess:

I have heard that it has been reported in England that I ravish'd this Lady, and then used her most barbarously;

but they wrong me, for I never offer'd any Thing of that Kind to her, I assure you; nay, I was so far from being inclin'd to it, that I did not like her; and there was one of her Ladies who I found much more agreeable to me, and who I was afterwards something free with, but not even with her either by Force, or by Way of Ravishing.[34]

The lower-class Mughal women, however, did not receive such treatment. Defoe's narration states,

after the first Heat of our Men was over, what was done, was done quietly, for I have heard some of the Men say that there was not a Woman among them but what was lain with four or five Times over, that is to say, by so many several Men, for as the Women made no Opposition, so the Men even took those that were next them, without Ceremony, when and where Opportunity afforded.[35]

Whatever the truth was, these writings demonstrate just how little regard men paid towards the different treatment high- and low-ranking women received.[36]

Family was an essential tool in pirates' attempts to escape death sentences. In some cases, they could be pardoned based on the testimony of positive character witnesses. If someone was able to testify that the accused pirate had a history of honourable behaviour, such as regular work, familial support, sober and honest living and being established in their community, the judge and jury could use that information to sway their decisions towards mercy.[37] This worked in favour of the pirate Henry Glasby when his wife, Elizabeth, spoke for him during his trial. Not only did she vouch for his character, but she turned her attention to the pirate's quartermaster and asked him if he had seen her husband actively robbing their victims. 'No,' he responded. 'He is a very good Man, and we never venture him on board, being suspicious that he designs to make his Escape for he endeavoured it once before.'[38] In the end, there was enough positive evidence for Glasby to be acquitted.

Benjamin Parr, one of the forced men on Captain Roberts's ship, testified that he had no choice but to obey because he had a wife and five children and needed to stay alive for their sakes. He was acquitted. One of the other forced men on Roberts's ship, Robert Hayes, would not be so lucky. Hayes claimed that he told Roberts he had a wife and child and hoped to be spared. He was forced to sign the pirates' articles and swore to Roberts that he would be his 'Mess-mate'. However, one of the other prisoners, William Darling, provided compelling evidence that Hayes voluntarily participated in robbing a ship only two days after their capture. Despite Hayes's marital status, he was found guilty of piracy and hanged.[39]

Piracy had a significant impact on families, due to the social ostracism wives and children faced if their husbands wound up on the gallows; they left too many ruined widows, orphans and families.[40] Condemned members of Stede Bonnet's crew lamented the tragedy that would befall their families. One member claimed: 'my Wife and Children are now perishing for want of Bread in New-England. Had it been only myself, I had not matter'd it so much, but my poor Family grieves me.'[41]

Many pirates understood this and tried to either spare their wives humiliation or comfort their families. The pirate Walter Kennedy was an Englishman under the command of Bartholomew Roberts and loyal to his captain's articles. He was eventually captured, sent to Marshalsea Prison in London and sentenced to death at Execution Dock on 21 July 1721. Kennedy never claimed to be innocent, but admitted that his life as a pirate was wicked and unhappy because he and his crew were always fleeing from capture. According to the ordinary, the spiritual chaplain and advisor to condemned people in prisons, Kennedy was ready to die and had made his peace with God. He said he was relieved that he only had a wife to leave behind rather than children too. However, on the day of his execution, Kennedy appeared to be 'extremely terrify'd and concern'd at the near Approach of Death' and begged for water at the scaffold. He finally managed to compose himself and publicly professed his guilt. His one request was that his wife be spared from the consequences of humiliation and scandal, insisting that she was a pious and virtuous woman who was always against his 'vices'.[42]

Wives and other family members had the closest personal relationships with pirates, and so might fall under suspicion – and consequent social ostracism – on their husband's or other relative's arrest. A condemned pirate knew what his reputation would do to his wife and children and might hope that 'no Reflections might be made upon his Innocent Family'.[43] Captain Kidd's wife, Sarah Bradley Cox Oort Kidd, was arrested after his execution. Lord Bellomont put her in jail and seized all her property on suspicion that she knew where Kidd had hidden his loot. She repeatedly denied any knowledge about her husband's spoils. Bellomont ultimately found that he had insufficient evidence to imprison her, so she was released. Sarah was lucky in that she was able to regain her freedom, property and a modicum of dignity, but her life was never easy. She and her servants were under constant social scrutiny as suspected protectors of pirates.[44]

One of the few things pirates could do before their death sentence was to write a consoling letter to their loved ones.

A 23-year-old pirate captain named Joseph Halsey was found guilty of murder on the high seas and wrote a letter to his mother to both comfort her and assure her of his innocence:

> don't make yourself uneasy, for God's sake, mother, I am only going out of the world a little sooner for it, and I am in hopes to rest with my Maker, for ever and ever, time without end. But this world is only a small space of time for man to dwell in, and as I die innocent, I hope God will find me rest. And mother I am in hopes to meet you in heaven, and my father, brother, and sisters, and all ... I am very sorry mother, to think I should be call'd so soon out of this world by an untimely end, for I had always hopes of helping you, and should have done very well, had it not been for these rogues. It has cost me all my wages, venture, and life. – Don't make yourself uneasy, for it cannot be help'd; I'll send you home my shirts, buckles, and hats. Remember me.[45]

William Lawrence was another pirate captain sentenced to death. He had placed his children into his mother's care before setting off to sea. He wrote a letter to his mother on the day of his execution and assured her that he was prepared for his death. The core of his letter was to implore his mother to 'be father and mother, as well as a grandmother, over my dear and tender infants, in whom, I hope that God may grant such honest principles and morals in their hearts'.[46] Words such as these were the least pirates could do to save their families.

The fate of pirates could mean the difference between the life and death of a community. Pirate havens in places such as Tortuga, Port Royal and Nassau left legacies that thrived even after the expansion of the Royal Navy into these areas. Married pirates put everyone's lives at risk, leaving family members in the desperate situation of trying to secure their release. A significant example is when a group of more than forty wives in Jamaica came together and presented a large petition to Queen Anne to secure their husbands' pardons. They argued that pardoning these men would benefit the Crown for numerous reasons such as the following:

1. First by this Generall Pardon a great many of the Lives of her Majesties good Subjects will be freed from danger from them, and the Trade of the good Nation open'd to all those parts of the world.
2. Her Majestie will have the Benefit of Service of a Great many of her Subjects (that are now uselesse) towards the taking of the Spanish West Indies and the Gallyons which they are very well used to.
3. Her Majestie will have the benefit of a great deale of Riches, which they do freely offer themselves, which is a fourth part of their riches.
4. This Nation [Jamaica] will reap a great advantage in the Currency of their wealth which is much wanted, And the poor wives and Relations of these Men receive their Comforts and Supports of Life.
5. And lastly the great hindrance to this good work having been the ill treatment of many who have adhered to former officers of mercie. As Burgis, Brent, Whooler, Hirks, with many other [pirates], who were some cleared by the late King Williams Proclamation, and other after . . . They the said Pirates and Buckaneers will thankfully Embrace the said Pardon and give the said Allowance to defray the

Charges in gratifying those persons the Trustees shall think fit.

Unfortunately, Queen Anne did not heed their pleas. All of the men were executed, leaving the women and their families in poverty.[47]

One of Roberts's codes specifically stated that no violence was to be carried out against women, but this was an unfortunate reality among pirates, particularly in the Indian Ocean and towards indigenous women. Pirates tried to deny this. William Philips, who may have been a member of Henry Avery's crew, confessed to killing 'about fourteen or fifteen of the Admirall of Mecca's men', but claimed that 'there were no women of any quality on board nor any ravished as is reported, therefore if anything of that kind was done it was done by some of the ships that are still out.' The reality, according to historian Ed Fox, is that there were many rumours of atrocities committed against Arab and Indian women by Avery's men. Another of Avery's crew even admitted that women were abused by the pirates, but would not go into detail.[48] Violence against women shows up in other survivors' recollections. Richard Lazenby, a man kidnapped by pirates named Seagar and Taylor, wrote a narrative describing his ordeal. One of his observations was about the pirates' conduct. The pirates arrived on the island of Aminidivi off the coast of India. 'They then sent their boat ashore which returned giving a good account of abundance of water and a large village. But, at the sight of the ships, the inhabitants fled off in boats to the neighboring Islands leaving abundance of women and children hidden in the bushes, which the Pirates found and forced to their barbarous inclinations.'[49] Edward Teach was known to have relations in every port. According to Captain Charles

Johnson, he had fourteen wives, one of whom lived on Ocracoke Island. Johnson wrote in *A General History of the Pyrates* that after Teach spent the night with his fourteenth wife, he invited 'five or six of his brutal Companions to come ashore, and he would force her to prostitute herself to them all, one after another, before his Face'.[50]

Rape was an unfortunate reality among pirates and commonly occurred after pirates sacked coastal towns. There pirates were not beholden to the strict rules on their ships and ran amok. In the aftermath of a battle, men who were fired up with fear, blood and greed without any discipline or supervision – and likely drunk – would commit rape if they could get away with it. Rape rarely occurred on ships, where the pirates were much more closely supervised. Before he became governor of the Bahamas, Woodes Rogers was a privateer and took pride in his crew's respectful behaviour towards women, meaning that they groped women for hidden jewellery rather than stripping them.[51]

The sailor Edward Barlow kept a meticulous journal of his voyages between 1659 and 1703 and recorded a rape he committed against a servant woman named Mary Symons while he was stationed on land. He wrote that he took her

> much against her will, for indeed she was asleep but being gotten into the bed I could not easily be persuaded out again, and I confess that I did more than what was lawful or civil, but not in that manner that I could ever judge, or in the least, think that she could prove with child, for I take God to witness that I did not enter her body, all though I did attempt something in that nature.

He tried to justify his attack by saying, 'I found by her that women's wombs are of an attractive quality and dangerous for a young man to meddle with.' He went back to sea towards Jamaica and when he returned to England he discovered she was pregnant, so he married her. Unfortunately, she died in childbirth after he went out to sea again.[52]

It was very unusual for women to participate openly on a pirate ship, if they were there at all. Women were often banned from pirate ships for practical reasons. They were seen as bad luck, as sources of conflict or as breaches in the male social order of maritime solidarity.[53] The idea of their being bad luck is interesting because it was more of a misconception. Bad luck in regard to women dates back as far as the ancient Roman era. Old folk tales spoke of 'sirens of the sea', dangerous, beautiful women who left the water to enchant and seduce sailors before dragging them down to the bottom of the ocean. This legend eventually evolved into a superstition that women generally brought bad luck – not just on the ship. This Roman legend, however, contradicts ancient Greek literature that describes water as a female element, which gave women power often denied to men. According to Greek legend, the Great Goddess of the Cretans symbolized fertility and protected sailors during their journey.

Mermaids were other female-driven seaborne creatures meant to disrupt sailors. They were portrayed as beautiful symbols of death and of men's ambivalence toward women. Like Eve from the Bible, the mermaid was a temptress, and her tail represented the Garden of Eden while her hair symbolized an insatiable sexual appetite. Like the siren, the mermaid lured sailors to their death or drove them to such distraction that they would abandon their duties and put the whole ship in danger. Interestingly, the origins and inspirations of sirens and mermaids are unknown, but they were likely the reason why people came to believe women might be bad luck on ships.[54]

Women were generally assumed to be hardy and chaste workers without any agenda of taking power away from men. Men believed that their presence had the potential to bring a harmony to a ship as their femininity reminded them of a maternal figure. Women wanted to be their equals but because they were mythologically portrayed as destroyers of men, they were always kept separate.[55] Men had to create these types of female stories because they had to legitimize their belief that women were too incompetent to be effective seafarers. It was more beneficial to create characters placed in the realm of myth than it was to acknowledge reality.[56]

Richard Whitbourne meets New World mermaids, engraving from
Theodor de Bry, *Decima tertia pars historiae Americanae* (1634).

Life at sea was difficult and Rackham had trouble under-standing why Mary Read would volunteer for piracy, especially since capture meant certain death. She replied,

> As to hanging, it is no hardship, for were it not for that, every cowardly Fellow would turn Pyrate, and so infest the Seas, that Men of Courage must starve. That if it was put to the choice of the Pyrates, they would not have the Punishment less than Death, the Fear of which to keep some dastardly Rogues honest; that many of those who are now cheating the Widows and Orphans, and oppressing their poor Neighbours, who have no Money to obtain Justice, would then rob at Sea, and the Ocean would be crowned with Rogues, like the Land, and no Merchant would venture out; so that the [Piracy], in a little Time, would be not worth following.[57]

There is truth in this statement. If there was no great risk, then any sailor could claim to be a pirate. Entering piracy by her own free will, Mary breached the barrier for women at sea.[58]

Anne Bonny and Mary Read were the exception to the rule as openly female pirates. Most women on pirate ships would have been disguised as men. The easiest part of their deception would be binding their breasts. The next simple task was to take advantage of the dirt and sweat that plagued every sailor. These hid any obvious feminine features. All ships had some young boys in their employ who could be as young as nine or ten years old. They were welcome additions because they were quicker and more agile than older men. Their youth was another advantage because they could be trained in seafaring skills and master them much faster. Most women would pass as adolescent boys, with their lack of facial hair and shorter stature.

Clothing was also a simple matter. Sailors' clothing was ideal for hiding a feminine body shape because it was large and baggy. A typical outfit was a loose shirt with a waistcoat and jacket, worn with baggy trousers. This type of clothing allowed for freedom of movement to climb ropes and go up and down ladders. They were easy to mend, clean and dry because they would not drag like skirts. The final item of clothing was a handkerchief worn around the neck for additional sun protection. Long hair was not an issue either. Sailors often tied their hair back into a ponytail. Assimilation was easy and the dress gave women more physical and mental comfort.[59]

The toilet, on the other hand, was a much more complicated issue. Toilets were typically buckets or even the open sea, as men urinated over the ship's railing. Defecation took place in large boxes or carved holes through which the waste would drop into the ocean.[60] The latter was easy enough, but urination, not so much. A common solution for women was a small funnel made out of a horn or a piece of metal that they could place into their trousers to use as a makeshift spout.[61]

Menstruation is the most obvious complication, but it might not have been as much of a problem as one might assume. The arduous work and simple diet may have stopped their periods completely. If a woman was young enough, the onset of menstruation might be delayed by a couple of years because of this line of work. Even if a woman had her period on the ship, she could still hide it by wearing dark-coloured trousers or by using the absorbent strips of cloth that women used in general. Sexually transmitted infections such as gonorrhea and other ailments such as piles were common among sailors and would sometimes leave bloodstains on their clothing. A bloodstain here or there would not be a major cause of suspicion.[62]

⚓

RELATIONSHIPS BETWEEN PIRATES both on and off the ship are intriguing and complicated. Questions about their sexuality persist. Pirates are seen as transgressive figures, and it is easy to theorize that many pirates were homosexual because they lived in an environment outside the rules of society. While there certainly were gay pirates, it is impossible to identify them or discover how many there were. *Matelotage* was a legal agreement by which pirates could make sure that their goods were protected and redistributed by a trusted friend to either the rest of the crew or their family. Whether or not some *matelotages* were a result of love is an interesting discussion, but it is impossible to draw any conclusion.

Women and their relationship to piracy are an even more complicated subject. They were brutalized, loved and cared for by pirates. Some were even allowed on ships, but this was an exception to the rule because most pirates outright banned them. But it is important to note that pirates' wives had an important impact on pirate life whether they were on the ship or not. A female presence did exist on ships, however, through mythology and folklore commonly remembered by sailors all over.

Pirates' relationships in all contexts are an important area of study because their bonds helped to guarantee their safety and survival by keeping them loyal to each other. They sought to avoid conflict where possible, and this helped them succeed in their endeavours.

5

SAFETY, WEAPONS
AND PIRATES'
BATTLE TACTICS

'The [Pirate] shall not keep his Arms clean, fit for an
Engagement, or neglect his Business, shall be cut off from
his share, and suffer such other punishment as the Captain
and the Company shall think fit.'
Articles on board the *Revenge*

It goes without saying that pirates could not survive without
their ship, but this could sometimes be their downfall. The
ship was not simply their home and mode of travel, but the
symbol of their power. Whenever they came upon a vessel ripe
for the taking, they did all they could to capture it before immediately sailing off to find a bigger and better one.

The process of maintaining a ship was an arduous one
that took a significant amount of time, especially if looking to
keep the vessel in the best shape possible. Bartholomew Sharp
detailed this process in his journal when he and his crew sailed
in the East Indies. They had suffered some damage after a battle
but received assistance from some of the locals, which allowed
them to make the necessary repairs:

An. Dom. 1681. May 9 Mund. Those Indians told us, That
up another River, lived a Shipwright, who was building
two new Ships. This was welcome news to us; so we went
up to the Carpenters Yard, and friendly desired the chief
Builder, and seven of his Workmen, to go on Board us,
and help us to cut down our Ship: He also helped us to
a Canoe load of Spikes, and Iron Work, which our Ship
wanted to fit her with . . .

We shortened our Main-Mast, six foot, made new
Cross and Trussel-trees to it. Shortened our fore mast
five foot, and made new Cross and Trussel-trees. [By the
head.] . . .

Made our Main, our Fore-Top-Mast, our Fore, our
Main-Top-Mast. Cut off her upper Deck, and sunk her
quarter Deck; she was six Foot ten Inches high, between
Decks, and we left her something more than four Foot
in the Waste.

All this we did in 10 Days, and she was fit for the
Sea, and we had done sooner had not wet weather
hindered us.[1]

The design of the ship could be the difference between survival and failure. Pirate ships were extremely varied, and the
crew often had to improvise to make them as efficient as possible.
Ships had to be exceptionally seaworthy, since pirates sailed
around the Atlantic for extended amounts of time fighting
and braving extreme storms. The ideal ship had to be fast enough
to attack and sail off before the victims could respond and catch
up. It also had to be big, with numerous guns, to be as threatening as possible. The larger the ship, the quicker its targets
surrendered.[2]

If the crew captured large merchant ships or galleons (if they were lucky), they had to remove carved works and cut down roundhouses and quarterdecks to make the ships snug for rough passages, lighter and more weatherly. Canoes and small boats were fitted so the pirates could venture further out to sea when necessary. The adjustments were not perfect, however. They each posed their own risks. Short hauls made for cargo were slower and not as weatherly as long, narrow ones. Stronger ships with closely spaced timber to support heavy guns and cannon fire were heavier. Lighter ships were faster but more vulnerable to cannon fire and guns. They could not support the large crew required to overwhelm larger prey by boarding and they were too weak to fight ship-to-ship against well-armed and well-manned merchant ships. Even so, smaller ships, between 30 and 60 tonnes, were more desirable. They were well suited to most necessary tasks, easier to maintain, easier to capture and less of a financial risk.[3]

Large, heavily armed ships gave pirates a certain prestige. However, size could be a problem. They could not always find a port that could support them. A large ship also limited the number of safe shores in which to hide and careen. If pirates sailed in large ships, they had to remain in active posture, constantly deployed. The only way they could hide in smaller inlets or creeks was if they switched out their large ships for shallow-draft vessels like sloops. No matter what, though, any ship of any size required the same maintenance and care.[4]

One of the best examples of a large, prestigious prize was the capture of the *Whydah*, a 300-tonne British slave ship complete with eighteen guns captained by the Dutchman Lawrence Price. It was new, only two years old, which meant it had many years ahead of it. In April 1717, the *Whydah* landed at Port Royal,

'Commerce thus guarded Spain insults no more; But flys dismay'd when British Thunders roar', engraving from *The American Traveller* (1741) showing a British warship during the War of Jenkins' Ear firing on a Spanish ship.

Jamaica, and unloaded five hundred enslaved people. Price was more than aware of the risk of pirate attacks, especially since he sailed in one of the largest and wealthiest ships in the Atlantic. The pirates Samuel Bellamy and Paulsgrave Williams got word of the *Whydah* and decided to make chase. Capturing this ship would make them the wealthiest and most powerful pirates of the age.

Captain Price understood that he was being pursued by the pirates because Bellamy flew his pirate flag, which displayed 'death's head and bones across'. The chase only lasted for three days, but took place over 300 nautical miles. Price realized it was fruitless to try to outrun the pirates. They had faster ships, and he was outmanned. Price half-heartedly fired a couple of guns before ordering the *Whydah* to heave to and surrender.

This proved to be a massive success for Bellamy and his crew. The *Whydah* was newer than their own ships, the *Sultana* and *Marianne*, and had loads of room to carry all kinds of supplies. Best of all, it was loaded with cash and valuable goods. In exchange for the enslaved people at Port Royal, Captain Price had received sugar, indigo, Jesuit's bark (used to treat symptoms of malaria) and a huge quantity of silver and gold worth between £20,000 and £30,000. Bellamy decided to make the *Whydah* his flagship and since Captain Price had surrendered without a fight, the pirate gave him the *Sultana* along with £20 worth of silver and gold to 'bear his charges'.[5]

Pirates needed a large crew to keep their ships in tip-top shape for maximum efficiency and safety. There was endless work to be done on a ship and routines were important to prevent idleness, which could lead to discontent. Common routine tasks were weighing and letting go of anchors; setting, reefing, furling and drying sails; striking topmasts; scrubbing and scraping the decks;

cleaning the head; tallowing the masts and strakes; pulling or picking oakum (tar that gathered on ropes); wetting the planks to keep the caulking tight; and shifting provisions. The more skilled pirates were tasked with mending sails and rigging, steering and navigating. Many pirates spent downtime studying ship-handling. The workday had to be divided up into shifts to keep the routine afloat. A typical day at sea was divided up into four-hour watches over a 24-hour period, usually noon to noon. The exception was the watch between 4 a.m. and 8 a.m., which was divided up into two two-hour watches (dog watches) to allow a rotation, so the same seamen did not stand watch at the same time every day.[6] One of the best ways to make sure their labour force never dwindled was to coerce forced men into the hard work. Bartholomew Roberts was known to force many of his prisoners to do menial work such as fixing the sails or flags.[7] Not only was this backbreaking, but performing these duties on a pirate ship was also likely to give an unwilling pirate a guilty sentence. Participation, no matter what kind, was still an act of piracy.

A man named William Petty was captured specifically because he had been a sailmaker on his previous ship. Roberts promised Petty that he would only be needed for a day or two to help make repairs. Petty was no fool and protested, to no avail, claiming later that he was brought onto the ship against his will. The carpenter's mate on Roberts's ship gave Petty the necessary materials to mend the sails and the quartermaster ordered him to start immediately. Petty claimed he had no choice but to participate, but unfortunately, he was pronounced guilty and executed.[8] According to a witness against Roberts and his crew, another prisoner named Adam Comrie was also forced to mend the sails; 'they kept the poor Fool always at Work on the Sails as a Slave.' This witness statement did not result in a guilty verdict for Comrie, but he was transferred to Marshalsea Prison.[9] It is unknown whether he was ultimately found guilty or acquitted.

A less experienced pirate had to learn extremely quickly on the job. He had to know the difference between stem and stern, port and starboard, along with distinguishing the difference between backing, reefing, balancing, furling and loosening the sails. He also had to familiarize himself with splices, hitches and knots, and the difference between cat-harpins and nippers, belaying pins and cabin-hooks. The various types of vessels he had to know included brigs, snows, schooners, shallops, sloops, men-o'-war and more. Rigging, masts and sails were part of the vocabulary list and the pirate had to understand basic ship manoeuvres such as beating against the wind, tacking and boxhauling.[10]

Understanding the elements was just as important. Trade winds and their patterns, different types of breezes, slatches, cats' paws, gales and fresh gales were part of the common vernacular. The pirate would encounter 'fair winds' that favoured the ship's movement on course and 'foul winds' that hindered it. Terms associated with oceans and seas, their currents, calms, swells and breakers, were essential, along with weather terminology for different types of storms, squalls and tempests, and the 'scud' clouds and their formation. If the pirate was charged with navigation, he had to learn the different constellations in order to estimate the ship's location and direction.[11]

Ships had little interior space and it was often taken up with cargo or ballast. Pirates had cramped living quarters, making the space a dense community. Seamen often had a sea chest in which their clothes and bedding were stored. They provided their own bedding, if they were lucky enough to have it, and slept in a canvas hammock that was often 3 by 6 feet (90 by 180 cm), hung horizontally. As they lay in their hammocks, they might sing or tell tales and play cards by candlelight.[12]

Pirate ships contained numerous animals as well, some with uses and many without. Rats, cockroaches and maggots infested virtually every ship in the maritime world. Sea worms might eat through the hull, which could cause immense damage over time. However, some ships might be lucky enough to have a dog, cat or parrot for entertainment, companionship and pest control. Even better, they might have some animals to provide steady food, such as cattle, sheep, goats and pigs. If pirates did not have them, they could plunder these animals from other ships.[13]

One of the most important items on a ship was gunpowder. The worst damage to a ship often came from spilled powder. If any fires occurred during battle, the powder could catch and cause a massive explosion. To avoid this risk, gunpowder always had to be closely monitored. It needed to be kept in excellent condition, which was quite a challenge. If the powder was of poor quality, the guns might misfire. Dry powder sparked, but wet powder would not. Even if the powder dried, it would never be of good quality again. Pirates wore cartouche boxes on their belts or shoulder straps, many of which carried cartridges of powder. They were compact – only about 15 centimetres wide and 10 tall (6 by 4 in.) – so they would not hinder anyone's movement, but were still accessible in battle. Despite their small size, these boxes also carried flints to snap sparks, powder measures, paper for making cartridges, a horn or flask of powder, linen for cleaning, oil for the gun's barrel and lock, extra balls in a ball bag, tompion for muzzles and to prevent water from getting inside a gun, priming wire, beeswax, a priming brush, a ball screw to remove musket balls and a screwdriver.[14]

Pitch, or tar, was another item that had to be carefully watched because it was extremely flammable. Part of the ship's carpenter's job was to make sure everything stayed in the best shape. An accident was a punishable offence. The logs from HMS *Phoenix* describe a terrible incident due to this material. On 7 April 1718, the log states,

> Yesterday an accident happen'd by the neglect of the Carpenter and his people, who were healing some pitch in the Fore Castle which boiled over and sett the ship on Fire but was soon extinguished; I Confin'd the Carpenter for neither him self not any of the Crew attended the pitch when on the Fire neither had any direction from my Self or any of his Superior Officers to make use of any att this time.[15]

Weapons were life, death and identity to pirates; so much so that Alexandre Exquemelin wrote, 'They name the musket their arm.'[16] Also known as a *fusil boucanier*, the musket was a long-barrelled, large-bored and club-butted flintlock that harkened back to pirates' days as hunting buccaneers. Muskets were lifelines when smaller ships were devoid of cannons. If pirates managed to fire accurately, they could have the upper hand in battles with little difficulty. They could do more damage with muskets at close range than a single round-shot cannon ball.[17] However, muskets had their challenges with loading and firing. Although it was a simple process, one mistake under the pressures of battle could cause a misfire and injury or even death. The process for loading a musket is as follows: the pirate half-cocks their hammer and safety position as he takes a cartridge out of his cartouche box. He rips open the top of the cartridge with his teeth, pours in a small amount of powder and closes the frizzen (the metal upright that strikes the flintlock before firing). The rest of the powder is poured down the barrel, followed by a ball, which is pushed down with a small ramrod at least three times to secure it. Once he is certain that the musket is fully loaded, the pirate lowers it to waist height, draws the hammer back to full cock, raises the musket to his shoulder, aims and fires.

The whole process could take an expert shooter up to twenty seconds. In a battle situation, however, a pirate could rush through the process or delay it under the mental strain.[18] If his mouth watered, the powder could get wet and not fire. If his hands were shaking, he might drop the cartridge altogether or bungle the ramrod and miss the mouth of the musket. Ideally the pirate would have at least two fully loaded muskets on his person to expedite the process.

Firing range was equally important. The maximum range for a musket was between 360 and 460 metres (400–500 yards), although true fatal effectiveness peaked at about 230 metres (250 yards). The impact would generally incapacitate the targeted victim. Some pirates, such as Blackbeard, were able to press on despite musket shots.[19]

Clean and well-cared-for weapons were the line between life and death in battle. If a weapon misfired or a sword broke, a horrendous injury or a fatal blow could result. Pirates kept their pieces in top shape, but unfortunately so did their victims. A man named Jonathan Barlow made sure that one of his crewmates had a proper pistol when the pirate Nicholas Simonds and his crew boarded his ship. The mate snapped the trigger of his gun at one of the approaching pirates who 'drew a Pistol from his side and snap'd at the Mate'. This must have gone against Simonds's orders, because when he realized that his pirate had tried to kill the sailor on his would-be prize, Simonds 'came out into the Stearage with a Pistol [and] shot the Pirate through the Body and kill'd him'. Barlow took advantage of his distraction and led his men below, where they managed to capture another pirate and successfully retake their ship.[20]

Pirates spent a large amount of time maintaining their weapons because they were essential for their trade and survival. Arms were cleaned, cared for and well oiled to prevent rusting. The sea air made this a constant threat and weapons could decay without warning. Soaked linen was used to keep the musket clean and oiled, but it was a tedious process. Muskets and other firing arms were coated in a form of black lacquer, which stained everyone's hands black or brown. Overuse caused the frizzen to soften and require hardening through heating treatments. The middle of battle was no time to discover one's trigger was rusted and locked.[21]

The most common weapons on a pirate ship were pistols and cutlasses. Pistols were close-range weapons, meant to be fired only once at a range of no more than 2.75 metres (3 yards). The barrels were 30 centimetres (1 ft) long, so they made excellent clubs after a bullet was discharged. Some pirates carried several pistols on their body. Blackbeard wore 'a sling over his shoulders, with three braces of pistols, hanging in holsters, like bandoliers'.[22] Another pirate was reported to carry four pistols in battle.[23] Cutlasses had short, sturdy blades with a strong protective hilt usually made from iron or brass. The shorter blades allowed for small, fast thrusts rather than more intricate sword-fights.[24] Their small size also meant they were ideal to be kept on the pirate's person during times of extreme physical duress

N. C. Wyeth, *'One more step, Mr Hands,' said I [Jim Hawkins], 'and I'll
blow your brains out!'*, 1911, oil on canvas for Robert Louis Stevenson,
Treasure Island (1911).

in compact spaces. Like the pistol, the cutlass was ideal for close
combat. Pistols and cutlasses were so important that they became
emblems on some pirates' flags, as reported in the *American
Weekly Mercury* in 1726. A group of pirates off the coast of
Curaçao flew 'with their Black Silk Flag before them, with the

François l'Olonnais holding a cutlass, engraving from A. O. Exquemelin, *The Buccaneers of America* (1678).

Representation of a Man in full Proportion, with a Cutlas in one Hand and a Pistol in the other Extended'.[25]

Blackbeard's final, epic battle culminated in a fight with the coastguard Lieutenant Maynard and his associates off the coast of North Carolina in 1717.

Maynard and Teach themselves two begun the Fight with their Swords, Maynard making a thrust, the point of his Sword went against Teach's Cartridge Box, and bended it to the Hilt, Teach broke the Guard of it and wounded Maynard's Fingers but did not disable him, where upon he Jumpt back, threw away his Sword and fired his Pistol, which wounded Teach. Demelt struck in between them with his Sword and cut Teach's Face pretty much; in the Interim both Companies ingaged in Maynard's Sloop, one of Maynard's Men being a Highlander, ingaged Teach with his broad Sword, who gave Teach a cut on the Neck.

Once he was wounded, Blackbeard yelled, 'Well done, lad!' The Highlander replied, 'If it not be well done, I'll do it better.'

Blackbeard's head on the end of the bowsprit, engraving from Charles Ellms, *The Pirates Own Book* (1856 edn).

At that, he thrust his sword and 'gave [Blackbeard] a second stroke, which cut off his Head'.[26]

There is little known about pirates' fighting techniques with their cutlasses. The weapon was suited to basic cuts, thrusts and parries similar to those used with the broadsword or in fencing. The goal was to hit the opponent without causing any injury to oneself by controlling the victim's blade or deliberate thrusting, which left that cutlass-wielder vulnerable. Cutlasses only had an 85-centimetre (34 in.) blade, which is why pirates were partial to them. Broadswords were much longer and took up too much room on the body. Practising with broadswords was a difficult endeavour because pirate ships were crowded not only with people but with items such as 'cannon[s], bitts, masts, rigging, coamings, hatches, and scuttles, not to mention the many implements and accessories of war strewn about'. There was just too little room.[27]

Ships were armed with cannons, known as guns, of various sizes for battle, which defined the pirates' vessels. By the eighteenth century, English guns were named by the weight of their shot, and ranged anywhere from 4 to as large as 16 pounds (7 kg). Other European ships could have guns up to 24 pounds (11 kg). These weapons were usually made of iron or bronze, but the latter was rare because it was extremely expensive. Round shot was the most common form of cannon ball and was used against hulls and masts at further distances. If a ship was meant to fight at close range, the cannons were fitted with two shots, intended to damage rigging and rudders. If the pirates were lucky, they might have bar shot, made of iron bars fitted together. This was especially damaging to rigging and sails and was sometimes even aimed at men. Case shot was extremely effective for longer-range firing – up to 250 metres (275 yards).[28]

Howard Pyle, *So the Treasure Was Divided*, 1905, oil on canvas.

Willem van de Velde the Younger, *An Action between English Ships and Barbary Corsairs*, c. 1695, oil on canvas.

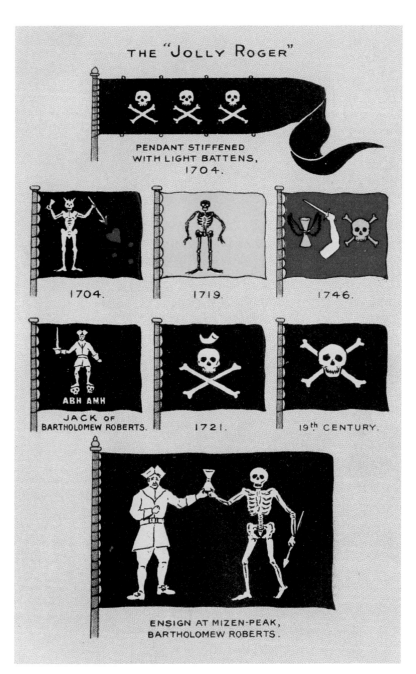

Jolly Roger flags, illustrations from Basil Lubbock,
The Blackwall Frigates (1922).

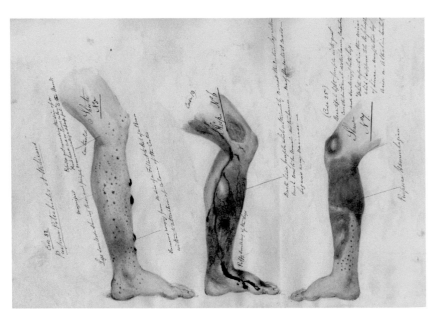

Watercolour illustrations of scurvy symptoms by Henry W. Mahon,
a ship's surgeon on the *Barrosa*, a British convict ship, *c.* 1841.

David Teniers the Younger, *Tavern Scene*, 1658, oil on panel.

Illustrated cover by
N. C. Wyeth for Robert
Louis Stevenson, *Treasure
Island* (1919 edn).

Frederick J. Waugh, *The Buccaneers*, 1910, oil on canvas.

Howard Pyle, *An Attack on a Galleon*, 1905, oil on canvas.

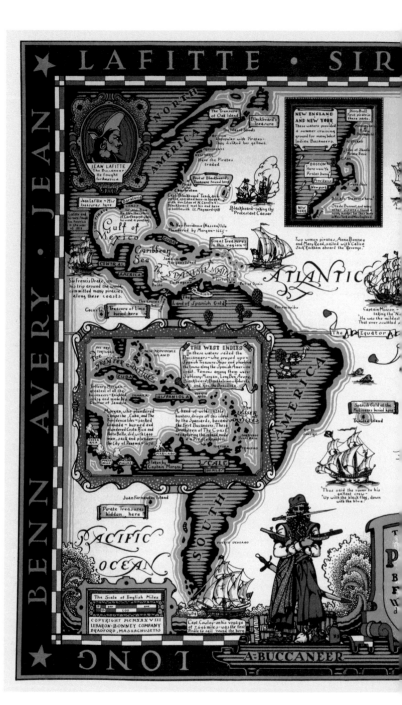

Map of the famous pirates, buccaneers and freebooters who roamed the seas during the 17th and 18th centuries, 1938, designed by Darby Harbold.

Sea monsters in a detail of Olaus Magnus, *Carta marina* (1539).

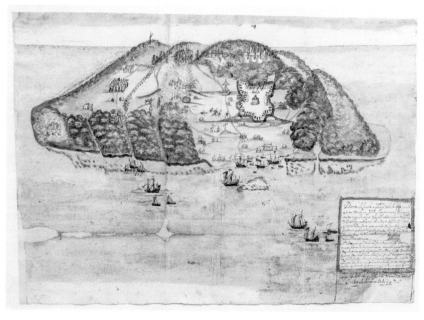

Plan of the island and fortifications of Tortuga, 1654,
colour wash and ink on paper.

Cannons were mounted on bed carriages with wheels to allow for movement and reduce recoil. Eighteenth-century cannons had some limitations in that they were only managed with two tackles, which were hooked from the carriage to the eyebolts.[29] While cannons were extremely effective in damaging other ships, they posed a great risk to the crew because gunners were always right in the line of enemy fire.[30] Swivel guns were a type of cannon used on smaller ships and were muzzle-loaded, like muskets. These were smaller and intended to specifically target people on the enemy ship.[31]

All these weapons were necessary for the impending battles. Before the engagement began, there was a scurry of activity on the pirate ship as every officer and sailor readied themselves for the fight. Hammocks were stowed in the hold or mounted against the walls of the ship to provide extra protection against cannons and splinters. Various types of canvas and cloth were run along the rails all around the ship to give pirates some visual protection so they could lead a stronger surprise attack. The gunners had some of the most important jobs because they oversaw the readying and loading of the cannons. Two to three men, on average, worked with each gun while an officer stood ready to command anywhere between five and ten guns at a time. They set out large hogsheads of water and spread wet blankets and sheets next to them. The gunners had to check each individual cannon to make sure they were dry and could fire shot. Like muskets, they prepared gunpowder, shot, cartridges, rammers and handspikes to load each gun. Not only that, but gunners had to protect against fires from either their own guns or any that might hit their ship. Whenever they could, they would deliberately spill water onto the deck in the hope that it would stay wet enough to prevent catching fire. In the meantime, the carpenter made sure to check the pumps and prepared shot plugs and lead sheets to protect against any holes. The surgeon waited in the cockpit of the ship, ready to treat the wounded, as they would undoubtedly start pouring in minutes after the battle commenced. Finally, the captain would ready the crew with a hearty speech, and everyone would take a dram of liquor to fortify their courage. Once battle began, the ship would be completely destroyed. If the enemy was powerful enough, they could smash their foes' vessel into pieces.[32]

Fear tactics were one of the most effective ways to guarantee success in a fight and the first step was displaying the pirate flag. This not only served to identify them as pirates, but signified the pirates' rejection of nationality and society, their terror and unique social world. The pirate flag had many names: the colours, the bloody flag, black flag, the banner of King Death and the Jolly Roger.[33] There are different theories as to the origin of the term 'Jolly Roger'. One is that it was an anglicized version of *jolie rouge*, meaning 'pretty red', which was used to describe the red or bloody flag. It is also possible that the word 'jolly' may have referenced the smiling appearance of a skull.[34] Another suggestion is that it came from the name of a Tamil pirate captain, Al Raja, who operated in the Indian Ocean. Yet the name 'Roger' is significant because it held several meanings for pirates. Before the flag became known as the 'Jolly Roger' it was known as the 'Old Roger', which was a colloquial term used for the Devil during the seventeenth and eighteenth centuries. Therefore the most likely theory is that it was derived from the Devil's nickname.[35]

The first pirate flags were red rather than the more familiar black and were recorded in the seventeenth century as being primarily used by French buccaneers. By the end of the seventeenth century, however, black flags came into existence. Each colour had a specific meaning. Red meant the pirates would give no quarter, which meant no mercy and that they intended to kill. Black indicated that pirates would give quarter and avoid death as much as possible. These meanings were later recorded in a 1721 French flag book. Under the image of a red flag was written '*Pavillon nomme Sansquartier*', or 'Flag called No Quarter'.[36] The flags were initially solid colours but by the early eighteenth century numerous symbols were emblazoned on them, such as bleeding hearts, blazing balls, hourglasses, spears, cutlasses and skeletons, all of which symbolized death.[37] The first known use of a black flag was recorded in 1700, when a French pirate off the coast of Cape Verdean Island near Santiago, Chile, fought under 'a stable ensign with ... a death's head and an hour glass'.[38] By the 1710s and 1720s, decorated flags had become the norm. It was a great risk to carry flags such as these, but since pirates knew that their capture meant certain death anyway, there was no extra cost for carrying a Jolly Roger.[39]

One of the most feared situations was when the pirates used both flags, as was the case when Captain Peter Solgard was attacked by pirates in 1723. He was the commander of a ship called the *Grey-Hound* and came upon a Virginia merchant ship on 7 June 1723. The merchant warned him that pirates were in the area and that he himself had just been attacked by two pirates the day before. The pirates appeared to be headed toward Block Island, Rhode Island, so Solgard changed direction and headed north to pursue them. On 10 June, Solgard came upon two pirate ships and gave chase. The pirates prepared for the attack and raised the black flag, indicating that they would give quarter if Solgard surrendered. Solgard refused and the pirates 'fired each a Shot, and soon afterward they haul'd down their Black and hoisted Red flags'. Solgard knew this meant that the pirates would fight to the death, but he managed to defeat and capture them.[40]

The most famous pirate flag that we refer to as the Jolly Roger is the one with a skull and crossbones. For several centuries, this symbol has been synonymous with pirates in both historical analysis and popular culture, thanks to writers such as Robert Louis Stevenson.[41] Its origin is a bit of a mystery, but the skull and crossed bones, originally known as a death's head, has been a symbol for death since the Middle Ages. It appeared on tombs in churches and cathedrals and on gravestones in country court-yards. Ship's captains occasionally used the symbol in their logbooks to indicate the death of a crew member. By 1700, it had begun to appear on pirate flags in addition to the above-mentioned images. Individual pirate captains began to create their own versions of the skull and crossbones. Bartholomew Roberts had his men design a flag that showed his own figure standing on two skulls representing a Barbadian's head and a Martinican's head, to indicate his rage at authorities in those islands who attempted to capture him. 'Calico' Jack Rackham's flag had the skull sitting above a pair of crossed cutlasses.[42]

The skull and crossbones was designed and used by the pirate Samuel Bellamy after he captured the *Whydah*. He was eventually caught in a storm and crashed on the coast of Massachusetts, causing a mass frenzy among the locals, who tried to grab all the wealth that washed up onshore. Only eight members of his crew of over 150 men survived. All were captured and put on trial for piracy, and six were hanged.

Before the infamous crash, he attacked several other major ships with his large fleet. At their trial, one of the men on the stand, Thomas Baker, gave testimony as to how Bellamy attacked ships. Baker claimed that he never was one of Bellamy's pirates because he never signed the articles. He claimed that he begged Bellamy to be released but Bellamy threatened he would maroon the poor man on an island with just one bottle of water, one bottle of gunpowder and a single bullet for his weapon. Poor Baker had no choice but to be complicit with the pirates. He testified that when Bellamy's crew attacked a ship, they 'spread a large black Flag, with a Death's head and Bones a-cross, and gave chase . . . under the same Colours'.[43]

False flags were sometimes used as a method to lure ships towards pirates so they could initiate an attack. Maritime law stated that all ships had to fly their country's flag to identify themselves, especially to hail another passing ship. Pirates knew this and took advantage of it by carrying the flags of various countries. A pirate might use a French flag to hail a French ship in order to prevent that merchant from sailing away. If it went according to plan, the French ship would allow the pirate ship to come close enough for them to fire. At that point, the French ship could not escape.[44] The pirate Captain Massey was known to use this tactic to initiate a battle. According to the records of the High Court of the Admiralty, Massey 'hoisted English Colours and afterwards the black flag' before chasing and attacking a victim ship.[45] This worked well because by the time he commanded the black flag to fly, the approaching ship was too close to escape.

This tactic did not always work, however. Sometimes pirates either picked ships that were too powerful or hoisted their black flag too soon, leaving their victim with an advantage. Captain Louis Guittar was one such pirate, who came upon a British ship called the *Shorham*. According to the *Shorham*'s captain, he saw what appeared to be a pirate ship called *La Paix*, or 'the peace' (an ironic name for a pirate ship), at six o'clock in the morning. He immediately sent up the British flag to hail the pirates, who in return 'hoisted up blood red Colloures', meaning they would fight to the death without mercy. Aldred stated that upon this signal he prepared his attack, and the two ships fought until four o'clock that afternoon. Finally, the quartermaster, Peter Heyman, fired two shots into the pirate ship. The pirate ship changed out its bloody flag, 'hoisted up a flagg of truce and then fired no more guns'. Aldred's men boarded Guittar's ship. In total, 124 pirates were captured, between 25 and 30 were killed in battle and 'about 40 or 50 English Prisoners were redeem'd'.[46]

Pirates did offer their victims quarter, but only if they would surrender their ship or at least all the goods on it. John Missel, a pirate, led his crew onto a captured ship and forced it to sail to shore. Once they arrived onto the Massachusetts coast, they forced the English crew onto the land. One of the pirates fired his gun in the air and shouted at their victims to 'call for Quarter'. The pirates warned them that if they did not come back on board, submit to the pirates and take quarter, they would all be killed. One of the surviving Englishmen, Mr Doty, followed the pirates' instructions and came back on board, but was taken, threatened with death and tied up. The pirates shouted back at the other Englishmen that if they did not come on board 'they would cut [Doty] to pieces.' One of the Englishmen, Philip Mews, came back onto the ship but was immediately tied up. A pirate named James Mews (unrelated to Philip) 'held a Knife to his throat, and told him he would be the Death of him; And once Swore at him, saying God Dam your Blood, you shall not live a Minute longer, and struck him with the knife.' Luckily one of the other pirates intervened and Mews lived. Mews retaliated that evening and attacked one of the pirates. Mews 'called him Son of a Bitch, struck him several blows, and threatened to kill him'. The Englishmen ultimately managed to survive the attack, thanks to being on land. The authorities came and promptly arrested the pirates the next day.[47]

Newspapers often reported pirate attacks such as these, sparing no detail of the pirates' brutality. In 1721, the *British Gazetteer* published the account of a ship called the *Cassandra* that was taken by pirates. At just over 1,100 words, the article gave full details of the ship, what was taken and the pirates' actions on board. The pirates had attacked the *Cassandra* on the morning of 8 August 1720 and were described as men who gave no quarter, with 'their black and bloody Flags being all the time display'd'. Three of the *Cassandra's* crew were cut to pieces. After 48 days of captivity among the pirates, the company reached Bombay, where it was joined by two more English ships that helped dispose of the pirates: a crew of nearly four hundred men.[48]

In 1639, Jo Oakes published a book about English piracy during the reigns of King Henry VIII and Elizabeth I, with varying descriptions of their lives, attacks and cruelty. He invoked frightening images to paint pirates in the most devilish manner. To set up his narrative, he describes pirate attacks from as early as the reign of King Richard II:

> In the yeare one thousand three hundred seventy nine, in the second yeare of Richard the Second, who was then but a child; one Sir Oliver De Clicon a French Pirate, committed sundry out rages, and landed in divers places of this Kingdome, who did much harme; and lastly entred the river Thames, and so came up as high as Graves end, where he spoyled the Town without any resistance;

burning a great part thereof, and departed with great abundance of riches.

This attack is reminiscent of the Viking raids that had terrorized Britain since the ninth century. For at least three hundred years, Norsemen sailed south and razed towns across Scotland and down into northern England, going so far as to colonize some places such as Yorkshire. The word 'pirate' comes originally from the Greek word *peirates*, meaning 'attacker', so it is no surprise that this French pirate, de Clicon, is described as such even though his pillaging took place on land rather than on sea. However, as Oakes details next, by the fifteenth century accounts began to differentiate between those who raided on land and those who did so on sea, and even those who raided in both locations:

In the yeare one thousand foure hundred and eighteene, and the sixt of King Henry the first, certaine French men of warre, of whom the Vicount of Narbon was chiefe Captaine: committed a great spoyle upon our Coast, robbing our Marchants, and pillaging ye sea Townes and Villages, of which the King hearing, being then at a place cald Toke in Normandy, he send the Earle of March, the Earle of Huntington, with others to scower the seas, who encountred the foresaid pirats; and after a long and cruell fight, vanquished and overcame them; this battle was fought uppon the ninth of August, in which ye Vicount who was admirall of the Fleet, and one Captaine Mountney who was Vice admirall, were both of them surprised & taken prisoners, in which ships they found great treasure, which they had got by pillaging and robbing; which after served the King to pay his souldiers.[49]

Just a little over one hundred years later, Henry VIII would officially define pirates as those who murder and rob on the sea, while giving the Admiralty jurisdiction to hunt out all pirates. But this would not stop them.

Success very much depended on strategy. Ideally, a pirate would seek out a specific target while taking in all the surrounding variables, such as wind, weather, provisions and timing. Pirates preferred coastal areas rather than the open ocean because the vast area of the latter made it easy for their prey to escape and made the pirates more of a vulnerable target. With smaller ships, pirates could sail in and out of various inlets and along craggy coastlines as they stalked the trade lanes. While smaller and more narrow coastal areas could be more dangerous, they provided more opportunities to intercept prizes. They would remain just over the horizon to be invisible to those onshore. Their sails were set low to make it more likely that they would remain undiscovered. Sometimes they sent out reconnaissance vessels to see if there was anyone in the vicinity worth attacking. Once the conditions were right, they would strike.[50]

The element of surprise was one of pirates' greatest strategies. They used tactics of deception and trickery, which were very effective at sea. The purpose was to get their victims to surrender as quickly as possible. Ultimately, the pirates wanted to attack, raid and escape to avoid being captured or killed. The pirates Samuel Bellamy and Paulsgrave Williams, his partner, pioneered theatrical tricks to scare other sailors into surrender. In 1715, Bellamy and Williams sailed with Henry Jennings, a renowned privateer-turned-pirate from the War of the Spanish Succession.

They joined forces to capture the French merchant ship the *Sainte-Marie*. Bellamy was young but ambitious and sought to prove himself at all costs. They managed to corner the French ship in the bay Bahia Honda on the northwestern coast of Cuba. Bellamy and Williams led the attack and employed a novel, if not shocking, strategy. They and their men stripped naked and charged onto the ship wearing only their pistols, swords and ammunition boxes. This, plus some bursts of gunfire from Jennings's ship and Bellamy's threats of no quarter, caused the captain to surrender almost immediately. Jennings boarded the ship and tortured the French sailors until they revealed where they had hidden 30,000 pieces of eight onshore. Once the

Charles Vane, engraving from Captain Charles Johnson, *The History and Lives of All the Most Notorious Pirates, and Their Crews* (1725).

pirates retrieved the loot and brought it onto the *Sainte-Marie*, they declared themselves victorious.[51] This strategy became infamous and soon other pirates began using their own forms of theatrical intimidation, such as Blackbeard's smoking beard (he put lit candles into it before his attacks to make it appear that he had ascended from the depths of hell) and Anne Bonny and Mary Read's bare-breasted attacks. Rackham's former captain Charles Vane took this practice even further by subjecting his victims to torture.

Violence and fear tactics went beyond theatrics. Pirate attacks were brutal and especially terrifying when they came without warning. The pirate George Cusack ordered one of his crew members to attack a ship with the element of surprise. The pirate chose a victim and woke him up by 'striking him over the face with the flat of his Sword, and calling him Dog, Swearing several Oaths, using the Deponent in a very ill manner, and said the Ship was their own'. Cusack and his crew ransacked the ship and left them 'not so much as Victuals to maintain them for Twenty four Hours, having taken their sails, Cables and Anchors, leaving them to the mercy of the Sea, and one Main-sail; and having begged on their knees for their Fore-sail and Anchor'.[52] Similarly, the pirate Robert Read called his victims 'doggs' and threatened to shoot them and then hang them for all to see. He shot the chief mate dead, put a rope around his neck 'and hoysted him upon Deck', before throwing him overboard.[53]

Edward Teach was notorious for his use of terror to subdue his victims and claim victory. He was iconic because of his long, black smoking beard. However, he did not kill any victims and discouraged his crew from doing so as well. Captain William Wyer of the *Protestant Caesar* survived one of Blackbeard's attacks. He was captured on 5 April 1718 by a ship that had

'40 Guns 300 Men' and was 'called Queen Ann's Revenge, Commanded by Edward Teach a Pirate'. Wyers knew of Black-beard's reputation and immediately said that he would not fight because he feared being murdered. Blackbeard told Wyers that if he came on board the *Queen Anne's Revenge* he would come to no harm. However, once Blackbeard realized that Wyer's ship was from Boston, he immediately commanded his crew to burn it. Blackbeard hated New England, especially Boston, because he felt it was a place meant to kill pirates: 'he would burn all Vessells belonging to New England for Executing six Pirates at Boston.' Blackbeard sent several members of his crew onto the *Protestant Caesar*, who promptly set it on fire. On 12 April, Blackbeard unloaded Wyer and his crew onto a Rhode Island ship, where they found safety.[54]

Pirates had no qualms about leaving their victims to the fate of the sea. Captain Bartholomew Roberts, one of the most prolific pirates of the Golden Age of Piracy, was known for his ruthlessness and the large number of prisoners he took. One of them, Edward Evans, who was a cook on a ship called the *Porcupine* when Roberts took her, claimed that one of Roberts's men, Robert Haws, set the ship on fire. This left Evans and the rest of the *Porcupine*'s crew with 'the dreadful choice of perishing by Fire or Water'. Those who chose water rather than burning to death or becoming prisoners jumped overboard but were imme-diately attacked and torn apart by sharks. The pirates 'took a cruel satisfaction in looking on'.[55] Another survivor was held at gunpoint as the ship burned. He asked one of Roberts's pirate 'the Reason of such wicked Practices? He answered, it was for a fun.'[56]

Extreme violence was common in pirate attacks, which added to other sailors' terror. Pirates were known to throw their victims overboard or murder them in other brutal ways. The pirate James Williams ordered his crew to cut their victims' throats while one of the pirates threw a man overboard and another shot Oliver Forneau, the captain of their prize, the *George*.[57] Williams's pirate John Smith was later convicted for throwing the captain's mate, surgeon and clerk overboard during the attack.[58]

Sometimes newspapers spared readers the gory details. The pirate George Lowther was known to burn his victims until they surrendered their goods.[59] On one occasion he plundered a Virginia-bound ship captained by a man named Graves for all its 'fresh Provisions, Arms and Powder'. A brief blurb in the *London Journal* claimed that Lowther threatened Graves by 'flourishing his Sword several times over his Head, and said, I make no doubt but you expect to see me make my exit at Execution Dock, but by G--- I never will, for if I should be over-power'd here is that shall End me.' The article concluded, 'Many other stories are told of this Desperado too shocking to appear in print.'[60]

There were times when newspaper and other publishing editors were all too happy to include the goriest details possible. Brutality held a morbid fascination and attracted readers. The publication of a pamphlet called *The Tryals of Thirty-Six Persons for Piracy* described how a pirate named Charles Harris attacked the ship *Amsterdam Merchant*, which was commanded by John Welland, who testified against Harris and his crew at the trial. Not only did the pirates sail off with 'three Barrels of Beef, of the value of Seven Pounds, some Quantities of Gold and Silver of the value of One Hundred & Fifty Pounds, [and] one Negro Man Slave named Dick of the value of Fifty Pounds', they sank the ship (worth over £1,000) and 'and cut off the said Wellands right ear'.[61]

The *London Journal* reported on the most horrifying act a pirate could commit: forced cannibalism (forcing someone to eat human flesh). The idea of forced cannibalism had the potential to cause a community of readers to feel united in their disgust, outrage and morbid intrigue.[62] One could argue that forced cannibalism was acceptable in print because it did not humanize the pirates. George Lowther and his crew were said to have 'murdered 45 Spaniards in cold Blood' and 'cut off the said Master's Lips and broiled them before his Face' and made the poor man eat his own lips.[63] Sometimes a pirate ship would be referred to as the 'Flying Devil' because the ships were said to have 'none but Devils aboard her'.[64]

Despite the collective abhorrence for this act, forced cannibalism and bodily mutilation were common in London newspaper reports about piracy. Cannibalistic rhetoric has been used since the Middle Ages to outrage, inflame and rally public feeling against enemies and criminals.[65] John Upton was found guilty of piracy in 1729 after spending five years terrorizing merchant ships off the North American coast and throughout the West Indies. The crime for which he was on trial was the plunder of a merchant ship called the *Perry Galley* on 14 November 1725 under the command of Story King. Upton received the death sentence after a trial that lasted nearly four hours.[66] Several weeks later a detailed account of Upton's crimes was published in the *Daily Journal*. In this particular article, not only was the captain of the plundered ship said to have been strung up by the neck, but he was wounded in 'above 20 places'; then 'they cut his ear in order to broil it', coercing the man to eat it, 'and thrust a Cartridge filled with Gun-Powder into his Mouth, [with] which they threatened to blow his Brains out.'[67] Upton's crimes do not appear in the *Calendar of State Papers*, but this does not mean that they did not occur. This story was published in London three times.[68] These examples of mutilation and forced cannibalism went against human nature because they were not what would be termed 'agreed cannibalism': a last resort for sailors on the sea who were about to succumb to starvation, and which was common knowledge but rarely discussed openly.[69] Cannibalism was the utmost cultural sign of brutality and excess.[70] These were characteristics that pirates embodied, which infuriated their more 'civilized' contemporaries.

6

FOOD AND DRINK
ON THE PIRATE SHIP

'Every Man has . . . equal Title to the fresh Provisions, or strong
Liquors, at any Time seized, and may use them at Pleasure.'
Articles of Captain Bartholomew Roberts

A healthy diet was essential to a pirate ship's success and a
sufficient allocation of food and drink was necessary to
keep the crew safe and happy. Food and drink were directly tied
into the crew's survival 'in terms of morale and nutrition and,
ultimately, could determine the success or failure of the voyage'.[1]
This was so important that an 1841 treatise outlined rules and
regulations regarding provisions at sea. In general, every ship
entering an Atlantic voyage was required to have 'at least sixty
gallons of water, one hundred pounds of wholesome ship bread,
and one hundred pounds of salted flesh meat'. In fact, 'if the
crew of any vessel not so provided shall be put upon short
allowance of water, flesh, or bread, such seaman shall recover
from the master double wages for every day was so allowanced.'[2]

There was a long-standing ancient medical belief that a
human body contains four humours which must remain in total
harmony for health: blood, black bile, yellow bile and phlegm.
Blood was a hot and wet element, yellow bile was hot and dry,

black bile was cold and dry and phlegm was cold and wet. An excess of blood meant the body was too hot, which caused fevers. Too much yellow bile was related to stomach issues while extra black bile presented as melancholia (or depression). An excess of phlegm caused respiratory issues. If any of the humours became imbalanced, they upset the order of the rest. Avicenna, a tenth-century Persian physician, stated:

> One must not forget that the most fundamental agents in the formation of the humours are heat and cold. When the heat is equable, blood forms; when heat is in excess, bilious humour [yellow bile] forms; when in great excess, so that oxidation occurs, atrabilious [black] humour forms. When the cold is equable, serous [phlegmatic] humour forms; when cold is in excess so that [congealing] becomes dominant, atrabilious humour forms.[3]

Seventeenth- and eighteenth-century physicians believed food had a direct effect on the body's ability to keep the four humours balanced, and that it was cooked by the body in various organs that included the stomach, liver and heart. According to Thomas Aubrey, an eighteenth-century ship's physician and author of *The Sea-Surgeon; or, The Guinea Man's Vade Mecum*, blood was generated by the digestion of food, which also kept the humours 'nourished and sustained'.[4] Any food that could not be converted into one of the four humours was excreted.

However, the average eighteenth-century sailor did not eat well. Rations were salt meat and fish about four times a week along with some cheese, butter, peas and hard sea-biscuits. One popular treat was 'dough-boys', which were simply boiled dumplings that offered extra carbohydrates and protein and were cooked in seawater rather than in the precious freshwater supply. Fresh fruit and vegetables, especially citrus such as lemons and limes, were highly desired but hard to come by. As a result, scurvy ran rampant on ships, often showing up about two or three months into a journey.[5] It was a debilitating disease caused by a chronic lack of vitamin C, with symptoms such as fatigue, muscle aches, bleeding gums, loose teeth and rashes. Sailors did not know what caused scurvy, but they knew it was connected to a lack of fruit and vegetables.[6] The best thing they believed they could do to prevent the disease was to keep fresh meat on board whenever possible, along with cream of tartar and boiled concentrate of lemons and oranges.[7] Pirates, who spent most of their time near coasts in order to be able to replenish these types of goods, rarely had to worry about this affliction, but it still posed a great risk.

Quality food was essential not just for health, but for morale. Merchant and naval ships were notorious for their poor rations. One English seaman who had spent time on a Royal Navy ship opined: 'A hot country, stinking Meat, and maggoty Bread, with the noisome and poisonous Scent of the Bilge Water, have made many a brave English sailor food for Crabs and Sharks.'[8] Distributing food equally and providing some variety in the diet was a difficult task and often led to arguments among the crew, especially since there was a direct correlation between the quality of food and the success of the voyage. Even though some observed that naval ships were still better than merchant vessels, captains, mates, stewards and pursers – anyone responsible for distributing food and drink – was 'detested for their conniving and exploit-ative ways'. John Phillips referred to his previous captain, John Wingfield of the ship *Swallow*, as 'a Super Cargo Son of a B---h' and accused him of starving the men; 'it was such Dogs as he put men on Pyrating.'[9]

Sometimes sailors received as little as 400 grams (14 oz) of food a day, or were served beer 'as bad as water bewitched'. The food was on occasion so terrible that sailors refused it, saying that not even rats would eat it.[10]

Unfortunately, sometimes merchants had no choice but to limit rations to make food supplies last during voyages plagued by challenges such as extreme winds, storms or harsh currents. This was also a grand opportunity for captains to cut as many costs as possible. In this case they might decrease sailors' pay and replace it with food, known as 'punch-gut money'. Similar

John Phillips, engraving from Captain Charles Johnson, *The History and Lives of All the Most Notorious Pirates, and Their Crews* (1725).

to the way food was meted out to prevent scurvy, monthly fare during hard times was a pound of whatever meat was on hand (usually salt pork, salt beef, bacon or fish) four times a week along with cheese, peas, butter, biscuits and small rations of wine, brandy, small beer or rum. As much fresh food was given out as possible as soon as it became available. Once on land the sailors could go hunting and fishing to supplement their food stores.[11]

Sailors enjoyed a higher quality of food on pirate ships. Their diets were varied and usually contained 'Beefe, Porke, Pease, Fish, Oyle, Bisket, Beere', butter, brandy and oats if they were available.[12] Tropical fruits sometimes made their way onto their menus, such as bananas, plantains, pineapples, avocados, oranges and other citrus fruits.[13] If pirates landed anywhere outside of a port in the West Indies, they looked for one food source more than any other: turtles. Their flesh is rich in nutrients and was thought to be a cure for most ailments. Pirates extracted oil from the turtles' livers and flesh, which they believed was good

Henry Morgan destroys the Spanish fleet at Lake Maracaibo, Venezuela, engraving from A. O. Exquemelin, *The Buccaneers of America* (1678).

for treating muscle aches and strains. Their flesh was believed to be essential for an anti-scurvy diet (although the meat actually contains little vitamin C) and for all sorts of venereal diseases that they sometimes picked up on land.[14] Turtle meat was also quite versatile in that it could be boiled, roasted, fried, baked or stewed. Seamen caught various types of fish depending on their location, such as albacore, catfish, mullet, smelt, rockfish, grouper, dolphinfish, snapper, shellfish and even sharks.[15] Henry Morgan searched out various islands off the coast of Panama where meat was plentiful to supplement this diet. Drake's Isle was a favoured spot. The island was said to 'afford plenty of Goats, Fish, and of Turtle' to replenish their stores.[16] Food preparation was simple, with small hearths meant for just one kettle each, to maintain safety. The crew, depending on its size, was typically divided up into four messes, who ate three meals a day using just a knife and their hands.[17]

Water was always tricky. The initial rations, before setting out to sea, came from rivers, which were often heavily contaminated with waste. It was stored in wooden casks with lime to keep it fresh, but the barrels were at risk of rotting due to the salty sea air.[18] Their supplies could turn brackish, fill with algae and dwindle quickly.[19] If they did not make frequent landfall for water, their voyage could be doomed. If they found water, they had to take as much as they could in case they fell into scarcity again. Captain Henry Morgan used their time on land to hunt out water sources and turtles: in one successful venture the crew managed to scrounge up nine turtles and enough water to fill their barrels several times over.[20]

Without proper storage, pirates would become either seriously ill or malnourished. A standard pirate ship had a large hold that usually contained most of their food stores. The main hold 'was used for provision such as water, meat, beer, cheese and butter which required neither special care nor security'.[21] Various-sized casks contained water and beer, but these items were problematic because of their weight and how much space they occupied. Some non-pirate ships only carried a certain provision of beverages to last a specific amount of time, such as four months.

Cooking food had its own challenges. Hot food could only be prepared in an area that could safely contain a fire – especially during storms and attacks. The cook room, later referred to as a galley, had to be large enough to cook meals for many men, but it needed to take up as little space as possible. This location was the cook's territory and was reserved for himself and any assistants he might have. No one was allowed into the cook room without special permission from either the officers or the cook himself.[22] In the sixteenth century, food 'was prepared on hearths built of some fifty bricks and situated in the hold above the wet ballast as greater security against fire'.[23] This style lasted until the late seventeenth century. The bricks were placed around a pit to enclose kettles while leaving an opening on one side. The opening was

> closed by an iron door, which was hinged and could be bolted shut. Horizontal pipes ran through the brickwork, forward of the kettle. The ash pit also had an opening in the top to allow the smoke to escape through a funnel. Several layers of brick were placed under the ash pit, to keep the fire away from the wood of the deck.

This was the most basic type of firehearth and was suitable only for boiling. Parts were added to the structure to give scope for more sophisticated cooking. In the seventeenth and early eighteenth centuries, the brickwork on the aft side of the main stove formed a separate furnace, with iron racks for grilling. This was used for the officers' food.[24]

The cook room was completed by a stove that had a large chimney, since the room was always located below deck. The stove was built in two parts. The lower part 'extended from over the top of the oven and going up through the decks, and the upper part above the main deck which directed the smoke high enough to not offend those on the top decks'.[25] The safety and location of the cook room were so important that treatises were written in the 1630s and '40s on their care.

The quartermaster was usually in charge of how food was stored and retrieved. He followed strict rules to make sure that everything was handled with care so casks would not break and food would not be lost.[26] The quartermaster also had to make sure that the pirates ate their fill, keeping them happy, not hungry. According to a former pirate named John Plantain, 'Every Man is allowed to eat what he pleases. Then they put all under the care of their Quarter-master, who discharges all things with an Equality to them all, every Man and Boy faring alike; and even their Captain or any other Officer, is allowed no more than another Man.'[27] Quartermasters might supervise the ship's cook to make sure that food was equally distributed.

Pirates also had a healthier diet than people on other ships, thanks in part to their prizes. Through theft, pirates were able to replenish their stores between ports. This kept them healthier and more physically fit than many other sailors. Strength and stamina were the difference between life and death as a pirate, especially when considering the physical peril of battle. In addition to food, alcohol was important on a ship for morale and medicinal purposes. Pirates were given rations of rum and wine. These, along with curfews, kept alcohol consumption under control so order could be maintained on the ship.

Alcohol, especially rum, has long been associated with pirates. The spirit has shown up in popular culture, such as Robert Louis Stevenson's ditty 'Yo-ho-ho and a bottle of rum!' in *Treasure Island*. Rum had several uses on board. Since water developed a foul taste over time, rum was a nice palate-cleanser. Distilled from sugar, it stayed sweet in wooden casks. It also did not take up much room. Thanks to its high alcohol content, they did not need to store nearly as much of it as they would beer and wine because it satiated their need for inebriation.[28]

A very popular drink for pirates was punch rather than grog, which would not gain popularity until the mid-eighteenth century. Punch was full of cheap ingredients that could be easily stored on board. Captain Kidd's favoured recipe included rum, water, lime juice, egg yolk and sugar, with some nutmeg sprinkled on top. In general, however, punch was much simpler on most pirate ships. It contained just four ingredients: 'One of sour, two of sweet, three of strong, four of weak'. The sour was lemon or lime juice (great to combat scurvy), the sweet was sugar, the strong was rum and water made up the weak component. Spices were used to modify the flavour further should one wish. The beverage is still a popular choice today in Caribbean resorts or themed bars and restaurants.[29] During his privateering days, Woodes Rogers wrote in his journal that sailors enjoyed a drink called flip, which consisted of beer, rum and sugar warmed up and served in a tin can. Bumboe was also popular among sailors: it was a rum punch that had been popular since the Middle Ages, and consisted of rum, water, sugar and nutmeg.[30]

Other spirits were also popular on ships. In general, the primary beverages at sea were alcoholic. Northern Europeans drank brandy and ale while those in North American waters drank rum and ale. Wine was very desirable, especially canary, sherry, Madeira, claret and Rhenish, if pirates could obtain them (although they were usually reserved for officers).[31]

Alcohol was used to give prisoners an incentive to join the crew and allowed pirates to provide hospitality to stay in good favour. Stede Bonnet was known for plying his prisoners with food and drink. Two such prisoners were a man named John Killing, later a witness in the trial against Bonnet, and his captain, who were both locked in a cabin on their own ship as the pirates plundered their goods. After some time, two of Bonnet's pirates came into their cabin to offer them some of their own pineapple (a fruit long known to symbolize hospitality) so they could all eat together. Killing said he had no appetite, so the pirates asked him what kind of alcohol they had on board. 'I told them some Rum and Sugar,' Killing said during the trial. The pirates gathered up ingredients to make punch and together all four men drank and sang songs.[32]

It goes without saying that a healthy diet was key to any mariner's survival and pirates were fortunate in that they were able to replenish their stores more often than other sailors. This kept them physically healthier than their victims, which may account for their successes. This does not mean they did not have their vices. While alcohol was seen as an essential part of their diet, some captains recognized the risks that spirits could pose to their voyages.

7

PIRATES' VICES

'He that shall be Guilty of Drunkenness in the Time
of an Engagement, shall suffer what Punishment the
Captain and majority of the Company shall think fit.

He that shall be found Guilty of Gaming, or playing at Cards,
or Defrauding or Cheating one another to the Value
of a Royal of Plate, shall suffer what Punishment the
Captain and majority of the Company shall think fit.'
The Articles of Capt. Edward Low the Pirate, with his Company

Vices were sometimes necessary for good morale, but on
ships two were often seen more as problems than solutions:
drinking and gambling. Drunkenness led to disorder and poor
judgement, while gambling caused anger and further unrest.
The latter was rampant on many ships.[1] In fact, it was just as
common as drinking. Backgammon was a particular favourite,
along with dice and cards, on which men placed cash bets.[2]
These habits were such an issue that Bartholomew Roberts wrote
a clause in his articles to specifically ban both drinking and
gambling.[3] Other pirates adopted similar policies to maintain
order. Jacob du Bucquoy, who was the pirate John Taylor's

prisoner, described the regulations as being 'in order to preserve the peace and union necessary between members of the brotherhood'. To maintain this peace, 'quarrels and insults are forbidden, likewise religious disputes; for the same reason gambling for money is also forbidden.'[4]

On the morning of Captain Kidd's execution on 23 May 1701, he was so 'enflam'd with drink' that he could barely speak, which filled the Ordinary of Newgate (the chaplain of Newgate Prison, who offered spiritual care to prisoners condemned to death) with 'unspeakable grief'.[5] The night before his execution, Kidd assured the ordinary that he lived in repentence of his sins and hoped 'to be sav'd through the Merits of Christ'. Kidd expressed his confidence in God's mercy, but the author was not convinced. Kidd 'reflected more upon others, than upon himself, and endeavoured to lay his Faults on his Crew and others, in the same Manner he did when upon his Trial'. He had a brief reprieve when he was hanged, because the rope snapped, and he fell to the ground shaken but still alive. The fall shook him out of his stupor and he was 'in a much better Temper than before'. He allowed the minister to pray with him as he climbed back onto the ladder. When Kidd finally died, the Ordinary of Newgate left 'with a greater Satisfaction than I had before, that he was Penitent'.[6]

Kidd's drunkenness at the scaffold coupled with the ordinary's lamentations reflected changing ideas about polite behaviour. In the eighteenth century, the idea of 'polite society' emerged and gained a foothold in Britain, and these cultural patterns spread to the British American colonies. 'Politeness' was associated with improvements in moral and social standards. The idea extended to all social classes thanks to the printing industry and a rise in literacy. It grew even further thanks to the increasing number of the middling folk who profited well enough from trade to develop a luxurious lifestyle. This, in turn, created a fixation on manners and the cultivation of new and ritualized forms of behaviour that were necessary for coexistence with an increasingly complex urban environment. Eighteenth-century polite society associated alcohol with poor conduct and bad reputations. Extreme drunkenness was considered antisocial behaviour in which a person could not exercise any self-control, which is what separated man from beast.[7] In North America, public drunkenness was one of the most offensive behaviours in polite society.[8]

Yet drinking remained a very popular habit on ships. Stolen spirits had to be guarded lest pirates drank them all. Idleness often interrupted work; long hours increased boredom and feelings of uselessness. Land-based workers and citizens did not understand this and believed that all sailors – pirate or not – were lazy and therefore prone to sinful behaviour. Some people felt that if pirates made themselves useful to society, they could re-enter the grace of God. The *Boston-Newsletter* printed articles urging its readers to 'instruct, admonish, preach and pray for them' because pirates were without salvation.[9] An Englishman named Hugh Jones, who published his observations of Virginian culture and society, suggested how they might solve their piracy problems. Jones described Virginia as a place where profane and immoral behaviour was heavily discouraged, but the behaviours were not suppressed very efficiently because the colony had no ecclesiastical court.[10] He argued that pirates were competent seamen, but lacked the steady employment necessary to keep them honest. If sailors were given more honest work through-out the plantations, the number of pirates would decrease and eventually they would be successfully eradicated.[11]

Excess drinking was considered to be both indecent and irreligious: to be either was illegal in the British North American colonies, especially New England. A crime against God was said to be a crime against society; a crime against society was an offence against God. Criminal codes were designed to enforce public and private morals. Early American ideas of crime stemmed from moral and religious origins rather than just economic and political roots. Britain and the colonies had officials responsible for the formulation, implementation and demonstrations of the norms in their respective fields.[12] According to a New England publication called *Abstract of the Laws*, proper decorum dictated that one must not appear drunk in public lest one face a large fine and spend hours in the stocks. Even though this was published in 1797, seventy years after the end of the Golden Age of Piracy, polite ideas about social behaviour were still prevalent in North America and the laws against drinking continued to be enforced. These also regulated alehouse-goers: if they were found to be publicly inebriated, their favoured drinking establishments could be shut down for up to three years.[13] They did not inhibit sailors and pirates, who often found life at sea so lonely that their only respite was spending their money in taverns on drink and women.[14]

The British West Indian colonies also had laws against drunkenness. Lechery ran amok on the plantation islands, which required the Council of Trade and Assemblies to establish social laws to regulate behaviours as they did in England. Jamaica, similar to the New England colonies, passed laws specific to social conduct. Acts were passed as early as 1664 to curb 'tippling, cursing and swearing'.[15] By the 1670s, drunkenness was such a problem that one of the quays in Port Royal became known as

'Drunkard's Key' because of the many pirates and privateers who frequented the area after unpacking their plundered goods.[16] In 1701, British officials ordered the governor of Jamaica to punish 'drunkenness, debauchery, swearing and blasphemy, and admit none to public trusts and employments whose ill-fame and conversation may occasion scandal'.[17] Strict laws were passed to punish drunkenness but to little effect.[18]

It took a couple of decades to establish order in Jamaica. The Acts of Assembly passed a law banning alehouses and taverns from selling alcohol without the requisite yearly certificates that allowed liquor licences. Once established, the person in charge of the said alehouse or tavern had to prevent any and all 'disorders committed in his said House or any Thing there done contrary to the Laws of England or this Island'. However, it is unknown how well these laws were actually enforced in the former 'Sodom of the Sea'.[19]

Drinking sometimes meant the end of pirates' careers. The pirate Edward Low banned drinking on his ship altogether. Article nine of his pirate code read: 'He that shall be guilty of Drunkenness in time of Engagement shall Suffer what Punishment the Captain and Majority of the Company shall think fit.'[20] Drunk pirates might lose their mental faculties, make rash decisions or find themselves under arrest after a blackout. Not only that, but excessive drunkenness was a real danger to ships' crews on both pirate and legitimate sailing vessels. When a pirate ship stole a vessel off the coast of Massachusetts, they found large stores of various spirits and 'got themselves Drunk and Asleep', which allowed the captain of the stolen ship to steer her ashore and have the pirates arrested.[21] In another instance, a French pirate named James Mews found himself taken captive because of his drinking. After his ship was taken by English pirates, he 'went to Breakfast, and Drank so much' that he did not realize more of them had boarded his ship. 'When he came to be sober, he found himself bound in the Hold of the Sloop, and he was kept tied until he came to Boston in the Sloop.'[22]

The most detailed example is the capture of Captain Jack Rackham and his crew in October 1720. After several small prizes, the pirates finally managed to capture a vessel that held a significant amount of wine. Instead of saving it to sell, the men decided to celebrate their victory by drinking it all. They sailed into a Jamaican cove called Negril's Point and laid anchor. Wine and rum flowed freely as they sang songs, smoked, laughed and played raucous pranks on each other. Rackham's wife, Anne Bonny, and the other female crew member, Mary Read, were the only two to not partake in the celebrations. They warned the men that drunkenness would leave them defenceless. The women were correct. Unbeknownst to them, a pirate-hunter named Jonathan Barnet had been tracking them for some time and was lying in wait watching the party from a distance. The governor of the Bahamas and the governor of Jamaica had both issued warrants for Rackham's arrest and were offering significant rewards, so Barnet could expect a good payout.

The pirate hunter could hear the sounds of celebration and knew that the pirates would likely end up too drunk to resist him. Sure enough, after Barnet hailed the *Revenge*, Rackham scrambled to ready his crew for battle. The pirates stumbled and swore but managed to load one of their swivel guns and fire it at Barnet's ship.[23] This did not deter the pirate-hunter and his men swarmed onto Rackham's ship. In a drunken panic, Rackham ordered his men below deck, leaving just Bonny and Read on board to defend them all. Read reportedly shouted at the pirates, 'If there's a man among ye, ye'll come up and fight like the man ye are to be!'[24]

She fired her gun into the hold, injuring some of the men, and even killed one.[25] Unfortunately, the battle was over almost immediately. No matter how skilled the women were at fighting, they could not hold off Barnet's entire crew. They were captured and transported to St Jago de la Vega, Jamaica, to stand trial. Rackham was found guilty and executed on 18 November 1720 in Port Royal.

Edward Teach took a different approach. He encouraged his large crew to celebrate recent wins by drinking themselves into oblivion. In the meantime, he had gathered forty of his most trusted crew with a plan to abandon Bonnet, take a pardon in North Carolina and lie low until they could set out again with less notoriety.

The plan worked. Once they landed on the coast of North Carolina, Teach took his men inland and successfully took the pardon. As a condition of receiving the pardon, Teach betrayed Bonnet by naming him and the rest of the crew. The next morning, Bonnet awoke to find Teach gone and realized his betrayal. In a panic, the crew frantically attempted to get back out to sea, but their ship was trapped on the shoals. Bonnet turned tail and abandoned his crew; he escaped during the night to find work with a new pirate crew.

The remaining pirates felt they had nothing to lose. They went inland, raided the nearest city's stores and enjoyed another raucous night of drinking. Two days later, while they were in an unconscious drunken stupor on the *Revenge*, they awoke to find themselves surrounded by Admiralty officials and placed under arrest.

Bonnet managed to continue his piratical career for a short period of time. He joined forces with the pirate Charles Vane, who was infamous for his cruelty, before he managed to take another ship for his own. Unfortunately, being the unskilled sailor he was, Bonnet was soon captured off the coast of South Carolina. He died via public execution in Charles Town on 10 December 1718.[26]

On the other hand, drinking could be a saviour to those who were forced into piracy. One could only hope that pirates might drink themselves into oblivion so the prisoners could make their escape. A man named John Filmore was kept prisoner for nine months, along with several other men, before he finally had the opportunity to escape his captors after a night of drinking. After a successful capture, the pirates 'had a grand carouse, eating and drinking, and spending the day in such diversions as their gross inclinations desired'. This finally presented Filmore and the other prisoners with the 'favourable opportunity' he had been waiting for 'to extricate us from our suffering'. Filmore gave the following testimony about his experience:

> It was late in the evening before the pirates retired to rest, and White and one more of the pirates got in the caboose, as drunk as beasts, and lay down before the fire; a favorable opportunity now seemed to offer for us to improve in conferring upon some means for our escape. We got together, held a consultation, and concluded to risk our lives in trying to work our deliverance, concluding that we had better die in so just a cause . . .
>
> Our plan being thus concerted, I went down into the caboose, where White and John Rose Archer, a desperate fellow who had been taken in one of the prizes, and immediately joined the pirates, laid on the floor, as before mentioned, drunk as beasts. I took fire and burnt these two villains in the feet, while they lay senseless, so badly

as to render them unable to be upon deck next day. There were only four now left of the old pirate gang, and give who had joined them since, besides the two I had rendered incapable of injuring us.[27]

Drinking has always been a social bonding activity and it was no different on a pirate ship. Alcohol was used as a means of entertainment and resistance. Pirates rebelled against the strictures of society through transgressions: blasphemous speech, drunkenness, robbery and violent encounters without fear of death.[28] Naturally, seventeenth-century buccaneers were said to be fond of tobacco and drink. Caribbean towns encouraged these vices. Port Royal, Jamaica, was home to no fewer than nineteen taverns, which were all registered between 1665 and 1693, the year the Royal Navy took control of the island.[29] Rum and wine were consumed copiously and drinking proved to be an excellent way to increase morale and create camaraderie. Bartholomew Roberts encouraged all his crew throughout his fleet to drink bountifully for their entertainment. This was especially important when he captured men and forced them into his crew, because once they had partaken, they were real pirates. As a result, most of Roberts's men were condemned regardless of how they came to be on his ship.

Many of Roberts's pirates claimed on the stand to have been forced and that they had no choice but to be among the pirates. However, eyewitness accounts that described their apparent camaraderie through drink could have deadly consequences, as was the case with Roger Scot from Captain Roberts's crew on the ship *Elizabeth* commanded by John Sharpe. Scot claimed he was one of Roberts's many victims who had no choice but to become part of Roberts's crew if he wanted to survive. However, one of the crew's witnesses, who had already been acquitted, Charles Manjoy, stated that he saw Scot, 'whom he knows very well on board of the Elizabeth . . . carousing and drinking with the pirates'. This indicated that Scot, indeed, found good company among the pirates, and even if he did not actually participate in any raids, he still appeared to be a loyal pirate. Whether or not it was a ruse on his part intended to give him a better chance of survival did not matter. Joseph Mansfield found himself in a similar situation. He said he was forced at gunpoint to join Roberts's crew but during their raids he would be too drunk to participate. However, the fact that he drank with the pirates was enough. The court found both men guilty, and they were sentenced to be hanged.[30]

This seemed to be the case with many of the forced men on Roberts's ship. Abraham Harper claimed his innocence, but a man named Harry Glasby spoke against him to say that once Harper came aboard Roberts's ship, the *Onslow*, he appeared to fall right into the pirate life. 'When the Quarter-master called for Drink or anything else, he with a merry Countenance always readily obeyed him.' Harper claimed that this was merely for self-preservation, but when Glasby testified that Harper also took part in every raid, his sentence was sealed. He was bound for the noose.[31]

Glasby proved to be an excellent eyewitness, and helped to condemn another man from Roberts's crew. He testified against a man named Robert Johnson, who did appear to actively resist becoming a pirate for quite some time. According to Glasby, before Johnson was forcibly taken, the pirates coerced him into drinking with them for his survival, but once he was too drunk to hold any coherent thoughts, they hoisted him onto Roberts's ship, the *Fortune*. However, Johnson quickly 'became a forward

Man, and was in Action, by the Quarter-master's Command'. Despite his protests, Johnson was sentenced to death.[32]

Drunkenness brought on a lack of judgement that caused the downfall of both victim and pirate. The Irish pirate captain Philip Roche was known to use alcohol to subdue his victims, a notable example being the French captain Henry Owsley. Owsley gave his liquor stores to Roche's pirates. Being extremely drunk himself, he then excused himself to go up onto the deck to urinate. Roche's pirates all got uproariously drunk and those who were well enough began fighting Owsley's crew to the death. During the hubbub, Owsley was standing at the ship's rails when two extremely drunk pirates named Slade and Dent snuck up behind him and threw him overboard. At their trial, the pirates claimed that they saw Owsley simply fall overboard to his death.[33] However, at this point it was recognized that this was a common practice that Roche employed, so the pirates were executed.[34]

MARINERS WERE PRONE TO excessive drinking. Alcohol was an excellent source of entertainment to alleviate long stretches of tedium. Pirates drank as a social bonding activity. Other sailors often drank to numb themselves against their rigorous labours and as a mental escape. It did not help that drinking water had to be heavily rationed, so wine, beer and spirits had to be consumed in greater quantities.[35] This led to rampant alcoholism, which on naval ships incited punishments specially reserved for drunkenness.[36] It was such a problem that the General Court in Boston prohibited sailors from consuming all spirits because the habit resulted in 'the great dishonour of God, and reproach of religion and governments here established, which also oftentimes occasions much prejudice and damage to the masters and owners of such ships and vessels to which they belong'.[37] Not only that, some pirate captains recognized the risks that excessive drunkenness caused on ships. Therefore, pirates had to find other ways to pass the time.

8

ENTERTAINMENT AND CULTURE ON THE PIRATE SHIP

'The Lights and Candles to be put out at eight-a-Clock at Night: If any of the Crew, at that Hour, still remained enclined for Drinking, they were to do it on the open Deck.'

'The Musicians to have Rest on the Sabbath Day, but the other six Days and Nights, none without special Favour.'
Articles of Captain Bartholomew Roberts

Pirates often had a good amount of downtime when not making repairs, cleaning or fighting. With all rigours and dangers that existed on the pirate ship, entertainment was essential for survival. Music and games provided much-needed relief and escapism for the pirates and helped form bonds of brotherhood.[1] Games such as cards and dice (except on the ship of Bartholomew Roberts, who considered them to be gambling), singing, playing instruments and dancing were all common forms of entertainment. Roberts took music so seriously that one of his articles specifically allowed musicians a day of rest on the Sabbath. The sea shanties sung by pirates have remained popular ever since. Having fun on the ship allowed sailors to get any feelings of restlessness or boredom out of their system, which made the atmosphere much better overall. 'Musicians played such melodies that the days passed most agreeably.'[2] In addition to sea shanties, maritime lore, legends and superstitions were told over and over to pass the time and to keep sailors', including pirates', own mythology alive. Without such pastimes, boredom would set in, which could lead to destructive behaviours that would endanger a ship.

Music was vital to life at sea and musicians often numbered among pirate crews. These included fiddlers, harpists, pipers, drummers and trumpeters. Some of them composed and sang songs that were meant to be humorous, usually making fun of British officers and other officials.[3] It is impossible to know how many pirates were lucky enough to have musicians because they either destroyed or did not keep records. However, Roberts was confirmed to have two musicians in his crew after his ship, the *Royal Fortune*, was captured. One of them was named Nicholas Bratter, a fiddler captured from a ship called the *Cornwall Galley* and forced to join the crew and sign the articles. However, in his defence at his trial it was said that 'the prisoner was only made use of, as music, which he dared not refuse.' Bratter was acquitted.[4]

And what would good music be without singing? Ballads and shanties were sung on ships to alleviate boredom and have a good time. Sailors loved ballads because they were celebrated in many of them. Since the seventeenth century, English ballads had depicted seamen as defenders of the nation.[5] Pirates certainly saw themselves as defenders of their own nation (the ship) and were happy to sing songs in which they were the heroes.

Ballads were also used to tell stories about pirates in an entertaining fashion. These were often sung to simple tunes, which made them easy to memorize, allowing them to spread far and wide. 'The Elegy of Captain Kidd' is one of the most famous to tell the story of a pirate. It tells the story of his piracy and capture in a way that gives its audience a moral lesson. The elegy begins:

> When any Great and Famous Man does Die,
> The World expects to have an ELEGY
> Produc'd, to his Immortal Memory:
> The End of which, we know, is to declare
> What those Great Deeds and Noble Actions were
> Which did Complete his Noble Character.

After his introduction, the ballads go on to provide detail about his actions, portraying him as a brave, albeit brash, man:

> Kidd was a Man of such undaunted Spirit,
> He'd face Hell-Gates, and all the Devils in it,
> Were't possible to STEAL: A Golden Prize
> Did so bewitch his Heart, and charm his Eyes!
> When on the Seas proud Waves he boldly rid,
> All stroke to fly the Great and Mighty KIDD
> So terrible was He, where e'er he came
> To ROB, or PLUNDER, that his very Name
> Would cause a Trembling Fear and Dread in those
> Who were his Friends, as well as his Foes.

This would rile up an enthusiastic audience. Here was a pirate who would face the Devil himself and rob the greatest ship of all time in a savage manner, but there was still a greatness to him. However, he is a cautionary tale:

These Actions rais'd his Face and made him Great;
Still climbing high'r, he fell by his own Weight:
GOOD FORTUNE left him, and his Pow'r failed him,
The DEVIL (ready for him), Gaol'd and Hang'd him,
To no one's Sorrow, rather by Joy display;
Who weeps to see a conquer'd BEAST OF PREY.

Finally, the ballad ends with a warning for dramatic effect:

Ready, Near this Tomb don't stand;
Without some Essence in thy Hand;
For here KIDD's stinking Corps does lie,
The Scent of Which may thee infect;
He Base did Live, and Base did Die,
Therefore his Tomb and Corps reject.
Put by he in WHITNEY's Grave did lie,
That all might Piss on him, as they pass'd by:
One rais'd his Face, by Robbing on SHORE,
The Other on the SEA. – Both now no more.[6]

Pirates may not have sung about one of their condemned brethren, but songs about the lives of sailors and pirates, no matter how exaggerated, were a popular choice on board.

Sea shanties were like ballads in that they were sung to simple tunes so they could be easily reproduced, but unlike ballads they were specifically intended for the maritime world and sung by sailors. They were the work songs of sailing men and were often improvised. Sometimes they included verses from other shanties. Topics included women, love, drinking, tough and hungry ships, mates, shanghaiing, waters and even revolutions. The majority were called 'sing-outs', and were based on the yells that sailors made when hauling ropes hand over hand. Other shanties were rowing songs, which became popular as early as the fourteenth century, in which sailors sang songs with phrases such as 'heave ho!' to illustrate the hard work at sea. Even the word 'shanty' has maritime origins. It likely came from words such as 'chant', 'chanter' and 'chanty', which later became slurred into 'shanty'. Sailors were known to distort words and almost create their own specific language on ships and the word for this type of song was no different.[7]

Songs were part of celebrations, including successful captures. George Cusack's crew were known to sing and make merry after a successful capture. According to one of Cusack's forced men, the pirates drank and sang their victims to hell in celebration. One of the crew's favourite songs was about how they knew their lives would lead them into hell, but at least they would have fun on their way there:

> Hang sorrow, let's cast away care,
> The World is bound to find us:
> Thou and I, all must die,
> And leave this World behind us.
> The Bell shall ring, the Clark shall sing,
> The Good old Wife shall wind us.
> The Sexton shall lay our Bodies in Clay
> Where the Devil in Hell shall find us.[8]

Songs like these, although morbid, helped prepare pirates for the inevitability of their demise. In this, they were all united and their fear was taken away.

Sometimes the guise of food, music and merrymaking was used as a form of torture for pirates' victims. Richard Hawkins,

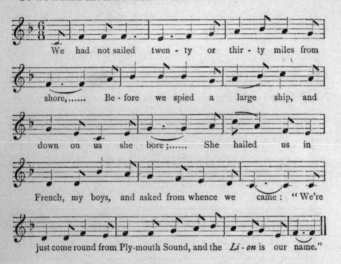

THE *LION* MAN-O'-WAR.

A very popular song at Portsmouth is "The *Lion* Man-o'-War." The following are a few of the words :—

"Are you the *Lion* man-o'-war, as we suppose you be?"
"We are the *Lion* man-o'-war, as you shall quickly see."
"Then haul your colours from the mast, and come along with me,
Or we'll sink the *Lion* man-o'-war at the bottom of the sea."

We had not sailed twen-ty or thir-ty miles from shore,...... Be-fore we spied a large ship, and down on us she bore ;...... She hailed us in French, my boys, and asked from whence we came : "We're just come round from Ply-mouth Sound, and the *Li-on* is our name."

'The *Lion* Man-o'-War', sea shanty from Laura Alexandrine Smith, *The Music of the Waters* (1888).

who was captured by the pirate Francis Spriggs, told the *British Gazette* that the pirates 'wanted a little more Diversion for Mischief' after they captured his ship. Hawkins was sent to the pirates' cabin for a meal. However, instead of proper food, the pirates inflicted torture upon him.

What should be provided for me but a Dish of Candles, which I was forced to eat, they having a Pistol at my head, and a naked Sword to my Breast, whilst others beat me with Swords call'd Tuks [a long, thin, double-edged sword]. After that I had to eat to their Satisfaction, I was buffeted and thump'd forwards to the Bag, among the rest of the Prisoners, who had much the same Fare as myself.

Hawkins's terror did not stop there. The pirates decided to continue their fun by subjecting him to 'sweating', another form of torture, which included music as a tool for a fright.

The Manner of a Sweat is thus: Between Decks they stick Candles round the Mizzen-Mast, and about twenty-five Men surrounded it with Points of Swords, Penknives, Compasses, Forks, etc. in each of their Hands: Culprit enters the Circle; The Violin plays a merry Jig; and he must run for about ten Minutes, while each Man runs his instruments into his Posteriors.[9]

James White, who was captured and tortured by Bartholo-mew Roberts and his crew, was forced to play music once the pirates realized he had the requisite skills. White 'appeared to be decrepid and ill-shapen, unfit for any purpose', but he was 'forced to comply . . . to obey their Orders' to play music or else he would be beaten even more. Not only that, but he also had to surrender all his seaman's wages to the pirates in exchange for maintaining the status of a 'forced man', leaving him completely vulnerable when they eventually dropped him off at an unnamed port.[10] Thanks to White's testimony, he was acquitted of piracy at the later trial.

Two more witnesses from Roberts's ship also described how pirates coupled music with cruelty. James Barrow, a forced boy of only sixteen, drank with the pirates and plundered a ship alongside them. Barrow was coerced into capturing live fowls from their prize to help make a grand dinner. He 'sung at Supper Spanish and French Songs out of a Dutch Prayer-Book; and [Barrow] beat one of the Ship's Company for coming to see what they were doing'. Even though Barrow clearly decided to join in with the pirates (whether it was because he wanted to or it was out of survival), he was not sentenced to death because of his young age. Instead, he was thrown into Marshalsea Prison for an undisclosed amount of time.[11]

Jack Rackham's crew also used drinking and singing to celebrate and relax after a successful attack. One of the survivors of Rackham's attacks, Ogleby, took advantage of one of the pirates' parties. Ogleby's captain had an opportunity for his crew to make their escape, but Ogleby suggested that they wait a night or two. 'Saturday night would be a good time, for then they would be merry with drinking,' and they could negotiate their release while Rackham was too happy and drunk to make a coherent decision. The plan worked and Ogleby would later become one of the chief witnesses at Rackham's trial.[12]

As with any profession, boredom descended on a pirate ship at various intervals. Their ships could be isolated for longer stretches and the pirates, close-knit in their community, would sometimes have nothing to do. Boredom could lead to discord, so captains sometimes created 'busy work' to keep their men occupied. These jobs could include scrubbing the deck or picking oakum. The latter chore was especially tedious. Larger vessels had tarred ropes, which had to be replaced after the tar eventually washed away. The pirates had to cut the rope into short strands and pick them all apart until they were down to their individual fibres. Then the material was rolled and twisted back up. Later, this rope might be used for caulking a ship. The job took hours and tore apart fingertips and fingernails, no matter how calloused and weathered the pirates' hands were from their general hard work.[13]

Tedious labour, long stretches at sea and the need for community inspired many pirates to tell tales, many of which spread from port to port. Most of these tales, known as 'yarns', were about adventures of shipwrecks, 'bloody battles, tyrannical officers or determined resistance'. Sailors and pirates had to learn how to live with and endure harsh, dangerous and even deadly conditions. Telling tales could teach them lessons about what to do in a storm, battle or shipwreck with levity. Even more important, this was also a way for them to build common values to strengthen their bond. The stories were long and told with flair, giving them a theatrical quality, with complex narratives that were funny, outlandish and full of fantasy and community. Every time pirates landed at port, their stories spread and were told elsewhere at sea, leading to a growth of major maritime lore.[14] The tales taught sailors about resistance, which inspired many of them to turn to piracy.

Another mark also told pirates' and sailors' tales: the tattoo. The art of the tattoo is ancient, but it had become associated with the maritime world by the eighteenth century. Many sailors tattooed each other by pricking the skin repeatedly with a form of pigment, such as ink or gunpowder. Tattoos were more than just skin art. They were identifiers in case the men died at sea or were captured. Soon tattoos began to illustrate other meanings. Anchors were a common way to show someone's successful initiation into sea life. Hearts often represented loved ones back home, while other symbols such as trees might mean liberty, which was a very popular theme among sailors and pirates during the Golden Age of Piracy.[15]

Some of the most pervading myths in maritime lore are those concerning women. There is a common misconception that women were seen as bad luck on ships. The stigma against women dates as far back as ancient Greece. Old sea tales spoke of 'sirens of the sea', or beautiful yet dangerous women who came out of the water to seduce sailors with song before dragging them to the bottom of the ocean. They were described as half-woman, half-bird creatures with the 'ability to so bewitch men with the sweetness of their song that the listeners forgot everything else and died of hunger'.[16] In Homer's epic poem the *Odyssey*, sirens sang a seductive song that bewitched sailors into diving into the sea. Odysseus stuffed wax into the sailors' ears and tied himself to the mast to avoid a deadly fate.[17] Their origins are a mystery, and yet their lore exists to this day. The sirens' seductive songs were most likely the cries of seals and manatees.[18] Over time, these female figures came to be seen as unlucky.

These creatures lured men to their deaths and drove them to such distraction that they would abandon their duties and endanger their crew, so the stories said. But the mermaid had different qualities to the siren. Their female charms were enchanting and beguiling. The term 'mermaid' can be interpreted as a 'maiden of the sea' who fulfilled sailors' yearning for female company, even though these beings caused nothing but doom.[19] Over the centuries, these legends became myths and were eventually diluted into the idea that women are bad luck on ships. The origin of the mermaid myth comes from stories of water sprites, known as undines, in European folklore. Stories said that undines could attain a human form if she married a mortal and had a child. This would give her a soul and the sufferings all humans endured.[20] (This tale was, of course, repurposed by Hans Christian Andersen in his story 'The Little Mermaid'.)

Numerous cultures have their own version of this half-woman, half-fish creature. According to Peter Jeans, a scholar of maritime lore, the Irish believed in a race of demons who lived in the sea, known as Formorians, while the ancient Babylonians told tales of a fish god, Oannes, who came out of the sea every day to give humans their wisdom. Norse mythology is the opposite, in that Ran, the wife of the god of the sea, ensnared sailors with a net to drown them.

The most familiar vision of mermaids comes from the ancient Syrians, who worshipped a sea goddess called Atargatis, a half-fish half-woman who derived her power from the moon to control the tides. She had a musical instrument and always held a mirror to admire her reflection. Sailors gravitated toward this myth because it was believed that Atargatis abated storms and calmed rough seas with her songs.

It appears that the mermaid might not have been a malevolent female figure meant to doom sailors for much of history. A major change began in ancient Greece, where the goddess of love, wisdom and beauty, Aphrodite, came from the ocean, or 'the source of all biological desire', tempting the weak spirit. Even the goddess's name, Aphrodite, can be traced to the term *aphro-genia*, meaning 'foam-born'. The early Christian Church took this myth and that of the siren to preach that they represented nothing more than the Devil's temptations of men with lust, which must be resisted at all costs.[21]

Many pirates' tales were about sea monsters, which symbolized the deep dangers in the ocean. These stories prevailed for centuries and were so significant that early cartographers included images of them on maps. A Swedish cartographer and ecclesiastic named Olaus Magnus drew a map of Scandinavia in 1539 and included images of a large tentacled monster that came to be known as the Kraken.[22] This was a sea monster that likely originated in Norse mythology, because the first description of it comes from Erik Pontoppidan's *Natural History of Norway*. The Kraken was said to be able to drag the largest and most powerful ships to the bottom of the sea by either using its tentacles or a creating a whirlpool. The word 'Kraken' comes from the Old Swedish term *kraken* and the Danish word *krage*, which both describe tree branches that resemble such a monster. Pontoppidan described the Kraken as 'a mile and a half wide'. Sometimes it slept on the seabed until the fires of hell became too hot and it was forced to surface. Olaus Magnus said the Kraken lounged at the surface, resembling an island. He claimed that its skin looked so much like the shingle of a beach that sailors would land on it, only to be eaten.

The Kraken was most likely based on an octopus or large squid. There are numerous images and accounts from the eighteenth century that describe a large octopus wrapping its tentacles around a ship and dragging the vessel and its unlucky passengers into the ocean depths. There were also reports of sailors being attacked and drowned by octopuses or squids. Whatever the reality, the Kraken remained and continues to be a large facet of maritime lore.[23] It demonstrated the unmapped mystery and terror of the ocean that all mariners faced.[24]

Magnus also documented a monster known as the Soe Orm:

A very large Sea-Serpent of a length of upwards of 200 feet and 20 feet in diameter which lives in rocks and in holes near the shore of Bergen; it comes out of its cavern only on summer nights and in fine weather to destroy calves, or hogs, or goes into the sea to eat cuttles, lobster, and all kinds of sea crabs. It has a growth of hairs of two feet in length hanging from the neck, sharp scales of a dark brown color, and brilliant flaming eyes.[25]

Other myths that captured pirates' imaginations included the *Flying Dutchman* and Davy Jones's locker. In sailing lore, the *Flying Dutchman* is a ghost ship doomed to sail the seas for all eternity. The first mention of it in print comes from John MacDonald's 1790 publication, *Travels in Various Parts of Europe, Asia, and Africa During a Series of Thirty Years and Upward*:

> The weather was so stormy that the sailors said they saw the *Flying Dutchman*. The common story is that this *Dutchman* came to the Cape in Distress of weather and wanted to get into harbour but could not get a pilot to conduct her and was lost and that ever since in very bad weather her vision appears.[26]

The *Flying Dutchman* has its origins in a Dutch story about a sunken ship. The story goes that a Dutch man-o'-war sank in a storm off the Cape of Good Hope. There were no survivors. Its consort ship managed to survive the storm and re-outfitted itself before going back to the same location. While at sea, the night watch reported that a ship was headed directly towards them at full speed, as if she intended to crash into them. But then the ship disappeared. One of the sailors identified her as their ill-fated consort, or at least her apparition. Over time, the story evolved to include an eighteenth-century Dutch captain who defied the sea; his demise was a result of his own arrogance. As punishment, he and his crew were doomed to sail for eternity. This symbolized a warning to sailors and represented the idea that death chases all at sea.[27]

John Tenniel, 'Davy Jones's Locker', engraving from
Punch; or, The London Charivari, CIII (10 December 1892).

The phrase 'Davy Jones's locker' has an unknown origin but
is still prevalent in pirates' and other sailors' superstitions with
several different meanings. Its first mention may have been in
Daniel Defoe's *Four Voyages of Capt. George Roberts*, which
recounts how Roberts was attacked by the pirate Edward Low.

When it became obvious that Roberts was about to be taken, one of the crew members 'told them they should not, for he would toss them all into Davy Jones's Locker if they did'.[28] The locker was known to be the Devil disguised as the spirit of the sea.[29] Others have said it was the grave of sailors who died in open water. The term may have originated from the biblical story about Jonah and the whale in that the 'locker' (the whale) was 'kept and confined'.[30] A 1682 publication of sermons mentions Jonah when discussing sailors' deaths: 'Of any, that has been in extreme peril, we use to say he has been where Jonah was.' In Norway, it was said that 'if a sailor is killed in a sea-skirmish, or falls overboard and is drowned, or any other fatality occurs that keeps his remains in the "great deep", his surviving crew-mates speak about him as one who has been sent to Davy Jones's Locker.'[31]

The term was used in newspapers well into the nineteenth century. In 1819, a ship called the *Socorro* sailed out of Campeche, Mexico, and attacked an English ship off the coast of Cuba. When the second in command of the ship went aboard the English vessel, he declared that 'he would be shown where the money was hidden, or he would send the whole of the [crew to] Davy Jones's Locker'. The event turned violent but in the end the *Socorro* only acquired a barrel of beef and pork, four bags of mixed goods, 100 pounds of rice, some candles and other practical items.[32]

Both the *Flying Dutchman* and Davy Jones's locker were born out of fear. Pirates and other sailors were terrified to die at sea. Some even refused to learn how to swim. If a sailor fell overboard and drowned at the beginning of a voyage, it signalled that the endeavour was doomed to fail.[33] These superstitions were the crux of pirates' beliefs – even more so than religion.

Eighteenth-century ideas about religion permeated society. The elite population thought of it as the handmaiden of social control.[34] People, especially in British North America, took a moral stance against crime and piracy. It is important to examine the religious and social contexts of Britain and the Americas to understand why there was such an emphasis on pirates' behaviour and irreligiosity. Sailors had a general apathy towards religion thanks to tough and dangerous work at sea. Religion was not a priority in such an environment. There was simply no time or desire to bother with religion while away from church and home. Their work included long periods of idleness and boredom. Long hours without any prizes led to boredom, restlessness and feelings of uselessness. Land-based workers, who did not have that experience, did not sympathize with mariners. They felt that they were lazy, which led to their drinking and whoring. Many people felt that if sailors, and pirates in particular, were given more honest work, especially in the plantation colonies, the number of pirates would decrease. (Better still, they could be sentenced to hard labour.)[35]

New England was very focused on religious behaviour. The influx of English Puritans who sought religious freedom cemented strong religious ideas in the colonies. It is no surprise that American colonists focused on pirates' irreligiousness more than observers did in England. Religious values and moral codes were prevalent throughout these settler societies and religion was front and centre to law and order. Crime was regarded as a sin, so New England courts functioned as guardians of biblical precepts.[36]

Personal conduct had a fundamental relationship to home, society and the nation; piracy was a crime against all three. Ideas about men's conduct and the importance of manners and civility shaped the way British leaders and society members perceived pirates.[37] These ideas influenced North American laws.[38] South Carolina had regulations to control excessive drinking among mariners and sailors in 1703.[39] Swearing and blaspheming, another popular activity among pirates, became a criminal offence in England in an attempt to curb social ills. Pennsylvania, the Quaker colony, had laws specifically against these behaviours since the colony was founded in 1682.[40]

Edward Teach was known for his extreme hairstyle. He wore his hair long and his long, black beard was said to reach halfway down his chest. During the 1600s, beards were very common among men of all classes, but this changed at the turn of the eighteenth century. Beard- and moustache-wearing started to decline in the 1680s as masculinity was redefined. Masculinity emerged into aesthetic ideals of neatness and elegance, inspired by new fashions in the French court of King Louis xiv. Polite society added to this fashion. The new bodily ideal for men was neat and elegant. According to the historian Alun Withey, 'the clean-shaven face became a *sine qua non* of male appearance. Where once beards had exemplified male power and strength, such ideas now shifted to the shaved face.' Symmetry was important for a polite appearance and beards took it away. Shaving became an act of control and was intended to remove a mask, 'enabling facial features to be seen and "read"'. Not only that, but a clean-shaven face was also seen as honest because it opened the person up. Having both long hair and a thick beard 'would obscure virtually the entire head and face, leaving nothing open for scrutiny'.[41] Teach deliberately rejected this fashionable and polite style to intimidate and harass his victims. He openly subverted society in total defiance of social norms.

A letter written by 'a gentleman in New England' to his friend in Glasgow expressed his disgust towards pirates. He stated that there was 'no love for men such as pirates, robbers, publicans and sinners'.[42] The explorer Jacob du Bucquoy was captured by the pirate John Taylor and recorded his experiences in a short memoir. He, like the gentleman in New England, expressed his disgust at pirates' behaviour:

> These men, who lead a gross or even bestial existence, live and die like animals. In all the time that I, to my great displeasure, spent with them, I never saw them engage in the visible practice of any religion whatsoever. They take oath on the Bible, but they never read it. The only custom they observe which seems to show any respect towards God was that whenever they are able they rest on Sundays. When one of them dies they chant a psalm or canticle while escorting the body, but that is rather a custom left over from their earliest education than a sign of their submission to God.[43]

These types of judgements were of no concern for pirates, however, because they did not see themselves as religious men, nor did religion matter to them. They used their irreligiosity to horrify their victims into submission. When the pirate George Cusack attacked a ship, he threw out all the victimized crew's papers 'and could not be perswaded to save a great large Bible that constantly lay upon the great [Captain's] Cabbin Table, from the mercy of the Waves'. The crew begged Cusack to save it, but Cusack replied, 'You Cowards, what do you think to go to Heaven and do such Actions as these? No I will make you Officers in Hell under me.' At that, Cusack threw the Bible overboard as he said, 'Go though thy may Divinity, what have we to do with thee?'[44]

Pirates saw themselves as removed from any form of authority, particularly the Church. Cursing, swearing and blaspheming defined pirate speech.[45] Without homes and churches to discourage this behaviour, sailors fell into these speaking habits, which naturally transferred onto pirate ships.[46] Cursing and swearing changed over time: in the medieval period, swearing by God or a saint was the most common; during the Renaissance era, people swore by things rather than at things, until people became the target. By the seventeenth century, as the Reformation changed religious piety and culture, swearing went out of fashion and became a social ill.[47] Naturally, pirates did not care for such niceties. Bartholomew Roberts was said to have sworn at a British official 'like any Devil'. In response, the British officer fell to the ground 'swearing and cursing as fast or faster than Roberts; which made the rest of the Pirates laugh heartily'.[48] The fact that they could elicit such a reaction from their persecutor was ironic and, frankly, hilarious. Newspapers described pirates' speech as barbarous, foul, scandalous and insolent.[49] These papers encouraged people to 'instruct, admonish, preach and pray for them' as they led 'wicked and vitious lives'.[50] Thomas Tew, a pirate from the West Indies who made the rounds in the Indian Ocean and Red Sea during the late seventeenth century, gained a reputation for having a particularly contemptible vocabulary. Colonial authorities frequently commented that he had a 'vile habit of swearing' and this opinion was even sent to King William III of England, shocking not just colonial officials but the royals.[51]

The Acts of Assembly in Jamaica were so concerned with this social problem that they issued laws against bad language:

outward profanity or blasphemy meant to 'dishonour Almighty God'. The Supreme Court of Jamaica was set to dole out the appropriate punishment. The fine for blaspheming was 'Twenty Pounds Current Money of this Island, or more, at the Discretion of the Court, for every such Offence'.[52] Anyone found guilty could be barred from employment in various arenas to prevent future embarrassment or scandals.[53]

Words and phrases such as 'damn' and 'son of a bitch' were common among pirate speech during attacks. This shook victims to their core. 'Damn' was one of the worst things you could say in the eighteenth century.[54] The use of the word put the speaker on the same level as the Lord, because only God had the power to condemn someone to hell and to damn. In essence, pirates were placing themselves on a level with God as they cursed at their victims.[55] Common use of the word 'bitch' dates to the fourteenth century. The phrase 'biche-son' appeared in 1330 and Shakespeare used a variant of it in *King Lear*. 'Son of a bitch' was not only a terrible insult but a direct blow that struck any man to his core, because the phrase insulted his mother and everything she represented. Not only that, the phrase dehumanized people. 'Bitch' meant 'dog', as it does today. In referring to someone as a dog, which pirates sometimes did in their insults, they were insinuating that the person was lowly, dirty and not Christian (although that may not have mattered much to pirates). Calling someone a 'son of a bitch' also attacked a mother's sexuality. In this context, 'bitch' referred to a prostitute, one who was as low as a dog, therefore implying that the mother was no better than a whore and engaged in bestial behaviour.[56]

Despite all this, pirates seemed to find religion when they faced death. If captured pirates were sent to London for their trial and subsequent execution, they were thrown into Newgate

Prison. There they would receive a visit from the Ordinary of Newgate, the spiritual chaplain who offered advice and urged criminals to repent. The ordinary then published his findings and observations for general consumption. His purpose was to teach readers the consequences of crimes and immoral behaviours through the lens of piracy. These publications were lucrative endeavours.[57] They were published on a regular basis from 1684 under the control of the City of London.[58] These were sold for three or six pence, much more expensive than newspapers, and the print runs were into the thousands. Ordinaries could expect up to £200 annual profit.[59] As a result, these sources can be questionable in terms of their intentions, but they provide a detailed view into the condemned pirates' state of mind.

The accounts followed a specific format. First, the ordinary provided a summary of the names and crimes of the person sentenced to death. His sermon followed the summary and detailed his accounts of his visits with the prisoners, which included some biographical sketches. Finally, he recorded their final confessions and behaviour at their executions. The goal was to prove that 'redemption was available to all' and that they could be reintegrated into the spiritual community through prayer.[60]

Paul Lorrain was the ordinary for Newgate Prison when Captain Kidd was thrown into a cell. Lorrain took a special interest in the man but was frustrated because Kidd resisted confessing to any sins or crimes. On the day of his execution, Lorrain took Kidd to the prison chapel for prayers and a chance to confess, but 'the hardness of Capt. Kidd's heart was still unmelted.' Kidd promised to make a full confession at the gallows, but as previously mentioned, when he arrived at Execution Dock, he was too drunk to make a coherent speech and rambled on about his innocence. However, there appeared to be a moment of divine intervention when the rope around Kidd's neck snapped. He fell to the ground, still very much alive. Lorrain used the opportunity to give Kidd one more chance to confess.

> When he was brought up and tied again to the tree, I desired to leave to go to him again, which was granted. Then I showed them the great mercy of God to him in granting him (unexpectedly) this further respite that so he might improve the few moments now so mercifully allotted to him in perfecting his faith and repentance. Now I found him in much better temper than before.

Kidd still would not confess, but Lorrain felt he had done his job to the best of his ability and had 'a greater satisfaction than I had before that he was penitent'.[61]

The pirate Walter Kennedy's final days in Newgate provide good detail as to his spiritual state of mind. He never claimed to be innocent of piracy, but admitted that his life as a pirate was wicked and unhappy because he and his crew were always fleeing from capture. On the day before his execution, Kennedy told the ordinary that he was ready to die and had made peace with God. However, on the morning of his execution, Kennedy appeared to be 'extreamly terrify'd and concern'd at the near Approach of Death' and begged for water at the scaffold. He managed to compose himself and confessed himself to be guilty.[62]

Captain John Massey was executed with Philip Roche in 1723 because they were both convicted of piracy at the same trial, but the two men were quite different in attitude. The Ordinary of Newgate observed that Massey was extremely penitent and spent much of his time in prayer and reading Scripture. Even after his sentence, Massey 'was in no Ways concern'd or appear'd

Captain Kidd hanging in chains, engraving from
Charles Ellms, *The Pirates Own Book* (1856 edn).

to be uneasy about it', implying that he had made peace with his fate. He carried this devout attitude to Execution Dock, where he was described as decent, gracious and penitent, 'Courage attending him to the last Moment'.[63] Philip Roche was not quite as openly devout as Massey while in prison. The ordinary claimed that Roche had 'no Concern or Uneasiness, nor in the least apprehensive suffering for his Offence' because he was promised a pardon for naming three of his accomplices. Unfortunately for him, he only received a reprieve and was sentenced to hang on 14 August 1723.[64] According to the ordinary, Roche became more subdued as the date of his execution drew nearer, 'appeared very serious and attentive' and desired the ordinary's company to read him Scripture. On the morning of his execution, however, Roche refused to go to chapel. He claimed that he depended 'on the Church of Rome for Pardon for his Crimes' as he had been raised Irish Catholic. Unfortunately, the resurgence of his faith did little to ease his conscience, as he could not make a speech at the scaffold, 'being faint and confus'd and in a Consternation'.[65]

In North America, a reverend named Cotton Mather made it his life's mission to sell religious and moral regulations via his sermons against piracy. As a third-generation preacher, Mather gained an enormous following in New England. Cotton's first foray into the execution sermon came about in March 1686 when a man named James Morgan was found guilty of murder and sentenced to hang. Nearly 5,000 people in Boston attended the public execution, because it was the first hanging in seven years and people were desperate to satisfy their morbid curiosity. Mather later wrote in his diary that people were so moved by his words that they 'very greedily desired the Publication'.[66] The result was the first of his many sermon publications, *The Call of the Gospel*, in 1686, which proved to be an instant success. This solidified Mather's place as Massachusetts's religious leader and moral backbone for the next forty years.

Piracy became his main interest as it increased around the turn of the eighteenth century. He took it upon himself to warn young people away from the temptation to turn pirate by appealing to biblical commandments and religious upbringings. He admonished the pirates on the scaffold that their behaviour 'Kills your Distressed Parents, and makes their Hearts even to stoop with Heaviness, to see that you are Irreclaimable from your Enormities, and that none of their Commands or Counsels, will prevail with you, to Reform your Disorderly Living'. Unlike the ordinary of Newgate, Mather believed that pirates were irredeemable and could never receive true salvation: 'Have not their Last Speeches most sadly Bewailed the Vile Speeches, with they have discovered Souls of Rottenness?'[67]

Mather sought to do more than just publicly condemn pirates. He aimed to completely dehumanize them. Although pirates could not be saved, Mather hoped to use their spiritual destruction to prevent the next generation from falling into piratical ways: 'Children, Will you not Begin Immediately to Live Religiously? . . . Oh, Take not up, first with a Lifeless Religion, and the Irreligious Life, which that will bring you to.'[68] His words were not only influential but stripped pirates of any remaining power and humanity they had left.

Survivors of pirate attacks also made serious comment on pirates' irreligiosity. One of the most detailed accounts of piracy is Philip Ashton's memoir of his captivity among pirates. He said that pirates were 'the worst Men of all'. The pirates were described as unholy degenerates who lived in utter disregard of their basic morals:

I soon found, that any Death was preferable to being
link'd with such a vile Crew of Miscreants, to whom it
was a Sport to do Mischief; where prodigious Drinking,
monstrous Cursing and Swearing, hideous Blasphemies,
and open Defiance of Heaven, and Contempt of Hell
itself was the constant Employment, unless when Sleep
sometimes abated the Noise and Revelings.[69]

However, Ashton noted that the pirates' cavalier attitudes disappeared one evening when they faced real danger while their
ship nearly capsized during a dangerous storm. 'The Poor
Wretches had no where to go for Help, for they were at open
Defiance with their Maker, and they could have much little
Comfort in the Thoughts of their Agreement with Hell.'[70] He
vividly described the pirates' fear of imminent death as the storm
continued to pummel the ship:

They evidently feared the Almighty, whom they defied,
lest He was come to torment them before their expected
Time. And tho' they were so habituated to Cursing and
Swearing, that the Dismal Prospect of Death and this
of so long Continuance could not correct the Language
of most of them, yet you might plainly see the inward
Horror and Anguish of their Minds, visible in their
Countenances, and like Men amazed or starting out of
Sleep in a Fright, I could hear them every now and then
cry out, Oh! I wish were at home![71]

What Ashton does not seem to consider, however, is that any
sailor's worst fear is drowning. No matter their thoughts about
God, heaven, hell or anything else religious, it is likely that

any storm would make the bravest pirate dissolve into a form of prayer.

The question about pirates' religiosity leads to another query: what about religious holidays? Did pirates observe anything like the Sabbath or Christmas, even though they were irreligious? Bartholomew Roberts mentions the Sabbath in his articles: 'The musicians to have rest on the Sabbath Day.' However, there is no mention of the Sabbath regarding the rest of the crew. Observing the holy day varied from ship to ship but it was generally for practical purposes rather than religious ones. The pirate Captain Watling ordered his crew to 'keep the Sabbath' when he was given the position during a time of crisis. The command was not intended to give a day of rest in service of the Lord but to let everyone have a day off so they could regroup and re-create a semblance of order. His previous commander, a man named Sawkins, was known to throw dice overboard when he saw them being used on the Sabbath (although since gambling was banned on most pirate ships, this may have just been coincidence). The actual function of the Sabbath and prayer was a mere formality or a familiar social ritual ingrained from childhood rather than authentic religious observance.[72]

Holidays were another matter, particularly Christmas. Regardless of a pirate's religious devotion, Christmas had always been a time for family, along with observance. Life at sea could be very lonely and most pirates entered the life with the knowledge that they would likely never see their families again. So naturally, the pirates had to make each other their family. Christmas was an excellent time for them to get rip-roaringly drunk to forget this sadness and to also enjoy each other's company. Jack Rackham's crew spent their Christmas together 'drinking and carousing as long as they had any Liquor left'.[73]

The privateer and sometime pirate William Dampier wrote about celebrating Christmas on his journeys with Captain Charles Swan. In 1685, he said that he and his crew 'sent in two [canoes] . . . to get Fish, being desirous to have a Christmas dinner'.[74] The following year, the crew found themselves in Mindanao in the Philippines. The isolation was difficult on everybody, including the captain. To combat this, Swan said he 'desired all his Men to be aboard that Day [Christmas], that we might keep it solemnly together: And accordingly, he sent aboard a Buffaloe the Day before, that we might have a good Dinner.'[75]

What about Christmas traditions? Pirates did celebrate the holiday, but for morale purposes rather than religious ones. It was an opportunity to blow off steam both on land and at sea. Decorations were quite popular in the eighteenth century. Most homes used evergreen trees, but pirates, for the most part, only had access to tropical plants. While ashore as they looked for water, fruit and wild animals, they may have gathered some decorative foliage if they desired. In terms of a Christmas feast, boar's head was the meat of choice because pirates often hunted this animal when they went onshore in the Caribbean. If they were in a more inhabited location, they would seek out the nearest taverns and the company of people. Aside from these traditions, a pirate Christmas would be multicultural because of the diverse population on the ship. Many different religious traditions would be mixed in.[76]

Pirate captains sometimes made Christmas observance a priority. Captain Bartholomew Sharp, facing threats of mutiny, acquiesced to his crew and paused their voyage for a Christmas meal. They stopped at the Juan Fernández islands off the coast of Chile, which proved to be a place of plenty. Good food abounded, much to everyone's joy. They found the island to be

Captain Roberts's crew carousing at Old Calabar River, engraving
from Charles Ellms, *The Pirates Own Book* (1856 edn).

'a very refreshing Place to us both in respect to the Goats we
found here . . . [and] fresh Water wherewith we filled our
Vessels'. Several days later, more good fortune befell them, with
'a great store of Fish, and particularly Lobsters'.[77] The happiness
was short-lived, however. Despite the good food and water,
many of the crew were still unhappy and wanted to either go

back home to England or continue towards Spanish ships ripe for plunder. According to Basil Ringrose, who recounted the event,

> A part of the disaffected to Captain Sharp got ashoar and subscribed a Paper to make John Watling Commander, pretending liberty to a free election as they termed it, and that Watling had it by vote. The reason of this mutiny was that Sharp had got about 3,000 pieces of Eight, and was willing to come home that year, but two thirds of the Company had none left; having lost it at play; And those would have Captain Sharp turned out, because they had no mind as yet to return home. This Fewd was carried on so fiercely, that it was very near coming to a civil War, had not some prudent men a little moderated the thing.[78]

Watling, however, was killed in battle soon after and Sharp became the ship's captain once again.

Edward England, active in 1720, preferred to make merry on land by allowing his crew to spend their Christmas 'in Carowzing and Forgetfulness, and kept it for three Days in a wanton and riotous Way'. According to Captain Charles Johnson, who recounted their holiday in *A General History of the Pyrates*, they wasted

> their fresh Provisions in so wretched and inconsiderable a Manner, that when they had agreed after this to proceed to Mauritius they were in that Passage at an Allowance of a Bottle of Water per Diem, and not above two Pounds of Beef, and a small Quantity of Rice, for ten Men for

a Day, so that had it had not been for the leaky Ship, (which once they were about to have quitted, and had done, but for a Quantity of Arrack and Sugar She had on Board,) they must most of them have perished.[79]

A captured survivor later named Richard Lazenby recounted this holiday and noted the damage their celebrations caused:

they caroused, and kept their Christmas in a most riotous manner, destroying most of the fresh provision they had aboard, of which quite two-thirds was wasted. After three days of such debauchery and waste, they decided to go to Mauritius to repair the Victory, which was now in a bad way.[80]

The maritime world was rife with dangers whether one was a pirate or not. Sailors generally had shorter lifespans because of their work-life endangerments. It is hard to know exactly how long a mariner worked because they moved constantly from port to port more than any other urban dwellers, changed occupations and, because they were often among the poorest population, rarely left any traces of their lives on tax documents and land probate records. Not only that, so many of them died young, and were therefore even less likely to have their own legal records, that it was nearly impossible to keep track of them.[81] Mariners, especially pirates, were home for less than six months out of the year. When they were home, they passed their time idly: repairing their homes, prepping everything for winter via menial tasks such as chopping wood, working odd jobs for cash and settling any necessary business matters before setting out again.[82] Pirates, however, always on the run from the law, likely spent their time moving from place to place while stuck on land until they could mercifully return to the sea.

ENTERTAINMENT AND CULTURE gave pirates unity and an identity. Songs and ballads kept morale up and provided fun and merriment during downtime. Mythology and tales at sea were other forms of entertainment that also taught sailors lessons while educating them about the risks at sea. Tales of sirens, mermaids, the Kraken and the *Flying Dutchman* came to define the maritime world, and have bled into contemporary popular culture in franchises such as *Pirates of the Caribbean*. But besides the fun and fiction, habits and lifestyle also defined pirate culture. Drinking was a bonding experience and sometimes a socially acceptable habit if it was allowed on ship and if the pirates drank responsibly. Whether they practised religion is questionable, but pirates had their own culture, customs and traditions.

CONCLUSION

The End of the
Golden Age of Piracy

Piracy could not last forever. At the turn of the eighteenth century, British officials launched what became known as a War on Piracy – an extermination campaign to rid the seas of pirates once and for all. Captured pirates were transported to London for trial and then public execution, which took place at Execution Dock on the bank of the Thames in Wapping, East London. After the pirates Joseph Dawson, Edward Forseith, William May, William Bishop, James Lewis and John Sparkes were pronounced guilty, they were told:

> The Law, for the heinousness of your Crime hath appointed, a severe Punishment by an ignominious Death; and Judgement which the Law awards, is this, That you and every one of you to be taken from hence to the Place from whence you came, and from thence to the place of Execution, and that there you, and every one of you be Hanged by the Necks, until you, and every one of you be Dead.[1]

Traditionally, criminals were hanged at the Tyburn Tree in West London (on the corner of Hyde Park, right outside where Marble Arch tube station is today), but pirates were taken to the Thames at low tide to symbolize the place of their crime. This demonstrated that the crimes were committed within the jurisdiction of the High Court of Admiralty: all bodies of water up to the low-tide mark.[2] The trial itself was for show; most pirates were presumed guilty before they even entered the courtroom. This was evident when Captain Kidd was put on trial in May 1701. Justice Turton, who presided over the trial, addressed the jury after they presented their final piece of evidence:

> Gentlemen, the business you are to inquire into is the piratical taking of these ships. The witnesses have positively and directly proved not only the taking of the ships, but the seizing of the goods and selling them, and sharing the money. If these witnesses say true, as nothing appears to the contrary by the prisoners cross-examining them, or otherwise, they are not at all contradicted, or their credibility made questionable. They are as are most likely to know what was done, being with them in the whole voyage, and engaged with them in those enterprises. And if you have give entire credit to the witnesses, you will probably find these persons guilty of the piracy they are charged with, which I leave to your consideration.[3]

The language made it clear that Kidd's fate was predetermined. The jury would agree and deliver the expected punishment.

The public execution ritual was intended to demonstrate power over the criminal and appease the offended public.

Britain had to prove to both its own people and its competitors that it was powerful enough to eradicate the plague upon the ocean. The execution was theatre intended to torture the victim and entertain an audience. The pirate was carted from either Newgate or Southwark prison to Execution Dock, led by the silver oar of the Admiralty Court.[4] Once they arrived on the scaffold they had to give a 'last dying speech' in which they admitted their crimes, begged forgiveness and warned people away from their type of life.[5] Their public executions drew thousands of spectators.[6] They were also a form of torture. The rope was too short, so their necks would not break. Instead, the pirate would be strangled to death, which could take as long as an hour. Pirates received no mercy and their limbs jerked uncontrollably during their struggle, in a movement that became known as the Marshall's Dance. If they were lucky enough to have friends, family or sympathetic witnesses present, they might come forward to pull their legs until their neck broke and thus end their misery.[7]

Accused pirates who were sentenced to death were often executed in large groups for maximum efficiency. According to the ordinary of Newgate, at one time 52 pirates were arrested and then 24 of them were hanged together at Execution Dock, which he referenced in his writings several times between 1710 and 1718. In November 1700, 24 French pirates were all executed together. A large group execution would attract substantial crowds, and create quite the spectacle.[8]

The Admiralty Court was charged with handling all maritime affairs. At the turn of the eighteenth century, it was told to specifically target pirates. It had been a ruling body since 1260 but did not make significant strikes in enhancing its authority until the seventeenth century, after the Royal Navy fell into decay and neglect under the rule of King James I.[9] The sudden increase in piracy created a need for a more specific legal institution to focus on crimes offshore. Since the fourteenth century, the Admiralty's jurisdiction had lain over

> the Seas, or publique Rivers or fresh waters, streams, Havens or places subject to overflowing, whatsoever, within the flowing and ebbing of the Sea, upon the Shoares and Banks whatsoever adjoining to them, or either of them, from any of the said first Bridges whatsoever, towards the Sea, throughout our Kingdoms of England and Ireland, or our Dominions aforesaid or elsewhere beyond the Seas.[10]

The Offenses of the Sea Act (28 Hen., c.15), a statute under King Henry VIII passed in 1536, had both created the first piracy law and declared England to be an empire, bringing pirates within the king's justice no matter where the act was committed. This also rendered piracy unable to be tried by civil law. Admiralty lawyers were the ones who had to determine if there was a case. If so, the Admiralty issued a commission to a special court of oyer and terminer, which had common-law procedures and juries. The court was in London, which is why pirates had to be transported there.[11] The commission of oyer and terminer granted Admiralty judges the authority 'to enquire of, to hear, determine, and Punish all Crimes, Misdemeanours, and abuses . . . against the Dignity of the King, Peace of the Kingdom, and Security of the Subject'. Members of the Admiralty were 'Justices of the Peace and Gaol delivery in those cases where the Transgression is upon the water, so that they may enquire into all offences at Common Law as well as such misdemeanour and Abuses as are contrary to Antient

Laws and usages of the Sea'.[12] By 1677, the Admiralty Court had the power to execute pirates simply for being pirates.[13]

However, piracy continued to grow. In another effort to combat it, King William III issued the Act for the Effectual Suppression of Piracy in 1698. The proclamation offered 'a promise of Pardon made to all such Men serving in Pyrate Ships, who will Desert the same, and upon their doing so repair to any of the Governors or Commanders in Chief of the Plantations, or other Persons who have authority to Try Pirates'.[14]

As piracy increased, it became too difficult and expensive to transport all captured pirates to London, so Admiralty Courts were set up in British colonies in the Caribbean and North America under the second Act of Piracy in 1699. There were three types of colonies in North America: royal, proprietary and charter. Crown-appointed governors ran royal colonies, such as Virginia, with legal structures that mimicked England. Proprietary colonies, such as Pennsylvania, were established by land grants to wealthy investors for the purpose of attracting settlement for the production of goods. Charter colonies, such as Massachusetts, Connecticut and Rhode Island, were under legal bondage and severance in that residents were tied to the English law while having the freedom to create their own government.[15] Each type of government had their own methods of condemning pirates. Royal colonies, being the most similar to England, were the most severe. Proprietary and charter colonies, on the other hand, found lucrative opportunities to harbour and deal with pirates for their own monetary advantage. Colonists overall, therefore, were not pleased with the new Admiralty Courts because they had enjoyed autonomy in establishing their own courts and laws and these rights were now being infringed upon. If they did not comply, they could lose their charters.[16]

As piracy increased at the turn of the eighteenth century, officials in each colony were ordered to try pirates according to the king's laws in England.[17] Colonial discontent over this grew because they felt their monarch was ignorant of their geographic realities, lack of parliamentary representation and legal authority. It was not fair to have to change their laws and conform exactly to England when they could not speak for themselves overseas. Even if some colonies were lucky to have a representative, this could still prove to be a challenge because colonies were very topographically diverse. Officials from Berkeley County in the Carolinas complained that they were barred from electing the standard ten representatives of their county to Parliament. They felt that too large an area was ruled by too small a committee, because those elected to Parliament were solely from the major port city, Charles Town. The Lords Proprietors of Carolina complained about their legal restrictions in terms of trying and executing pirates: 'Is it just that all the inhabitants of Carolina should be subjected to laws made by members of Parliament chosen only by the inhabitants of Charlestown?' They argued that the king had denied them their promised right to assemble their own freeholders to make laws as they saw fit and that it would be a mistake to grant legal authority simply to Charles Town. To emphasize these concerns, officials often highlighted the king's geographic and practical ignorance of the colony: 'We do not think Charlestown a proper place for the seat of Government, for besides its unhealthiness, it is too much exposed that a few men could surprise the Governor, Council and Parliament in their beds.'[18]

Even without colonial grumblings about having new laws imposed upon them, there were still issues with the relationship between their economies and pirates. Virtually all of the New

England settlements were port towns and cities that depended on the maritime profession and trade. The strict trade controls established by the Navigation Acts created a large black market of goods that colonists could only get from pirates who dealt with local governors in exchange for goods, protection and money. Port-town citizens also felt a comradeship with pirates. Common-law juries were reluctant to convict pirates because they often identified with the accused, either through social or commercial ties.[19] The mid-Atlantic and southern colonies, such as New York, Rhode Island and the Carolinas, were more isolated than New England and were more receptive to illegal trading with pirates.[20] Letters between officials insisted that they needed more protection from the English government if they were expected to uphold their laws. They claimed that pirates destroyed merchant ships daily and that it was only a matter of time before pirates decided to land permanently and transfer their robberies to the shore, like the Vikings of old. This would cause 'the utter destruction and ruin of the trade of his Majesty's Plantation on the Continent'.[21]

Despite some governors' participation in piracy, most did not actually condone it in their colonies. The reality was that they were simply too ill-equipped and uninformed about how to proceed against people who aided and sheltered pirates.[22] Prior laws from Jamaica were reinstated, such as the Jamaica Act of 1683, which prohibited the island from trading with pirates.[23] Perhaps this law could be officially passed throughout the North American colonies? An order was passed in 1697 that gave governors the power to arrest, seize and secure all pirate ships and effects captured within North American jurisdiction.[24] However, merchants ignored any proclamations based on the Jamaica Act and continued to trade with pirates throughout North America.[25]

Even regular colonists opted to flout the rules. Philadelphia's residents, for example, reportedly supplied Captain Kidd's former crew's boats daily while he stationed himself offshore, and in return Kidd supplied them with plundered goods.[26] In Philadelphia, obstructions to the prosecution of illegal traders and pirates, along with the blatant disregard of the Navigation Acts, were a source of frustration to maritime authorities.[27]

The mid-Atlantic colonies were the most notorious for their relationship with pirates. The governor of Rhode Island refused to observe the Navigation Acts and instead permitted and encouraged illegal trade with pirates. Colonial administrator Edward Randolph told the Council of Trade and Plantations that Rhode Island was a 'receptacle for pirates, who are encouraged and harboured by its Government', and that its inhabitants aided pirates 'at all times'.[28] In the South, South Carolina was known to have a long history of friendly relationships with pirates to the point that the colony was referred to as a 'second Jamaica'.[29] During the mid-seventeenth-century wars against Spain, pirates often got their provisions from South Carolina, where they paid in cash and established friendly commercial relationships.

Citizens' loyalty was essential to uphold laws in addition to judiciary force. In varied settlements like those in the West Indies, nationalistic identities were complicated. Piracy and illegal trade created a breach between the colonists and the Crown, which caused conflicts between those who aided illegal trade against the Navigation Acts. This created a decades-long struggle over criminal and trade relations, which meant an intrusive Crown and an independent American legal identity.[30] When two members of Henry Avery's crew escaped imprisonment in Pennsylvania, they had the support of many colonists.

Sheriffs were unsuccessful in recapturing the fugitives, and some even refused to write warrants for their arrests.[31]

However, these conflicts eventually faded into being the exception rather than the norm. Even though not all colonies were pleased by these orders, they complied. New England, whose colonies mostly relied on maritime merchant trade, were vigilant in capturing, trying and executing pirates. Rhode Island successfully hanged more pirates than any other British colony in the Atlantic after new Admiralty Courts were established in 1700.[32]

When the Act for the Effectual Suppression of Piracy was revised in 1701, it included an additional clause offering a pardon to pirates if they gave evidence against their commanding officers or fellow crew.[33] While there were many pirates who took the pardon, including some infamous ones such as Edward Teach, Jack Rackham and Charles Vane, there were a substantial number of pirates who were loath to take advantage of it. Often, pirates who came forward did not go unpunished. Sometimes a pirate was sentenced to transportation or pressed into naval service rather than sent to the noose. In fact, transportation had been inserted into pardon conditions a little after 1660 and became routine until pardons were firmly established in 1718. By then, transportation had ceased to be an additional consequence for pardoned pirates.[34]

Even so, most pirates were granted their pardons without any additional punishments, including Robert Seely, who sailed under the pirate Henry Avery's command. This pardon was likely due to Seely's 'young age' (which was not specified); the ignorance of his youth may have allowed him to be 'carryed away by Henry Avery'.[35] In general, pardons were quite common during the eighteenth century; about half of those condemned to death for their crimes did not actually go to the gallows but were instead transported to overseas colonies or imprisoned indefinitely. A pardon was a chance for the monarch to demonstrate royal authority and appease public expectations for mercy. The hope was that a death sentence might frighten a criminal out of breaking the law ever again.[36] Any pirate who readily turned himself in would be guaranteed his pardon. The only exceptions to King William III's Act for the Effectual Suppression for Piracy were Henry Avery and Captain Kidd, because their acts of piracy were too notorious for them to be allowed pardons, regardless of their circumstances.[37]

After the end of the War of the Spanish Succession in 1714, requests for pardons decreased. Most pirates were privateers during the war and had been allowed to keep 80 per cent of the loot they stole from their victims. They feared that if they took a pardon, their goods and effects might be confiscated. In another attempt to entice pirates to turn themselves in, King George I extended the Act in both 1717 and 1718 and sent out orders to the governors of the various Caribbean islands and North American colonies not to seize any pirate's property if they came forward.[38]

Most pirates' executions in the Caribbean took place in the former pirate stronghold of Port Royal, Jamaica, in the years after the Royal Navy took back control of the island. Officials set up a Supreme Judicature directly modelled after the courts in England: 'The Judges of the Supream Court of Judicature shall have Cognizance of all Pleas Civil, Criminal and Mixt, as fully as the Kings Bench, Common Pleas, and Exchequer would have in England.'[39] Criminal courts were also organized similarly to the English judicial system. The supreme court, which tried all serious offences until 1758, was presided over by the chief justice and four assistant judges.[40] Death sentences had to be carried out within 28 days. The exception to the rule was those convicted in Port Royal, whose sentences were carried out within ten days. Similar to London, pirates in the Caribbean were often executed in groups. Approximately 10 per cent of all mass executions in British American colonies were pirates.[41] The main difference was the actual execution ceremony, because there is no record that details a specific ritual in the Caribbean. A silver Admiralty oar led the processions of condemned pirates in Boston and New York.[42] However, in the Caribbean, no oar was presented and the details of executions were slim. One report from 1665 tells of a group of twelve pirates who were condemned together after attacking one Captain Ensome, who only lost one man and imprisoned the pirates on his ship. Of those men, six were hanged together while three were acquitted.[43] The most detailed descriptions about these executions in the Caribbean are from *A General History of the Pyrates*, including Bartholomew Roberts's men in 1722. Those who were condemned to be executed were hanged. After their bodies were taken down, they were strung up in chains for all to see as a warning to other pirates.[44]

Because of the closer relationship between pirates and civilians, there were instances of strong reactions against pirates' deaths. In a letter to the Council of Trade and Plantations in England, governor Lord Hamilton described how a mob in Port Royal had rescued a pirate from the gallows. The pirate had robbed a Spanish ship and on the day of his execution another ship was robbed in Port Royal. The shock of these two events in the same day led Hamilton to issue a proclamation that promised a reward and a pardon to the person who came forward. Unfortunately, no discovery was made.[45]

ACTS OF ORGANIZED PIRACY ended in the late 1720s. For the rest of the eighteenth century, most incidents of piracy were individuals rather than fleets. However, the Golden Age of Piracy lived on in historical memory. Pirates became romantic figures over the decades, eventually evolving into pop-culture heroes. They were viewed as fascinating figures, 'purveyors of lawlessness'.[46] Their freedom was intriguing because of the lack of social mobility during the early modern era. Pirates have remained popular because of their 'it' factor – a strange magnetism that attracts both sexes. The 'it factor' is the effortless embodiment of contradictory qualities simultaneously: strength and vulnerability and innocence and experience.[47] They embodied these qualities, but they also contradicted them, because of their actions. They were attractive to early modern audiences because they were seen as unpredictable, which kept people's attention.

One of the ways this unpredictability manifested was through the idea of the 'ghost ship': a spectral vessel that sails unseen 'out there' in the mists of time, with a doomed crew seeking redemption from an ancient curse.[48] The notion of the ghost ship was born out of the fear that colonial authorities and colonists had about pirates. No one could predict where they would strike next and how calamitous their next assault would be. As the idea of the romantic pirate emerged by the end of the eighteenth century, the 'ghost ship' personified the pirates' last dying speeches: their final redemptions in life were translated into ethereal fictions. These public events came to exist in the collective memory: 'what remains of the past in the lived experience of groups, or what these groups make of the past'. Images of the past were meant to be made of the representations of a collective past produced within a specific community or the power of recollection vested in a group's institutional structures.[49]

Their strength lay in acting against the most powerful nations in the Atlantic world, but they were vulnerable because their lifespan was short, and their capture meant certain death if they were found guilty. They claimed innocence because they felt justified in their actions and had the undeniable maritime skills to be successful. But their mortality was a common bond.

Even after a pirate's death, he lived on for those who had witnessed his execution. Judge Samuel Sewall, the justice who oversaw the trial and execution of the pirate John Quelch and his crew in Boston, wrote in his diary:

> When I came to see how the river was covered with people, I was amazed. There were 100 boats or some 150 boats and canoes, so said Cousin Moody of York. Mr Cotton Mather came with Capt. Quelch and six others for their execution from the prison to Scarlet's Wharf. There they were taken into a boat and taken to a place of execution about halfway between Hanson's Point and Broughton's Warehouse . . . When the scaffold was hoisted to its proper height, the seven pirates were taken upon it. Mr. Mather prayed for them while standing in the boat. Ropes were all fastened to the gallows. When the scaffold was set to sink, there was such a screech of women that my wife heard it sitting in our entry next to our orchard, and was much surprised at it. Our house was a mile from that place.[50]

Execution Dock was memorable enough to be depicted in late eighteenth-century paintings of the Thames. A 1782 painting called *A Prospective View of the River Thames*, made by an unknown artist, depicted the view of the King's Arms at Blackwall,

Shooter's Hill, in Woolwich. Blackwall Yard appears on the left and Woolwich to the right of the centre, on the Thames's south bank, while Shooter's Hill appears on the far right. There is a small ship in the river, and right below its stern, the gibbeted body of a pirate can be seen as a warning to sailors.[51] The pirate is a lonely figure and barely noticeable upon first view. However, his inclusion tells us that the bloody history of the Thames did not leave historical memory.

People even knew about Execution Dock in the American colonies. In 1732, a pirate named John Ellis was captured and convicted of piracy, and met his death at the Wapping site. Both the *Boston Gazette* and *American Weekly Mercury* published the same letter from 11 March 1732, which stated, 'Yesterday the death warrant came down to Newgate, ordering the execution of John Ellis, the pirate, at Execution Dock on Monday next.'[52]

Pirates' legacies have been stamped permanently into the lexicon of popular culture since the Golden Age of Piracy thanks to works such as *A General History of the Pyrates*, which would inspire a whole generation of pirate literature. The author Daniel Defoe in particular ignited pirates' voices in works such as *Robinson Crusoe* (1719), *The King of Pirates* (1720), *Captain Singleton* (1720) and *Colonel Jack* (1722) – all of which were published at the height of the third round of the Golden Age. However, no publication would launch pirates into the permanent cultural memory like Robert Louis Stevenson's novel *Treasure Island*, published in 1883.

Stevenson was born in Edinburgh, Scotland, in 1850 and was surrounded by pirate stories and histories thanks to Scotland's colourful piratical past in port cities such as Glasgow. He knew these pirate tales and created a bedtime story for his children that transformed into a serial called 'The Sea Cook', which was later collated into the infamous novel for which he is best known. Every pop-culture image of piracy comes from *Treasure Island*: peg-legs, eye patches, walking the plank, treasure hunts and 'X marks the spot'. The novel became an instant sensation in Britain and America among both children and adults, girls and boys, men and women. By the early twentieth century, it had been adapted for stage and screen. *Treasure Island* would add to the pirate lexicon thanks to Disney's 1950 adaptation starring the Cornish actor Robert Newton, who played Long John Silver and exaggerated his native accent for the character. This became known as the 'pirate accent' and has been used in television and film ever since.[53]

The Pirates' Code had the same purpose in fiction and reality: to maintain order and safety on a pirate ship, but over time it has turned into a major piece of pirate lore that has taken on its own meaning. Despite changes and legends in popular culture, the code is essential in the study of piracy and the realities of pirates' lives. Even after the Golden Age of Piracy ended, the legends lived on, and they will remain in historical memory for years to come.

SELECT LIST OF PIRATES

Henry Avery (1669–unknown): English pirate known for activities in the East Indies, especially taking the large ship *Ganj-i-sawai*.

Samuel Bellamy (1689–1717): English pirate known for taking the largest and wealthiest slave ship in the West Indies, the *Whydah*. His ship foundered in a storm off the coast of Massachusetts on 26 April 1717. All, including Bellamy, perished, save for two members of his crew.

William Bishop (unknown–1696): English pirate who sailed with Henry Avery.

Stede Bonnet (1688–1718): Wealthy Barbadian plantation-owner-turned-pirate known for purchasing his pirate ship, the *Revenge*, and later sailing with Edward Teach (Blackbeard). After being abandoned by Teach, he escaped but was captured, and was executed on 10 December 1718.

Anne Bonny (1697–unknown): Irish pirate who sailed with her husband, 'Calico' Jack Rackham, in and around Jamaica. She was found guilty of piracy in November 1720 but received a stay of execution due to her pregnancy. The date of her death is possibly 1733, based on a recently uncovered death record from St Catherine's Parish, Jamaica.

Joseph Braddish (1672–1701): British American pirate from Massachusetts who mutinied against his captain on the ship *Adventure*. He was captured and executed with Captain Kidd on 23 May 1701.

Robert Culliford (1666–unknown): Cornish pirate who sailed with Captain Kidd. He may have been in a romantic relationship with fellow pirate John Swann. He was found guilty of piracy but not executed.

George Cusack (unknown–1675): Irish pirate who sailed around the Western European coast and the West Indies. He was executed for piracy on 18 January 1675.

Joseph Dawson (unknown–1696): English pirate who sailed with Henry Avery.

Edward England (1685–1721): Irish pirate who sailed around the west coast of Africa and the Indian Ocean. He was marooned and his cause of death is unknown.

Edward Forseith (unknown–1696): English pirate who sailed with Henry Avery.

Louis Guittar (unknown–1700): French pirate who sailed throughout the West Indies. He captured a ship called *La Paix* and was executed on 13 November 1700.

Benjamin Hornigold (1680–1719): English privateer-turned-pirate best known for transforming Nassau (Island of Providence, Bahamas) into an official pirate city before becoming a pirate hunter. He most likely died in a hurricane.

Henry Jennings (unknown–*c.* 1745): English privateer-turned-pirate best known for raiding the wreck of the Spanish treasure fleet in 1715 and then sailing around Jamaica as a pirate. He took a pardon and moved to Bermuda.

Walter Kennedy (1695–1721): English pirate who sailed with Bartholomew Roberts in the Caribbean and off the coast of West Africa. He was captured and executed at Execution Dock, London, on 21 July 1721.

William Kidd (1645–1701): Scottish privateer-turned-pirate. He is best known for capturing the *Quedah Merchant* in 1698 and claimed to have buried his treasure, which later turned out to be a hoax. He was executed at Execution Dock, London, on 23 May 1701.

Edward Low (1690–1724): English pirate who sailed throughout the Caribbean and was known for his ruthlessness and cruelty towards his victims. He was best known for capturing a ship called the *Fancy*. His crew marooned him in Martinique and the French executed him in 1724. He wrote his own set of pirate codes.

George Lowther (unknown–1723): English pirate also known for his cruelty who sailed with Edward Low. It is believed that he died by suicide rather than be captured.

William May (1689–1700): English pirate who sailed with Henry Avery. He was best known for capturing a ship called the *Pearl*. His cause of death is unknown.

Henry Morgan (1635–1688): Welsh privateer who later became governor of Jamaica. He was best known for his raid on Panama City. He died on 25 August 1688 and his cause of death is unknown.

John Phillips (unknown–1724): English pirate who was initially forced into piracy. He became captain of a ship called *Revenge* and captured 34 ships. He was killed off the coast of Nova Scotia in a surprise attack on 18 April 1724.

John Plantain (unknown–1728): English Jamaican pirate who sailed in the East Indies with Edward England. His cause of death is unknown.

Bartolomeu Português (1623–1670): Portuguese pirate who attacked Spanish ships around Campeche. He may have been the first pirate to write a set of pirate codes.

John Quelch (1666–1704): English pirate who was the first to be tried and executed without a jury. He was known for pirating off the coast of Marblehead, Massachusetts. He was captured and executed on 30 June 1704.

Jack Rackham (1682–1720): English pirate who sailed with Charles Vane and then became captain of the *Revenge*. His wife was the female pirate Anne Bonny. He sailed around Jamaica from August until October 1720 before being captured by the pirate hunter Jonathan Barnet. He was executed in Jamaica on 18 November 1720.

Mary Read (1685–1721): English pirate who sailed with Jack Rackham and Anne Bonny on the *Revenge*. She was found guilty of piracy in November

1720 and received a stay of execution due to her pregnancy. She died of 'gaol fever' in Jamaica on 28 April 1721.

Bartholomew Roberts (1682–1722): English pirate who sailed with Edward England before becoming a pirate captain. He was known for attacking various slave-trading ports on the coast of West Africa and became the wealthiest pirate who ever lived. He was killed by a stray bullet in battle on 10 February 1722. He wrote his own set of pirate codes.

Philip Roche (1693–1723): Irish pirate who sailed around northern Europe. He was known for killing all captains and crew members of captured ships. He was found guilty of piracy and hanged at Execution Dock, London, in August 1723.

Bartholomew Sharp (1650–1702): English pirate who sailed Central and South America and the Caribbean. He was known for capturing a ship containing over 60,000 pieces of eight. He was captured on St Thomas in the West Indies and executed on 29 October 1702.

John Sparkes (unknown–1696): English pirate who sailed with Henry Avery.

Francis Spriggs (unknown–1725): English pirate who sailed with Edward England and Edward Low. He took over England's ship after a mutiny and likely died in battle on an unknown date.

John Swann (unknown–1699): English pirate who sailed in the East Indies and may have been romantically involved with fellow pirate Robert Culliford. His cause of death is unknown.

John Taylor (unknown–1723): English pirate who was active in both the West and East Indies. He was involved with two captures: the *Victory* and the *Cassandra*. His cause of death is unknown.

Edward Teach, alias Blackbeard (1680–1718): English pirate who sailed under Benjamin Hornigold and then later as a captain with Stede Bonnet. He was best known for capturing the French slave ship *La Concord* and renaming it the *Queen Anne's Revenge*, and for barricading the port of Charleston, South Carolina. He was notorious for his unconventional looks and long, black beard. He was beheaded in battle off the coast of Ocracoke, North Carolina, on 22 November 1718.

Thomas Tew (unknown–1695): British American pirate in the East Indies known for attacking wealthy trading ships. He died in battle during his second voyage.

Charles Vane (1680–1721): English pirate who sailed under Henry Jennings before striking out as a captain. He was known for being cruel and ruthless to his victims and for attempting to blockade Nassau. Vane's ship was wrecked in a hurricane and he was stranded on an island until an English ship sailed by and rescued him. They recognized him as a pirate and imprisoned him in Jamaica, where he was found guilty of piracy. He was executed in Port Royal on 22 March 1721.

Palsgrave Williams (1675–after 1723): English pirate who sailed with Samuel Bellamy and was captain of the *Sultana*. Williams was known for forcing victims into piracy. He was not with Bellamy on the night of the April storm. He retired from piracy in 1723.

GLOSSARY

Articles: Set of rules that pirates were required to abide by. Also known as *pirate codes*

Boatswain: A petty officer in charge of maintenance on a ship, especially of the hull

Buccaneer: Similar to privateers, and often based out of Hispaniola and Tortuga during the seventeenth century. Many were French and preyed on the Spanish. They were known to roast meat on land and ship, hence their name, from the French word *boucanier*

Captain: The person with ultimate command and authority of a ship

Common Council: Event where the entire pirate crew came together to unanimously vote on decisions such as punishments

Cutlass: A short, slashing sword

First Mate: Second-in-command to a captain on a ship. Also known as the lieutenant

Flux: Diarrhoea

Frizzen: The L-shaped hammer of a small gun

Galleon: Large warship commonly used between the sixteenth and eighteenth centuries

'Going on the Account': Maritime slang for becoming a pirate

Golden Age of Piracy: A period of a high concentration of pirates that affected the Caribbean, East Indies and North America between approximately 1670 and 1730

Gun: A cannon

Gunner: The leader of the groups of pirates in charge of weapons and cannons on the ship

Letter of Marque: Document issued by a government to a privateer instructing them to attack specific ships

Lieutenant: Second in command to a captain on a ship. Also known as the first mate

Man-o'-War: A type of battleship

Matelotage: Civil unions among sailors and pirates in the seventeenth and eighteenth centuries

Pieces of Eight: Spanish dollars made from silver worth eight *reales*, commonly used as currency in the seventeenth- and eighteenth-century Caribbean

Pirate: One who robs and murders at sea indiscriminately without legal sanction

Pirate Codes: See *articles*

Privateer: One who attacks specific ships on government orders with a *letter of marque*

Prize: Pirates' capture and loot

Quartermaster: The crew member in charge of various responsibilities and decision-making activities such as distributing prizes and money and doling out punishments

Sloop: A small, single-masted boat, like a sailboat

Vessel: A steerable ship, not completely dependent on sails and wind direction

REFERENCES

INTRODUCTION: THE PIRATES' CODE OF HONOUR

1 Rebecca Simon, 'Historical Film as a Learning Tool: Pirates of the Caribbean', in Clio@Kings, originally published in 2015. This blog has been defunct for several years, but the author has her original document.

2 Peter T. Leeson, *The Invisible Hook: The Hidden Economics of Pirates* (Princeton, NJ, 2009), pp. 63–4.

3 *Tryals of Thirty-Six Persons for Piracy, Twenty-Eight of them upon Full Evidence were Found Guilty, and the rest Acquitted. At a Court of Admiralty for Tryal of Pirates, Held at Newport within His Majesties Colony of Rhode-Island and Providence-Plantations in America* (Boston, MA, 1723), in Joel H. Baer, *British Piracy in the Golden Age: History and Interpretations, 1660–1730*, 4 vols (London, 2007), vol. III, p. 191.

4 Captain Charles Johnson, *A General History of the Pyrates*, ed. Manuel Schonhorn (Mineola, NY, 1999), pp. 308–9.

5 Roberts was actually a teetotaller but acknowledged that alcohol could increase morale and productivity on his ships, so he allowed it.

6 Johnson, *A General History of the Pyrates*, pp. 212–13.

7 Ibid., pp. 350–51.

8 Extract from *The sixteen-year voyage in the Indies made by Jacob du Bucquoy, full of remarkable adventures, notably those which he experienced during his mission to the Delagoa River* (Harlem, NY, 1745), in Ed Fox, *Pirates in Their Own Words: Eye-Witness Accounts of the 'Golden Age' of Piracy, 1690–1728* (self-published, 2014), pp. 287–8.

9 Fox, *Pirates in Their Own Words*, p. 171.

10 Bartholomew Roberts died on 10 February 1722, just one month before this particular trial, which is why he was not named.

11 'A Journal of the Proceedings of the Court of Admiralty, held
   at Cabo Corso Castle, this 29th of March, 1722', in *A Full and
   Exact Account, of the Tryal of all the Pyrates, Lately taken by Captain
   Ogle, on Board the Swallow Man of War, on the Coast of Guinea*
   (London, 1723), in Baer, *British Piracy in the Golden Age*, vol. III,
   p. 88.

12 Ibid., p. 88.

13 Ibid., p. 100.

14 Ibid., pp. 104–5.

15 *The Tryals of Thirty-Six Persons for Piracy*, p. 182.

16 *The Proceedings on the King's Commission of Oyer and Terminer, and
   Gaol Delivery for the King of England, held at Justice Hall in the Old
   Bailey, on Wednesday and Thursday, being the 26th and 27th Days of
   May, in the Eleventh Year of His Majesty's Reign* (London, 1725), in
   Fox, *Pirates in Their Own Words*, p. 325.

17 *British Journal*, 8 August 1725, in Fox, *Pirates in Their Own Words*,
   pp. 299–300.

18 Marcus Rediker, *Villains of All Nations: Atlantic Pirates in the
   Golden Age* (Boston, MA, 2004), pp. 8–9, 49. See also Colin Woodard,
   *The Republic of Pirates: Being the True and Surprising Story of the
   Caribbean Pirates and the Man Who Brought Them Down* (Boston,
   MA, 2008), p. 1; Marcus Rediker, *Outlaws of the Atlantic: Sailors,
   Pirates, and Motley Crews in the Age of Sail* (Boston, MA, 2014),
   p. 64.

19 Alexandre Exquemelin, *The History of the Buccaneers of America*
   (London, 1771), pp. 3–4.

20 National Library of Jamaica (hereafter NLJ), MS 60, *Jamaica Council
   Minutes*, I, 'An Act declaring the Laws of England in force in
   this Island passed to the Council', 10 November 1664; NLJ, MS 60,
   Jamaica Council Minutes, III, 'At a Council Held at St Jago de la
   Vega', 14 March 1674.

21 Calendar of State Papers (hereafter CSPC) 15, Item 324,
   'Considerations offered by the Agents of Jamaica and the merchants
   trading thereto, to the Council of Trade and Plantations',
   16 October 1696.

22 CSPC 19, Item 180, 'Edward Randolph to the Council of Trade and
   Plantations', 19 February 1701.

23 Douglas R. Burgess Jr, *The Politics of Piracy: Crime and Civil
   Disobedience in Colonial America* (Chicago, IL, 2014), pp. 27–8.

24 CSPC 18, Item 15, 'Governor Sir William Beeston to the Council
   of Trade and Plantations', 5 January 1700.

25 CSPC II, Item 1313, 'A true and perfect narrative . . . delivered upon oath by Thomas Philips before Edwyn Stede', 18 October 1683.
26 Douglas R. Burgess Jr, *The Pirates' Pact: The Secret Alliances between History's Most Notorious Buccaneers and Colonial America* (New York, 2009), p. 17.
27 CSPC 19, Item 180, 'Edward Randolf the Council of Trade and Plantations', 19 February 1701.
28 CSPC 15, Item 1203, 'Jeremiah Basse to William Popple', 26 July 1697.
29 CSPC 15, Item 698, 'Council of Trade and Plantations to the Lords Proprietors of Carolina', 9 February 1697. See also Kris E. Lane, *Pillaging the Empire: Piracy in the Americas, 1500–1750* (Armonk, NY, 1998), p. 168.
30 NLJ, MS 1651/40, 'Petition of Merchants and Sugar Planters Against the Navigation Acts', 1735.
31 Lane, *Pillaging the Empire*, p. 168.
32 Exquemelin, *The History of the Buccaneers of America*, pp. 3–4; Marcus Rediker, 'Life under the Jolly Roger', *Wilson Quarterly*, XII/3 (Summer 1988), p. 156.
33 CSPC 19, Item 4, 'Rear Admiral Benbow to the Council of Trade and Plantations', 2 January 1701.
34 As quoted in Lane, *Pillaging the Empire*, p. 169.
35 Mark Hanna, *Pirate Nests and the Rise of the British Empire, 1570–1740* (Chapel Hill, NC, 2015), p. 126. Figures from CO 1/43, fol. 59, 'Account of What Passengers, Servants and Slaves Have Been Brought to This Island, June 25, 1671–March 1679'.
36 Woodard, *The Republic of Pirates*, p. 86.
37 Lane, *Pillaging the Empire*, p. 185.
38 CSPC 31, Item 311, 'Mr Gale to Col Thomas Pitt, junr, So Carolina', 4 November 1718.
39 CSPC 29, Item 331, 'Council of Trade and Plantations to Mr Secretary Methuen', 13 September 1716.
40 Ibid.
41 Rebecca Simon, *Why We Love Pirates: The Hunt for Captain Kidd and How He Changed Piracy Forever* (Coral Gables, FL, 2020), p. 140.
42 BL, Add. MSS 39946, fo 28, 'Deposition against Benjamin Hornigold'.
43 CSPC, VII/944, 1–10 June 1699.
44 Jamie L. H. Goodall, 'Tippling Houses, Rum Shops and Taverns: How Alcohol Fueled Informal Commercial Networks and Knowledge Exchange in the West Indies', *Journal for Maritime Research*, XVIII/2 (2016), p. 100.

45 Ibid., p. 99.
46 Ibid., p. 110.
47 Marcus Rediker, *Between the Devil and the Deep Blue Sea: Merchant Seamen, Pirates and the Anglo-American Maritime World, 1700–1750* (Cambridge, 1987), p. 81.
48 The exception to this rule was if they had already taken a ship and held some people captive; ibid., pp. 257–60.
49 Benerson Little, *The Sea Rover's Practice: Pirate Tactics and Techniques, 1630–1730* (Lincoln, NE, 2007), p. 31.
50 Rediker, *Villains of All Nations*, p. 79.
51 Paul Gilje, *Liberty on the Waterfront* (Philadelphia, PA, 2004).
52 CO 137/11/45iii, *Deposition of Abijah Savage, Commander of the Sloop Bonetta of Antigua before His Excellency Walter Hamilton* (20 November 1716); Eric Jay Dolin, *Black Flags, Blue Waters: The Epic History of America's Most Notorious Pirates* (New York, 2018), pp. 181–2.
53 *A Full and Exact Account, of the Tryal of all the Pyrates, Lately taken by Captain Ogle, on Board the Swallow Man of War, on the Coast of Guinea* (London, 1723), p. v.
54 However, Blackbeard would eventually sell the majority of them into slavery. *The Tryals of Major Stede Bonnet, and Other Pirates* (London, 1719), pp. 44–8.
55 *Tryals of Thirty-Six Persons for Piracy*.
56 *The Voyages and Adventures of Capt. Barth. Sharp and others, in the South Sea: Being a Journal of the same. Also Capt. Van Horn with his Buccanieres surprizing of la Veracruz. To which is added The true Relation of Sir Henry Morgan his Expedition against the Spaniards in the West-Indies, and his taking Panama. Together with the President of Panama's Account of the same Expedition: Translated out of Spanish. And Col. Beeston's Adjustment of the Peace between the Spaniards and English in the West Indies* (London, 1684), p. 79.
57 Dolin, *Black Flags, Blue Waters*, pp. 158–9.
58 *The Arraignment, Tryal and Condemnation of Capt. John Quelch, and Others of His Company, &c. for Sundry Piracies, Robberies, and Murder, Committed upon the Subjects of the King of Portugal, Her Majesty's Allie, on the Coast of Brasil, &c.* (London, 1704), p. 8.
59 Ibid., p. 15.
60 Ibid., p. 4.
61 *The Tryals of Major Stede Bonnet*, pp. 11, 38, 46.
62 *An Abridgement of the Laws in Force and Use in Her Majesty's Plantations* (London, 1704), p. 125.

63 Rediker, *Villains of All Nations*, p. 9.

64 *Piracy Destroy'd; or, A Short Discourse Shewing the Rise, Growth and Causes of Piracy of Late; with a Sure Method how to put a Speedy Stop to that Growing Evil* (London, 1701), pp. 3–5.

65 Rediker, *Villains of All Nations*, pp. 101, 132–3. See also Rediker, *Outlaws of the Atlantic*.

66 Rediker, *Between the Devil and the Deep Blue Sea*, p. 159.

67 For more discussions about religion on pirate ships, see Edward Kritzler, *Jewish Pirates of the Caribbean: How a Generation of Swashbuckling Jews Carved Out an Empire in the New World in Their Quest for Treasure, Religious Freedom, and Revenge* (London, 2009).

68 BL Egerton CH 7651, Island of Jamaica, Signet Warrants for various appointments, 1717–24.

1 WORK, LIFE AND WAGES ON THE PIRATE SHIP

1 Virginia W. Lunsford, 'A Model of Piracy: The Buccaneers of the Seventeenth-Century Caribbean', in *The Golden Age of Piracy: The Rise, Fall and Enduring Popularity of Pirates*, ed. David Head (Athens, GA, 2018), p. 139.

2 Alexandre Exquemelin, *The History of the Buccaneers of America*, trans. Alexis Brown (Mineola, NY, 2000), p. 70.

3 Captain Charles Johnson, *A General History of the Pyrates*, ed. Manuel Schonhorn (Mineola, NY, 1999), p. 117.

4 Lunsford, 'A Model of Piracy', p. 139.

5 Exquemelin, *The History of the Buccaneers of America*, p. 71.

6 *The Grand Pyrate; or, The Life and Death of Capt. George Cusack the Great Sea-Robber With an Accompt of all His Notorious Robberies both at Sea and Land. Together with His Tryal, Condemnation, and Execution* (London, 1676), pp. 6–7.

7 Ibid., p. 15.

8 *The Tryals of Joseph Dawson [et al.] . . . for several Piracies and Robberies by them Committed, in the Company of Every the Grand Pirate, near the Coasts of the East Indies; and several other Places in the Seas. Giving an Account of their Villainous Robberies and Barbarities* (London, 1696), pp. 132–3.

9 *The Arraignment, Tryal, and Condemnation of Captain William Kidd, for Murther and Piracy, upon Six Several Indictments . . . As also, the Tryals of Nicholas Churchill [et al.] . . . To which are added Captain Kidd's Two Commissions: One under the Great Seal of England, and the Other under the Great Seal of the Court of Admiralty* (London, 1701), p. 20.

10 *The Tryals of Joseph Dawson*, p. 22.

11 Ibid., p. 10.

12 Johnson, *A General History of the Pyrates*, p. 131.

13 Extract from *The sixteen-year voyage in the Indies made by Jacob du Bucquoy, full of remarkable adventures, notably those which he experienced during his mission to the Delagoa River* (Harlem, NY, 1745).

14 Benerson Little, *The Sea Rover's Practice: Pirate Tactics and Techniques, 1630–1730* (Lincoln, NE, 2007), p. 31.

15 Marcus Rediker, *Villains of All Nations: Atlantic Pirates in the Golden Age* (Boston, MA, 2004), p. 66.

16 Ibid., pp. 68–9.

17 Eric Jay Dolin, *Black Flags, Blue Waters: The Epic History of America's Most Notorious Pirates* (New York, 2018), p. 161.

18 Marcus Rediker, 'Life under the Jolly Roger', *Wilson Quarterly*, XII/3 (Summer 1988), pp. 159–60.

19 *The Voyages and Adventures of Capt. Barth. Sharp and others, in the South Sea: Being a Journal of the same. Also Capt. Van Horn with his Buccanieres surprizing of la Veracruz. To which is added The true Relation of Sir Henry Morgan his Expedition against the Spaniards in the West-Indies, and his taking Panama. Together with the President of Panama's Account of the same Expedition: Translated out of Spanish. And Col. Beeston's Adjustment of the Peace between the Spaniards and English in the West Indies* (London, 1684), p. 49.

20 *The Substance of this Examinations of John Brown &c.*, 6 May 1717, printed as the appendix of *The Trials of Eight Persons Indicted for Piracy* (Boston, MA, 1718), pp. 23–5.

21 Peter T. Leeson, 'The Economic Way of Thinking about Pirates', in *The Golden Age of Piracy*, ed. Head, p. 154.

22 Johnson, *A General History of the Pyrates*, pp. 440–51.

23 Lindley S. Butler, *Pirates, Privateers, and Rebel Raiders of the Carolina Coast* (Chapel Hill, NC, 2000), pp. 58–9.

24 HCA 24/132, *Gittus vs. Bowles* (1718).

25 Johnson, *A General History of the Pyrates*, p. 115.

26 Marcus Rediker, *Between the Devil and the Deep Blue Sea: Merchant Seamen, Pirates, and the Anglo-American Maritime World, 1700–1750* (Cambridge, 1987), pp. 118–19.

27 Dolin, *Black Flags, Blue Waters*, pp. 161–2.

28 Ibid., pp. 162, 164.

29 Rediker, *Between the Devil and the Deep Blue Sea*, pp. 121–3.

30 HCA 24/127, *Child vs. Clark* (1702); Rediker, *Between the Devil and the Deep Blue Sea*, p. 125.

31 Rediker, *Between the Devil and the Deep Blue Sea*, pp. 129–30.

32 Ibid., p. 142.

33 Ibid., p. 143.

34 Daniel Vickers, 'Maritime Labor in Colonial Massachusetts: A Case Study of the Essex County Cod Fishery and the Whaling Industry of Nantucket, 1630–1775', PhD diss., Princeton University, 1981, chap. 4.

35 Rediker, *Between the Devil and the Deep Blue Sea*, p. 146.

36 *The Lives, Apprehensions, Arraignments, and Executions of the 19 Late Pyrates . . . As they were Severally Indited on St Margarets Hill in Southwarke, on the 22d of December last, and Executed the Fryday Following* (London, 1609), pp. G–G2.

37 Kris E. Lane, *Pillaging the Empire: Piracy in the Americas, 1500–1750* (Armonk, NY, 1998), pp. 184–5.

38 Dolin, *Black Flags, Blue Waters*, p. 172.

39 *American Weekly Mercury*, 17 March 1720.

40 Peter T. Leeson, *The Invisible Hook: The Hidden Economics of Pirates* (Princeton, NJ, 2009), p. 11.

41 Ibid., p. 13.

42 Jennifer G. Marx, 'The Pirate Round', in *Pirates: Terror on the High Seas, From the Caribbean to the South China Sea* (East Bridgewater, MA, 1999), p. 141; *Flying Post*, 17–20 October 1696. For more discussion about wages, see Richard J. Blakemore, 'Pieces of Eight, Pieces of Eight: Seamen's Earnings and the Venture Economy of Early Modern Seafaring', *Economic History Review*, LXX/4 (2017), p. 12.

43 Captain Charles Johnson, *A General History of the Pyrates*, ed. Manuel Schonhorn (Mineola, NY, 1995), p. 244.

44 Ibid., pp. 53–5.

45 Craig Cabell, Graham A. Thomas and Allan Richards, *Captain Kidd: The Hunt for Truth* (Barnsley, 2010), pp. 95, 123; Graham Harris, *Treasure and Intrigue: The Legacy of Captain Kidd* (Toronto, 2002), pp. 21–3; Neil Rennie, *Treasure Neverland* (Oxford, 2013), p. 51. However, the connection between pirates and treasure has only been inseparable since the publication of Robert Louis Stevenson's novel *Treasure Island* (1883).

46 CSPC 17, Item 621, 'Governor Lord Bellomont to the Council of Trade and Plantations', 8 July 1699.

47 CSPC 17, Item 680, 'Governor the Earl of Bellomont to the Council of Trade and Plantations', 26 July 1699.

48 *London Post with Intelligence Foreign and Domestick*, 21–3 August 1699.

49 *London Post*, 6–8 September 1699.

50 BL, RP.8780, 'Autograph Letter Signed to Johnson Dickinson, discussing trade matters including an account of the remnants of Captain Kidd's crew and tales of buried treasure', Philadelphia, 9 July 1699.

51 BL, IOR/H/36, 'To Their Excellencies The Lords Justices of England The humble Petition of the Governour & Company of Merchants of London trading into the East Indies', 21 September 1699.

52 CSPC 18, Item 14, 'Letter from Lord Bellomont', 5 January 1700.

53 Robert C. Ritchie, *Captain Kidd and the War against the Pirates* (Cambridge, MA, 1986), p. 194.

54 *Post Boy*, 7–9 September 1699.

55 Samuel Sewall, *The Diary of Samuel Sewall*, ed. Mel Yazawa (Boston, MA, 1998), p. 6n.

56 *New-York Gazette*, 16 December 1765.

57 *New-Bedford Mercury*, 6 April 1837.

58 Dolin, *Black Flags, Blue Waters*, p. 172.

2 PUNISHMENTS ON THE PIRATE SHIP, PIRATE OR NOT

1 James S. Rankine, 'Pails, Pills, and Performances: Violence among Pirate Crews in the Golden Age', paper given at *The Problem of Piracy II: An Interdisciplinary Conference on Plunder across the Sea from the Ancient to the Modern* (online conference, 4–6 August 2021), p. 6.

2 HCA 1/18, f. 37, 'The Informant of Edward Evans', reproduced in Ed Fox, *Pirates in Their Own Words: Eye-Witness Accounts of the 'Golden Age' of Piracy, 1690–1728* (self-published, 2014), pp. 214–15.

3 Extract from *The sixteen-year voyage in the Indies made by Jacob du Bucquoy, full of remarkable adventures, notably those which he experienced during his mission to the Delagoa River* (Harlem, NY, 1745).

4 It should be noted that this article is not generally applied to pirates who are drunk. Ibid.

5 *A full and true Discovery of all the Robberies, Pyracies, and other Notorious Actions of that Famous English Pyrate, Capt. James Kelly . . . Written with His own Hand, During His Confinement in Newgate; and Delivered to His Wife, the Day of His Execution; Published by Her Order and Desire* (London, 1700).

6 Marcus Rediker, *Outlaws of the Atlantic: Sailors, Pirates, and Motley Crews in the Age of Sail* (Boston, MA, 2014), p. 71.

7 *The Proceedings on the King's Commissions of Oyer and Terminer, and Gaol Delivery for the Admiralty of England, held at Justice Hall in the*

Old Bailey, on Wednesday and Thursday, being the 26th and 17th Days of May, in the Eleventh Year of his Majesty's Reign (London, 1725), Reproduced in Fox, *Pirates in Their Own Words*, p. 326.

8 'A Journal of the Proceedings of the Court of Admiralty, held at Cabo Corso Castle, this April the 7th, 1722', in *A Full and Exact Account, of the Tryal of all the Pyrates, Lately taken by Captain Ogle, on Board the Swallow Man of War, on the Coast of Guinea* (London, 1723), reproduced in Joel H. Baer, *British Piracy in the Golden Age: History and Interpretations, 1660–1730*, 4 vols (London, 2007), vol. III, p. 126.

9 Ibid., p. 106.

10 'Narrative of Mr. Henry Watson, who was taken prisoner by the pirates, 15 August, 1696', CSPC 1696–1697, reproduced in Fox, *Pirates in Their Own Words*, p. 177. See also Benerson Little, *The Sea Rover's Practice: Pirate Tactics and Techniques, 1630–1730* (Lincoln, NE, 2007), p. 205.

11 *British Journal*, 8 August 1724, 22 August 1724.

12 Peter T. Leeson, *The Invisible Hook: The Hidden Economics of Pirates* (Princeton, NJ, 2009), p. 64.

13 Francis Grose, *A Classical Dictionary of the Vulgar Tongue* (London, 1788), p. 237.

14 Philip Gosse, *The Pirates' Who's Who: Giving Particulars of the Lives and Deaths of the Pirates and Buccaneers* (New York, 1924), p. 55.

15 Ibid., p. 113.

16 Captain Charles Johnson, *The General History of the Pyrates* (Mineola, NY, 1999), pp. 157–8.

17 Marcus Rediker, *Villains of All Nations: Atlantic Pirates in the Golden Age* (Boston, MA, 2004), p. 75.

18 Ibid., p. 76.

19 HCA 1/54 ff. 119–20, *The Information of Thomas Grant*, 28 April 1721.

20 HCA 1/54 ff. 123, *The Information of Edward Green*, 29 April 1721.

21 *The Grand Pyrate; or, The Life and Death of Capt. George Cusack the Great Sea-Robber With an Accompt of all His Notorious Robberies both at Sea and Land. Together with His Tryal, Condemnation, and Execution* (London, 1676), p. 16.

22 'A Journal of the Proceedings of the Court of Admiralty', p. 11.

23 Ibid., p. 101.

24 Ibid., p. 14.

25 Ibid., p. 100.

26 Eric Jay Dolin, *Black Flags, Blue Waters: The Epic History of America's Most Notorious Pirates* (New York, 2018), pp. 164–5.

27 Virginia W. Lunsford, 'A Model of Piracy: The Buccaneers of
the Seventeenth-Century Caribbean', in *The Golden Age of Piracy:
The Rise, Fall, and Enduring Popularity of Pirates*, ed. David Head
(Athens, GA, 2018), pp. 133–4.

28 Leeson, *The Invisible Hook*, p. 116.

29 Peter T. Leeson, 'The Economic Way of Thinking about Pirates',
in *The Golden Age of Piracy*, ed. Head, pp. 159–61.

30 *Weekly Journal or British Gazetteer*, 22 April 1721.

31 *London Journal*, 20 June 1724.

32 *Monthly Chronicle*, May 1729. This story was reprinted several times
over the years.

33 Angus Konstam, *Blackbeard: America's Most Notorious Pirate*
(Hoboken, NJ, 2006), p. 157.

3 HEALTH AND SAFETY ON THE PIRATE SHIP

1 Robert Louis Stevenson, *Treasure Island* (New York, 1994), p. 74.

2 Eric Jay Dolin, *Black Flags, Blue Waters: The Epic History of America's
Most Notorious Pirates* (New York, 2018), pp. 160–61.

3 Stevenson, *Treasure Island*, p. 11.

4 Sara Caputo, 'Treating, Preventing, Feigning, Concealing: Sickness,
Agency and the Medical Culture of the British Naval Seamen
at the End of the Long Eighteenth Century', *Social History of
Medicine*, XXXV/3 (2021), p. 6.

5 Rebecca Simon, *Why We Love Pirates: The Hunt for Captain Kidd and
How He Changed Piracy Forever* (Coral Gables, FL, 2020), pp. 34–5.

6 Ibid., p. 88.

7 Alexandre Exquemelin, *The History of the Buccaneers of America*,
trans. Alexis Brown (Mineola, NY, 2000), pp. 56–7.

8 Marcus Rediker, *Villains of All Nations: Atlantic Pirates in the Golden
Age* (Boston, MA, 2004), pp. 73–4; Marcus Rediker, '"Under the
Banner of King Death": The Social World of Anglo-American
Pirates, 1716–1726', *William and Mary Quarterly*, XXXVIII/2
(April 1981), pp. 203–27.

9 David McLean, 'Health Provision in the Royal Navy, 1650–1815',
in *The Social History of English Seamen, 1650–1815*, ed. Cheryl A. Fury
(Woodbridge, 2017), p. 121.

10 John Woodall, *The surgeons mate or Military & domestique surgery
Discouering faithfully & plainly ye method and order of ye surgeons chest,
ye uses of the instruments, the vertues and operations of ye medicines, with
ye exact cures of wounds made by gunshott, and otherwise as namely:
wounds, apos fumes, ulcers, fistula's, fractions, dislocations, with ye most*

easie & safest ways of amputation or dismembering. The cures of the scruery, of ye fluxes of ye belly, of ye collicke and iliaca passio, of tenesmus and exitus ani, and of the calenture, with A treatise of ye cure of ye plague. Published for the service of his Ma. tie and of the com:wealth (1617).

11 Rediker, *Villains of All Nations*, p. 73.

12 John Atkins, *The Navy Surgeon; or, Practical System of Surgery. With a Dissertation on Cold and Hot Mineral Springs; and Physical Observations on the Coast of Guiney* (London, 1742), p. 118; see Mark C. Kehoe, 'Amputation during the Golden Age of Piracy', in *The Pirate Surgeon's Journals: Tools and Procedures*, at https://piratesurgeon.com, accessed 16 November 2021.

13 Woodall, *The Surgeon's Mate*, pp. 157–8.

14 EXT 1/261 ff. 197–199, 'The Petition of John Massey and George Lowther'.

15 McLean, 'Health Provision in the Royal Navy', p. 110.

16 A TRUE RELATION OF *a most Horrid Conspiracy and Running away with the* SHIP ADVENTURE, *Having on Board Forty Thousand Pieces of Eight, and other Goods to a great Value. Together with the Cruel and Barbarous leaving and turning ashore upon the Island Naias, in the East-Indies, the Captain, and three Merchants which were Passengers, and Sixteen honest and able Seamen, Eight whereof miserably perished by Hunger and Hardship, and but Four of the Remainder yet come to England. Together with some short Account of what passed at the Trial and Condemnation of those who Committed that Fact* (London, 1700).

17 Ibid.

18 'A Journal of the Proceedings of the Court of Admiralty, held at Cabo Corso Castle, this April the 7th, 1722', in *A Full and Exact Account, of the Tryal of all the Pyrates, Lately taken by Captain Ogle, on Board the Swallow Man of War, on the Coast of Guinea* (London, 1723), reproduced in Joel H. Baer, *British Piracy in the Golden Age: History and Interpretations, 1660–1730*, 4 vols (London, 2007), vol. III, p. 30.

19 Benerson Little, *The Sea Rover's Practice: Pirate Tactics and Techniques, 1630–1730* (Lincoln, NE, 2007), p. 151.

20 Jeremy R. Moss, *The Life and Tryals of the Gentleman Pirate, Major Stede Bonnet* (Virginia Beach, VA, 2020), pp. 29–30.

21 *Tryals of Thirty-Six Persons for Piracy, Twenty-Eight of them upon Full Evidence were Found Guilty, and the rest Acquitted. At a Court of Admiralty for Tryal of Pirates, Held at Newport within His Majesties Colony of Rhode-Island and Providence-Plantations in America* (Boston, MA, 1723).

22 *The Arraignment, Tryal, and Condemnation of Captain William Kidd, for Murther and Piracy, upon Six Several Indictments . . . As also, the Tryals of Nicholas Churchill [et al.] . . . To which are added Captain Kidd's Two Commissions: One under the Great Seal of England, and the Other under the Great Seal of the Court of Admiralty* (London, 1701), p. 31.

23 'A Journal of the Proceedings of the Court of Admiralty', p. 30.

24 William Dampier, *Memoirs of a Buccaneer, Dampier's New Voyage Round the World* (London, 1697), p. 214. See Mark C. Kehoe, 'Treating Fluxes in the Golden Age of Piracy', *The Pirate Surgeon's Journals: Tools and Procedures*, https://piratesurgeon.com, accessed 16 November 2021.

25 William Cockburn, *The Nature and Cure of Fluxes: To which is Added, the Method of Finding the Doses of Purging and Vomiting Medicines for Every Age* (London, 1724), p. 131; Thomas Aubrey, *The Sea-Surgeon or the Guinea Man's Vadé Mecum* (1729), p. 72; see Kehoe, 'Treating Fluxes in the Golden Age of Piracy'.

26 James Yonge, *The Journal of James Yonge Plymouth Surgeon, 1647–1732*, ed. F.N.L. Poynter (Hamden, CT, 1963), p. 44.

27 Marcus Rediker, *Between the Devil and the Deep Blue Sea: Merchant Seamen, Pirates and the Anglo-American Maritime World, 1700–1750* (Cambridge, 1987), p. 197.

28 See David Stewart, *The Sea, Their Graves: An Archaeology of Death and Remembrance in Maritime Culture* (Gainesville, FL, 2011).

29 Captain Charles Johnson, *A General History of the Pyrates*, ed. Manuel Schonhorn (Mineola, NY, 1999), chapter on John Halsey.

30 Ibid.

31 Ambroise Paré, *The Workes of that Famous Chirugion Ambrose Parey*, trans. Thomas Johnson (London, 1649), p. 760.

32 Stewart, *The Sea, Their Graves*, p. 118.

33 Ibid., p. 117. See also Mark C. Kehoe, 'Dealing with the Deceased in the Golden Age of Piracy', *The Pirate Surgeon's Journals*, https://piratesurgeon.com, accessed 25 January 2022.

34 *The Metropolitan: A Monthly Journal of Literature, Science and the Fine Arts*, 1 (May–August 1831), p. 394.

4 SEX, SEXUALITY AND RELATIONSHIPS ON AND OFF THE PIRATE SHIP

1 B. R. Burg, 'Officers, Shipboard Boys and Court Martial for Sodomy and Indecency in the Georgian Navy', in *The Social History of English Seamen, 1650–1815*, ed. Cheryl A. Fury (Woodbridge, 2017), p. 90.

2 Laura Gowing, *Gender Relations in Early Modern England* (Harlow, 2012), p. 20.

3 Articles of War, in John D. Byrn Jr, *Crime and Punishment in the Royal Navy: Discipline on the Leeward Island Station, 1784–1812* (Aldershot, 1989), pp. 12, 203–10.

4 HCA 1/55, fol. 22, 'Information of Richard Mandewell', 1722; CO 137/14, *The Trials of Jack Rackham and Other Pirates* (London, 1721); Peter T. Leeson, *The Invisible Hook: The Hidden Economics of Pirates* (Princeton, NJ, 2009), p. 16.

5 Katherine Bone, 'Tortuga: Den of Pirates and Thieves', in 'Pirates and Privateers: The History of Maritime Piracy', ed. Cindy Vallar (2015), at www.cindyvallar.com.

6 CSPC 17, Item 530.VI, 'Copy of Deposition of Theophilus Turner'.

7 John Franklin Jameson, *Privateering and Piracy in the Colonial Period* (New York, 1923), p. 199.

8 B. R. Burg, *Sodomy and the Pirate Tradition: English Sea Rovers in the Seventeenth-Century Caribbean* (New York, 1995), p. 128.

9 HCA 1/98, f. 193, Agreement between Francis Reed and John Beavis, 10 March 1696, in E. T. Fox, *Pirates in Their Own Words: Eye-Witness Accounts of the 'Golden Age' of Piracy, 1690–1728* (self-published, 2014), pp. 73–4.

10 HCA 1/98, f. 171, Robert Collover to Mrs Whalley, 6 April 1699, in Fox, *Pirates in Their Own Words*, p. 77.

11 Colin Woodard, *The Republic of Pirates: Being the True and Surprising Story of the Caribbean Pirates and the Man Who Brought Them Down* (San Diego, CA, 2007), p. 139.

12 Alison Games, *Migrations and Origins of the English Atlantic World* (Cambridge, MA, 2001), pp. 46–7.

13 Peter T. Leeson, Peter J. Boettke and Jaymes S. Lemke, 'Wife Sales', *Review of Behavioral Economics*, I (2014), p. 352.

14 Marcus Rediker, *Villains of All Nations: Atlantic Pirates in the Golden Age* (Boston, MA, 2004), p. 117.

15 Captain Charles Johnson, *A General History of the Pyrates*, ed. Manuel Schonhorn (Mineola, NY, 1999), p. 164.

16 CO 137/14/9–30, *The Tryals of Captain John Rackham, and other Pirates. Who were all Condemn'd for Piracy, at the Town of St. Jago de la Vega, in the Island of Jamaica, on Wednesday and Thursday the Sixteenth and Seventeenth Days of November 1720. As also, the Tryals of Mary Read and Anne Bonny, alias Bonn* (St Jago de la Vega, Jamaica, 1721).

17 Jo Stanley, *Bold in Her Breeches: Women Pirates across the Ages* (London, 1995), p. 7.

18 Ibid., p. 8.

19 Margarette Lincoln, *British Pirates and Society, 1680–1730* (Woodbridge, 2015), p. 188.

20 CO 134/14, *The Trials of Captain John Rackham and Other Pirates* (London, 1721), pp. 27–8.

21 Johnson, *A General History of the Pyrates*, p. 6.

22 Gowing, *Gender Relations in Early Modern England*, p. 20.

23 Ibid.

24 Ulrike Klausmann, Marion Meinzerin and Gabriel Kuhn, *Women Pirates and the Politics of the Jolly Roger* (Montreal, 1997), pp. 212–15.

25 *The History and Lives of all the most Notorious Pirates and Their Crews* (London, 1725), p. 72.

26 Rictor Norton, 'Lesbian Pirates: Anne Bonny and Mary Read', *Lesbian History*, 14 June 2008, http://rictornorton.co.uk.

27 Stanley, *Bold in Her Breeches*, p. 155. David Cordingly also accepts that Anne and Mary had a sexual relationship. See David Cordingly, *Seafaring Women: Adventures of Pirate Queens, Female Stowaways, and Sailors' Wives* (New York, 2011), p. 82.

28 Jonathan Morris, 'Burgh Island Statue "Should Be Pilchards not Pirates"', BBC News Online, 16 February 2021, www.bbc.com. This was in response to controversy over a plan to place their statues in Devon, which was later abandoned.

29 CO 137/14, *The Trial of Captain John Rackham* (London, 1721), p. 19.

30 'By His Excellent Woodes Rogers, Esq Governour of New Providence, &c A Proclamation', *Boston Gazette*, 10 October 1720.

31 Johnson, *A General History of the Pyrates*, p. 53.

32 For a full account of Avery's life, see ibid., pp. 49–62.

33 Margarette Lincoln, 'Henry Every and the Creation of the Pirate Myth in Early Modern England', in *The Golden Age of Piracy: The Rise, Fall, and Enduring Popularity of Pirates*, ed. David Head (Athens, GA, 2018), p. 172.

34 Daniel Defoe, *The King of the Pirates: Being an Account of the Famous Enterprises of Captain Every, the Mock King of Madagascar. In Two Letters from Himself* (London, 1720), p. 58.

35 Ibid., p. 59.

36 Lincoln, 'Henry Every and the Creation of the Pirate Myth in Early Modern England', p. 176.

37 J. M. Beattie, *Crime and the Courts in England, 1660–1800* (Oxford, 1986), p. 440.

38 'A Journal of the Proceedings of the Court of Admiralty, held at Cabo Corso Castle, April the 2d, 1722', in *A Full and Exact*

Account, of the Tryal of all the Pyrates, Lately taken by Captain Ogle, on Board the Swallow Man of War, on the Coast of Guinea (London, 1723), in Joel H. *Baer, British Piracy in the Golden Age: History and Interpretations, 1660–1730*, 4 vols (London, 2007), vol. III, p. 100.

39 Ibid., pp. 146, 155.

40 *The Tryals of Major Stede Bonnet and Other Pirates . . . Who were all condemn'd for Piracy* (London, 1719), p. 11.

41 Ibid., p. 39.

42 'The Confession of Walter Kennedy, who was condemn'd at the Sessions of the Admiralty, for that he with other Pirates, had robb'd and plunder'd the Ship called the Loyal Rover, etc.', *A Select and Impartial Account of the Lives, Behaviour and the Dying Words of the most Remarkable Convicts from the Year 1700, to the present Time*, vol. I (London, 1760), pp. 232–7; *Weekly Journal; or, British Gazetteer*, 29 July 1721.

43 *Ordinary of Newgate*, 'Ordinary's Accounts: Biographies of Executed Criminals', London Lives, www.londonlives.org, accessed 30 August 2022.

44 Robert C. Ritchie, *Captain Kidd and the War against the Pirates* (Cambridge, MA, 1986), p. 229.

45 *The Ordinary of Newgate's Account of the Behaviour, Confession, and Dying Words of Capt. Joseph Halsey, Who was executed at Execution-Dock, on Wednesday the 14th of March, 1759, For the Murder of Daniel Davidson* (London, 1759), pp. 6–7.

46 Old Bailey Online (www.oldbaileyonline.org, version 6.0, 29 September 2021), Ordinary of Newgate's Account, February 1760 (OA17600211).

47 British Library, ADD. MS.61620, 'Petitions of Pirate Wives', November 1707, pp. 155b–156.

48 SP 63/358 ff. 127–32, *The Voluntary Confession and Discovery of William Phillips*, 8 August, 1696, in Fox, *Pirates in Their Own Words*, p. 32.

49 *The Narrative of Richard Lazenby, of London, Second mate of the 'Cassandra', Captain James Macrae, Commander, taken by the Pirates Seagar in the 'Fancy' and Taylor in the 'Victory' at Johanna in the Comoro Islands in July 1720*, in Fox, *Pirates in Their Own Words*, p. 280.

50 Johnson, *A General History of the Pyrates*, p. 76.

51 As recounted in Benerson Little, *The Sea Rover's Practice: Pirate Tactics and Techniques, 1630–1730* (Lincoln, NE, 2007), pp. 202–3.

52 Maev Kennedy, 'Sailor's Rape Confession Uncovered in 17th-Century Journal', *The Guardian*, 18 September 2018, www.theguardian.com.

53 Rediker, *Villains of All Nations*, p. III.
54 Rebecca Simon, *Why We Love Pirates: The Hunt for Captain Kidd and How He Changed Pirates Forever* (Coral Gables, FL, 2020), pp. 39–40.
55 Stanley, *Bold in Her Breeches*, p. 9.
56 Ibid., p. 14.
57 Johnson, *A General History of the Pyrates*, pp. 158–9.
58 Stanley, *Bold in Her Breeches*, p. 38.
59 Cordingly, *Seafaring Women*, p. 63.
60 David Cordingly, *Under the Black Flag: The Romance and Reality of Life among the Pirates* (New York, 1995), p. 69.
61 Cordingly, *Seafaring Women*, p. 64.
62 Ibid.

5 SAFETY, WEAPONS AND PIRATES' BATTLE TACTICS

1 *The Voyages and Adventures of Capt. Barth. Sharp and others, in the South Sea: Being a Journal of the same. Also Capt. Van Horn with his Buccanieres surprizing of la Veracruz. To which is added The true Relation of Sir Henry Morgan his Expedition against the Spaniards in the West-Indies, and his taking Panama. Together with the President of Panama's Account of the same Expedition: Translated out of Spanish. And Col. Beeston's Adjustment of the Peace between the Spaniards and English in the West Indies* (London, 1684), pp. 77–8.
2 Eric Jay Dolin, *Black Flags, Blue Waters: The Epic History of America's Most Notorious Pirates* (New York, 2018), p. 166.
3 Benerson Little, *The Sea Rover's Practice: Pirate Tactics and Techniques, 1630–1730* (Lincoln, NE, 2007), pp. 42–3.
4 Ibid., p. 45.
5 Examination of John Brown and Peter Cornelius Hoof', in *The Trials of Eight Persons Indited for Piracy &c. Of whom Two were acquitted, and the rest found Guilty. At a Judicial Court of Admiralty assembled and Held in Boston within his Majesty's Province of Massachusetts-Bay in New England, on the 18th of October 1717 and by several Adjustments continued to the 30th. Pursuant to His Majesty's Commission and Instructions, founded on the Act of Parliament–Made in the 11th and 12th of King William IIId. Intituled An Act for the more effectual Suppression of Piracy. With an Appendix, Containing the Substance of their Confessions given before Their Excellency the Governour, when they were first brought to Boston and committed to Gaol* (Boston, MA, 1718), p. 23; Dolin, *Black Flags, Blue Waters*, pp. 183–4.

6 Little, *The Sea Rover's Practice*, pp. 85–6.

7 'A Journal of the Proceedings of the Court of Admiralty, held at Cabo Corso Castle on the Coast of Africa, Monday April the 9th, 1722', in *A Full and Exact Account, of the Tryal of all the Pyrates, Lately taken by Captain Ogle, on Board the Swallow Man of War, on the Coast of Guinea* (London, 1723), p. 52.

8 Ibid., p. 41.

9 Ibid., p. 45.

10 Marcus Rediker, *Between the Devil and the Deep Blue Sea: Merchant Seamen, Pirates and the Anglo-American Maritime World, 1700–1750* (Cambridge, 1987), p. 163.

11 Ibid., p. 163.

12 Ibid., p. 160.

13 Ibid., pp. 160–61.

14 Little, *The Sea Rover's Practice*, pp. 65, 152.

15 'HMS Phoenix, 22 Feb–11 Apr 1718 Log Entries', Baylus C. Brooks, http://baylusbrooks.com, accessed 30 December 2021.

16 Alexandre Exquemelin, *The History of the Buccaneers of America*, trans. Alexis Brown (Mineola, NY, 2000), p. 89.

17 Little, *The Sea Rover's Practice*, p. 57.

18 Ibid., p. 60.

19 B. P., Hughes, *Firepower: Weapons Effectiveness on the Battlefield, 1630–1850* (New York, 1997), p. 11.

20 HCA 1/99, *The Trials of Nicholas Simonds et. al.*, Rhode Island, 24 February 1724.

21 Little, *The Sea Rover's Practice*, pp. 63–4, 86.

22 Johnson, *A General History of the Pyrates*, p. 84.

23 Refers to Captain Shipton off the Bay of Honduras in January 1725. *American Weekly Mercury*, 11–18 March 1725.

24 Little, *The Sea Rover's Practice*, pp. 68–9.

25 *American Weekly Mercury*, 15–22 February 1726.

26 *Boston News-Letter*, 16–23 February 1719; *Boston News-Letter*, 23 February–2 March 1719. See also Angus Konstam, *Blackbeard: America's Most Notorious Pirate* (Hoboken, NJ, 2006), p. 257.

27 Little, *The Sea Rover's Practice*, p. 68.

28 Ibid., pp. 137–9.

29 Ibid., p. 139.

30 William Dampier, *Memoirs of a Buccaneer: Dampier's New Voyage Round the World* (London, 1697), pp. 135–6.

31 Little, *The Sea Rover's Practice*, pp. 139–41.

32 Ibid., pp. 142–5, 151.

33 Marcus Rediker, 'Life under the Jolly Roger', *Wilson Quarterly*, xii/3 (Summer 1988), p. 156.

34 Dolin, *Black Flags, Blue Waters*, p. 171.

35 Cordingly, *Under the Black Flag*, p. 118.

36 Ibid., p. 117.

37 Ibid., p. 116.

38 As quoted in Dolin, *Black Flags, Blue Waters*, p. 171.

39 Peter T. Leeson, 'The Economic Way of Thinking about Pirates', in *The Golden Age of Piracy: The Rise, Fall, and Enduring Popularity of Pirates*, ed. David Head (Athens, GA, 2018), p. 159.

40 *Tryals of Thirty-Six Persons for Piracy, Twenty-Eight of them upon Full Evidence were Found Guilty, and the rest Acquitted. At a Court of Admiralty for Tryal of Pirates, Held at Newport within His Majesties Colony of Rhode-Island and Providence-Plantations in America* (Boston, MA, 1723), in Joel H. Baer, *British Piracy in the Golden Age: History and Interpretations, 1660–1730*, 4 vols (London, 2007), vol. iii, pp. 177–8.

41 Cordingly, *Under the Black Flag*, p. 115.

42 Ibid., p. 116.

43 *The Substance Examinations of John Brown* &c., 6 May 1717. Printed as the appendix of *The Trials of Eight Persons Indicted for Piracy* (Boston, MA, 1718), pp. 23–5.

44 Dolin, *Black Flags, Blue Waters*, pp. 169–70.

45 HCA 1/55 ff. 23–4, 'The Information of Alexander Thompson', 2 March 1722.

46 Bodleian Library, MS Rawlinson A 271, f. 44b, 'Deposition of Joseph Man', 11 June 1700.

47 *The Trials of Five Persons for Piracy, Felony and Robbery* (Boston, MA, 1726), pp. 23–4.

48 'The Account which the Captain of the Cassandra gives to the India Company . . .', *Weekly Journal or British Gazetteer*, 22 April 1721.

49 *A True Relation, of the Lives and Deaths of the Two Most Famous English Pyrats, Purser, and Clinton; Who Lived in the Reigne of Queene Elizabeth. Together with the particular actions of their Takings, and undertakings With other pleasant Passages which hapned before their surprizall worth the observing* (London, 1639), in E. T. Fox, *Scattergoods and Swaggering Rascals: Documents Relating to English Piracy of the Tudor and Jacobean Period* (self-published, 2015), p. 18.

50 Little, *The Sea Rover's Practice*, pp. 76–8.

51 Dolin, *Black Flags, Blue Waters*, p. 178.

52 *The Grand Pyrate; or, The Life and Death of Capt. George Cusack the Great Sea-Robber With an Accompt of all His Notorious Robberies both at Sea and Land. Together with His Tryal, Condemnation, and Execution* (London, 1676), p. 20.

53 HCA 1/55 ff. 132–3, *The Examination of Robert Read*, 3 April 1725.

54 *Boston News-Letter*, 9–16 June 1718.

55 'A Journal of the Proceedings of the Court of Admiralty, held at Cabo Corso Castle, this April the 6th, 1722', in *A Full and Exact Account, of the Tryal of all the Pyrates, Lately taken by Captain Ogle, on Board the Swallow Man of War, on the Coast of Guinea* (London, 1723), p. 39.

56 'A Journal of the Proceedings of the Court of Admiralty', pp. 70–71.

57 HCA 1/55 ff. 103–4, *The Examination of James Williams*, 27 March 1725.

58 HCA 1/55 ff. 105–6, *The Examination of John Smith*, 2 April 1725.

59 CSPC 33, Item 754.iv, 'Deposition of John Wickstead', 24 November 1723.

60 'We have this farther Account of Insolence . . .' *London Journal*, 24 August 1723.

61 *Tryals of Thirty-Six Persons for Piracy, Twenty-Eight of them upon Full Evidence were Found Guilty, and the rest Acquitted. At a Court of Admiralty for Tryal of Pirates, Held at Newport within His Majesties Colony of Rhode-Island and Providence-Plantations in America* (Boston, MA, 1723).

62 Merrall Llewelyn Price, *Consuming Passions: The Uses of Cannibalism in Late Medieval and Early Modern Europe* (New York, 2003), p. 7.

63 'London', *London Journal*, 20 June 1724.

64 *The Grand Pyrate*, p. 16.

65 Pryce, *Consuming Passions*, p. 7.

66 '6', *Monthly Chronicle*, May 1729.

67 'On This Day . . .', *Monthly Chronicle*, May 1729.

68 In addition to the *Monthly Chronicle*, the story also appeared in the *Daily Journal* (10 June 1729) and the *Weekly Journal or British Gazetteer* (14 June 1729).

69 'Agreed cannibalism' is a term used by historians to describe the act of shipwrecked sailors drawing lots to see who would be killed and eaten for the others' survival. There are no official maritime laws that sanction or prohibit drawing lots; instead it is known as a 'custom of the sea' in the event of a worst-case scenario for survival. There has not yet been a comprehensive study of this culture in the field of early modern maritime history. For studies about drawing lots and customs to the sea, refer to Nathaniel Philbrick, *In the Heart*

of the Sea: The Epic True Story that Inspired 'Moby Dick' (London, 2005); and Neil Hanson, *The Custom of the Sea* (London, 1998).

70 Peter Hulme, 'Introduction: The Cannibal Scene', in *Cannibalism and the Colonial World*, ed. Francis Barker, Peter Hulme and Margaret Iversen (Cambridge, 1998), p. 33.

6 FOOD AND DRINK ON THE PIRATE SHIP

1 Cheryl A. Fury, 'Heath and Care at Sea', in *The Social History of Seamen, 1650–1815*, ed. Cheryl A. Fury (Woodbridge, 2017), p. 198.

2 R. H. Dana Jr, *The Seaman's Manual; Containing a Treatise on Practical Seamanship with plates; A Dictionary of Sea Terms; Customs and Usages of the Merchant Service; Laws Relating to the Practical Duties of Master and Mariners* (London, 1841), p. 239.

3 Byron J. Good, *Medicine, Rationality and Experience: An Anthropological Perspective* (Cambridge, 1993), p. 105. See also Mark C. Kehoe, 'Food and Healthiness at Sea during the Golden Age of Piracy', *The Pirate Surgeon's Journals*, http://piratesurgeon.com, accessed 17 November 2021.

4 Thomas Aubrey, *The Sea-Surgeon or the Guinea Man's Vadé Mecum* (London, 1729), pp. 8–9.

5 David McLean, 'Health Provision in the Royal Navy, 1650–1815', in *The Social History of English Seamen*, ed. Fury, p. 111.

6 Kris E. Lane, *Pillaging the Empire: Piracy in the Americas, 1500–1750* (Armonk, NY, 1998), p. 193.

7 Erica M. Charters, '"The Intention Is Noble": The Western Squadron, Medical Trials, and the Sick and Hurt Board during the Seven Years War', in *Health and Medicine at Sea, 1700–1900*, ed. David Boyd Hancock and Sally Archer (Woodbridge, 2009), p. 21.

8 An English Sailor, *The State of the Navy Consider'd in Relation to Victualling* (London, 1699).

9 HCA 1/99 f. 102, 'Proceedings of the Court held on the Coast of Africa upon Trying of 100 Pirates taken by his Majesties Ship Swallow' (1722).

10 Marcus Rediker, *Between the Devil and the Deep Blue Sea: Merchant Seamen, Pirates and the Anglo-American Maritime World, 1700–1750* (Cambridge, 1987), pp. 126–7.

11 Ibid., p. 127.

12 Richard Ligon, *A True and Exact History of the Island of Barbados* (London, 1673), p. 119.

13 Benerson Little, *The Sea Rover's Practice: Pirate Tactics and Techniques, 1630–1730* (Lincoln, NE, 2007), p. 89.

References

14 Ibid., p. 209.

15 Rediker, *Between the Devil and the Deep Blue Sea*, p. 128.

16 *The Voyages and Adventures of Capt. Barth. Sharp and others, in the South Sea: Being a Journal of the same. Also Capt. Van Horn with his Buccanieres surprizing of la Veracruz. To which is added The true Relation of Sir Henry Morgan his Expedition against the Spaniards in the West-Indies, and his taking Panama. Together with the President of Panama's Account of the same Expedition: Translated out of Spanish. And Col. Beeston's Adjustment of the Peace between the Spaniards and English in the West Indies* (London, 1684), in Joel H. Baer, *British Piracy in the Golden Age: History and Interpretations, 1660–1730*, 4 vols (London, 2007), vol. I, p. 129.

17 William Funnell, *A Voyage Round the World* (London, 1707), p. 28.

18 McLean, 'Health Provision in the Royal Navy', p. 111.

19 Wayne Curtis, *And a Bottle of Rum: A History of the New World in Ten Cocktails* (New York, 2018), p. 52.

20 *The Voyages and Adventures of Capt. Barth. Sharp and others, in the South Sea*, p. 130.

21 Alexandre Exquemelin, *The Buccaneers of America: A True Account of the Most Remarkable Assaults Committed of Late Years Upon the Coasts of the West Indies by the Buccaneers of Jamaica and Tortuga (both English and French) Wherein are Contained More Especially*, ed. Basil Ringrose (London, 2015), p. 312, as quoted by Mark C. Kehoe, 'Organization of Ship's Food in the Golden Age of Piracy', *Pirate Surgeon's Journals: Tools and Procedures*, https://piratesurgeon.com, accessed 17 January 2022.

22 William Monson, *The Naval Tracts of Sir William Monson*, ed. M. Oppenheim (1913), vol. IV, pp. 64–5, as quoted by Kehoe, 'Organization of Ship's Food in the Golden Age of Piracy'.

23 John Keevil, *Medicine and the Navy*, vol. I: *1200–1649* (London, 1957), p. 72.

24 Brian Lavery, *The Arming and Fitting of English Ships of War, 1600–1815* (Annapolis, MD, 1987), p. 196, as quoted by Kehoe, 'Organization of Ship's Food in the Golden Age of Piracy'.

25 Ibid., as quoted by Kehoe, 'Organization of Ship's Food in the Golden Age of Piracy'.

26 Kehoe, 'Organization of Ship's Food in the Golden Age of Piracy'.

27 Clement Downing, *A Compendious History of the Indian Wars* (London, 1737), p. 108.

28 Curtis, *And a Bottle of Rum*, pp. 52–3.

29 Ibid., pp. 113–15.

30 Lane, *Pillaging the Empire*, p. 195.
31 Little, *The Sea Rover's Practice*, p. 90.
32 *The Tryals of Major Stede Bonnet and other Pirates* (London, 1719), in Baer, *British Piracy in the Golden Age*, p. 376.

7 PIRATES' VICES

1 Benerson Little, *The Sea Rover's Practice: Pirate Tactics and Techniques, 1630–1730* (Lincoln, NE, 2007), p. 202.
2 David Cordingly, *Under the Black Flag: The Romance and Reality of Life among the Pirates* (New York, 1996), p. 94.
3 Ibid., p. 110.
4 Extract from *The sixteen-year voyage in the Indies made by Jacob du Bucquoy, full of remarkable adventures, notably those which he experienced during his mission to the Delagoa River* (Harlem, NY, 1745), in E. T. Fox, *Pirates in Their Own Words: Eye-Witness Accounts of the 'Golden Age' of Piracy, 1690–1728* (self-published, 2014), p. 288.
5 'The Ordinary and his Account', Old Bailey Online, www.oldbaileyonline.org, accessed 21 July 2022.
6 'The Ordinary of Newgate his Account of the Behaviour and Dying-Words of Captain William Kidd and Darby Mullins, Condemn'd for Piracy', *A Select and Impartial Account of the Lives, Behaviour and the Dying Words of the most Remarkable Convicts from the Year 1700, to the present Time*, vol. 1 (London, 1760), pp. 1–4.
7 Anna Bryson, *From Courtesy to Civility: Changing Codes of Conduct in Early Modern England* (Oxford, 1998), pp. 3, 96.
8 See Daniel E. Williams, 'Puritans and Pirates: A Confrontation between Cotton Mather and William Fly in 1726', *Early American Literature*, XXII/3 (1987), pp. 233–51.
9 *Boston News-Letter*, 26 June–3 July 1704.
10 Hugh Jones, *The Present State of Virginia, Giving a particular and short Account of the Indian, English and Negroe Inhabitants of that Colony* (London, 1724), pp. 95–7.
11 Ibid., p. 149.
12 John E. Witte and Thomas C. Arthur, 'Three Uses of the Law: A Protestant Source of the Purpose of Criminal Punishment?', *Journal of Law and Religion*, X (1993–4), p. 433.
13 *Abstract of the Laws Against Sabbath-Breaking, Swearing, and Drunkenness* (Stockport, 1797).
14 Michael J. Crawford, ed., *The Autobiography of a Yankee Mariner: Christopher Prince and the American Revolution* (Washington, DC, 2002), p. 151.

15 NLJ, MS 60, 'An Act against tippling, cursing and swearing', *Jamaica Council Minutes*, vol. I, 8 November 1664.

16 NLJ, MS 60, 'The Deposition of John Yardley Master to the Ketch John's Adventure', *Jamaica Council Minutes*, vol. III, 5 July 1676.

17 CSPC 19, Item 647.ii, 'Instructions for Brigadier William Selwyn as Governour of Jamaica', 23 July 1701.

18 NLJ, MS 60, 'Instructions for our Right Trust and Welbeloved John Lord Vaughan', *Jamaica Council Minutes*, vol. III, 3 December 1674.

19 CO 139/8/8–9, *Act of Assembly Passed in the Island of Jamaica from 1681 to 1737 Inclusive* (London, 1738); Peter Linebaugh and Marcus Rediker, *The Many-Headed Hydra: Sailors, Slaves, Commoners, and the Hidden History of the Revolutionary Atlantic* (Boston, MA, 2013), p. 158.

20 *Boston News-Letter*, 1–8 August 1723.

21 'Bermudas, July 30', *London Gazette*, 21–4 September 1717; 'Boston, May 3', *Boston News-Letter*, 29 April–6 May 1718.

22 *The Trials of Five Persons for Piracy, Felony and Robbery* (Boston, MA, 1726), in Joel H. Baer, *British Piracy in the Golden Age: History and Interpretations, 1660–1730*, 4 vols (London, 2007), vol. III, pp. 221–2.

23 Joan Druett, *She Captains: Heroines and Hellions of the Sea* (New York, 2000), p. 92.

24 Little, *The Sea-Rover's Practice*, p. 33.

25 Druett, *She Captains*, p. 92.

26 Angus Konstam, *Blackbeard: America's Most Notorious Pirate* (Hoboken, NJ, 2006), pp. 184–7, 190–96.

27 *The Narrative of the Singular Sufferings of John Fillmore and Others on board the noted Pirate Vessel commanded by Captain Phillips: With an Account of their daring Enterprise, and happy Escape the tyranny of that desperate Crew, by capturing their Vessel* (Aurora, NY, 1837), in Fox, *Pirates in Their Own Words*, pp. 231–3.

28 Marcus Rediker, *Villains of All Nations: Atlantic Pirates in the Golden Age* (Boston, MA, 2004), pp. 132–3.

29 Kris E. Lane, *Pillaging the Empire: Piracy in the Americas, 1500–1750* (New York, 1998), pp. 96, 106, 152.

30 'A Journal of the Proceedings of the Court of Admiralty, held at Cabo Corso, this 31st of March, 1722', in *A Full and Exact Account, of the Tryal of all the Pyrates, Lately taken by Captain Ogle, on Board the Swallow Man of War, on the Coast of Guinea* (London, 1723), p. 19, in Baer, *British Piracy in the Golden Age*, p. 32; 'A Journal of the Proceedings of the Court of Admiralty, held at Cabo Corso Castle on the Coast of Africa, Monday April the 9th, 1722', ibid., p. 129.

31 'A Journal of the Proceedings of the Court of Admiralty, held at
Cabo Corso Castle on the Coast of Africa, this April the 7th, 1722',
ibid., pp. 126–7.

32 'A Journal of the Proceedings of the Court of Admiralty, held at
Cabo Corso Castle on the Coast of Africa, Monday April the 9th,
1722', ibid., p. 128.

33 HCA 1/55 ff. 36–41, *The Examination of Philip Roche*, 11 April 1723.

34 'Philip Roche, Executed on 5th of August for many Murders on
the High Seas and Piracy', Newgate Calendar, www.exclassics.com,
accessed 29 October 2021.

35 Lane, *Pillaging the Empire*, p. 195.

36 Christopher P. Magra, 'Faith at Sea: Exploring Maritime Religiosity
in the Eighteenth Century', *International Journal of Maritime
History*, XIX/1 (June 2007), p. 9.

37 Nathaniel B. Shurtleff, ed., *Records of the Governor and Company of
the Massachusetts Bay in New England*, vol. IV (Boston, MA, 1853),
pp. 2–3.

8 ENTERTAINMENT AND CULTURE ON THE PIRATE SHIP

1 John Appleby, *Women and English Piracy, 1540–1720: Partners and
Victims of Crime* (Woodbridge, 2013), p. 16.

2 Extract from *The sixteen-year voyage in the Indies made by Jacob
du Bucquoy, full of remarkable adventures, notably those which
he experienced during his mission to the Delagoa River* (Harlem,
NY, 1745).

3 Benerson Little, *The Sea Rover's Practice: Pirate Tactics and
Techniques, 1630–1730* (Lincoln, NE, 2007), p. 92.

4 HCA 1/99.3, 'Proceedings of the Court Held on the Coast of Africa';
see also David Cordingly, *Under the Black Flag: The Romance and
Reality of Life among the Pirates* (New York, 1995), p. 94.

5 Paul A. Gilje, *To Swear Like a Sailor: Maritime Culture in America,
1750–1850* (Cambridge, 2016), p. 7.

6 'An Elegy of Captain Kidd, who was Executed at Execution-Dock,
on Friday the 23rd of this Instant May, 1701', Maggs Brothers,
Proclamations Against Piracy, 1603–1701 (London, n.d.). The original
copy is in the National Library of Jamaica in Kingston, Jamaica.

7 Stan Hugill, *Shanties from the Seven Seas: Shipboard Work-Songs and
Songs Used as Work-Songs from the Great Days of Sail* (Mystic, CT,
1994), pp. 1–2, 4–5, 21, 32, 34.

8 *The Grand Pyrate; or, The Life and Death of Capt. George Cusack the
Great Sea-Robber With an Accompt of all His Notorious Robberies both*

at Sea and Land. Together with His Tryal, Condemnation, and Execution (London, 1676).

9 Richard Hawkins's account of his capture by Francis Spriggs, *British Journal*, 8 August 1724 and 22 August 1724.

10 'A Journal of the Proceedings of the Court of Admiralty, held at Cabo Corso Castle, April the 2d, 1722', *A Full and Exact Account, of the Tryal of all the Pyrates, Lately taken by Captain Ogle, on Board the Swallow Man of War, on the Coast of Guinea* (London, 1723), pp. 20–21.

11 'A Journal of the Proceedings of the Court of Admiralty, held at Cabo Corso Castle on the Coast of Africa, April the 12th, 1722', *A Full and Exact Account, of the Tryal of all the Pyrates* (London), pp. 63–4.

12 co 137/14/9–30, *The Tryals of Captain John Rackham, and other Pirates. Who were all Condemn'd for Piracy, at the Town of St. Jago de la Vega, in the Island of Jamaica, on Wednesday and Thursday the Sixteenth and Seventeenth Days of November 1720. As also, the Tryals of Mary Read and Anne Bonny, alias Bonn* (Jamaica, 1721).

13 Marcus Rediker, *Outlaws of the Atlantic: Sailors, Pirates, and Motley Crews in the Age of Sail* (Boston, MA, 2014), p. 13.

14 Ibid.

15 Ibid., pp. 17–18.

16 Peter D. Jeans, *Seafaring Lore and Legend: A Miscellany of Maritime Myth, Superstition, Fable, and Fact* (New York, 2004), p. 248.

17 Cristina Bacchilega and Marie Alohalani Brown, eds, *The Penguin Book of Mermaids* (New York, 2019), p. xx.

18 Jeans, *Seafaring Lore and Legend*, p. 248.

19 Ibid.

20 Ibid.

21 Ibid., p. 248.

22 Rediker, *Outlaws of the Atlantic*, p. 20.

23 Jeans, *Seafaring Lore and Legend*, pp. 280–82.

24 Rediker, *Outlaws of the Atlantic*, p. 20.

25 Jeans, *Seafaring Lore and Legends*, pp. 281–2.

26 John MacDonald, *Travels in Various Parts of Europe, Asia, and Africa During a Series of Thirty Years and Upward* (London, 1790), p. 276.

27 Rediker, *Outlaws of the Atlantic*, pp. 19–20.

28 Daniel Defoe, *The Four Voyages of Capt. George Roberts* (London, 1726), p. 89.

29 Francis Grose, *1811 Dictionary of the Vulgar Tongue*, extracted from Project Gutenberg, https://archive.org.

30 Peter Linebaugh, *The London Hanged: Crime and Civil Society in the Eighteenth Century* (London, 2003), p. xvii; Martha Grace Duncan,

Romantic Outlaws, Beloved Prisons: Unconscious Meanings of Crime and Punishment (New York, 1996), pp. 82, 85.

31 John Stephen Farmer, *Slang and Its Analogues Past and Present: A Dictionary, Historical and Comparative, of the Heterodox Speech of All Classes of Society for More than Three Hundred Years; with Synonyms in English, French, German, Italian, etc.* (London, 1890), p. 258.

32 *St. George's Chronicle and Grenada Gazette*, 18 September 1819.

33 Little, *The Sea Rover's Practice*, p. 91.

34 Gary B. Nash, *The Urban Crucible: The Northern Seaports and the Origins of the American Revolution* (Cambridge, 1986), pp. 128–9.

35 Christopher P. Magra, 'Faith at Sea: Exploring Maritime Religiosity in the Eighteenth Century', *International Journal of Maritime History*, XIX/1 (June 2007), pp. 5, 20; Hugh Jones, *The Present State of Virginia, Giving a particular and short Account of the Indian, English and Negroe Inhabitants of that Colony* (London, 1724), p. 149.

36 Douglas Greenberg, 'Crime, Law Enforcement, and Social Control in Colonial America', *American Journal of Legal History*, XXVI/4 (October 1982), p. 297.

37 For a discussion on masculinity and politeness, see Lawrence Klein, ed., *Anthony Ashley Cooper Third Earl of Shaftesbury: Characteristics of Men, Manners, Opinions, Times* (Cambridge, 1999); Lawrence E. Klein, 'Politeness and the Interpretation of the British Eighteenth-Century', *Historical Journal*, XLV/4 (2002), pp. 869–98.

38 For a discussion on politeness and North American religious society, see Daniel E. Williams, 'Puritans and Pirates: A Confrontation between Cotton Mather and William Fly in 1726', *Early American Literature*, XXII/3 (1987), pp. 233–51. For a discussion on drinking and drunkenness in North America, see Sharon V. Salinger, *Taverns and Drinking in Early America* (Baltimore, MD, 2002); James Nicholls, *The Politics of Alcohol: A History of the Drink Question in England* (Manchester, 2009); Susanne Schmid and Barbara Schmidt-Haberkamp, eds, *Drink in the Eighteenth and Nineteenth Centuries* (London, 2009).

39 Salinger, *Taverns and Drinking*, p. 39.

40 Robert Shoemaker, *Prosecution and Punishment: Petty Crime and the Law in London and Rural Middlesex, c. 1600–1725* (Cambridge, 1991), pp. 49, 61; Jack D. Marietta and G. S. Rowe, *Troubled Experience: Crime and Justice in Pennsylvania, 1682–1800* (Philadelphia, PA, 2006), p. 39.

41 Alun Withey, *Concerning Beards: Facial Hair, Health and Practice in England, 1650–1900* (London, 2021), pp. 34–6.

42 *Letter from a Gentleman in New England* (Boston, MA, 1742).

43 Extract from *The sixteen-year voyage in the Indies made by Jacob du Bucquoy.*

44 *The Grand Pyrate; or, The Life and Death of Capt. George Cusack the Great Sea-Robber With an Accompt of all His Notorious Robberies both at Sea and Land. Together with His Tryal, Condemnation, and Execution* (London, 1676), pp. 7–8.

45 Marcus Rediker, '"Under the Banner of King Death": The Social World of Anglo-American Pirates, 1716–1726', *William and Mary Quarterly*, XXXVIII/2 (April 1981), pp. 221–2, 227.

46 Michael J. Crawford, ed., *The Autobiography of a Yankee Mariner: Christopher Prince and the American Revolution* (Washington, DC, 2002), p. 151.

47 Gilje, *To Swear Like a Sailor*, pp. 10–11.

48 Rediker, 'Under the Banner of King Death', pp. 221–2, 227.

49 'A Letter from Portsmouth, Dated February 1', *New York Gazette*, 28 March 1757; 'Further Advices by the Packet, London, June 1', *New York Gazette*, 14 August 1769.

50 *Boston News-Letter*, 26 June–3 July 1704.

51 CSPC 16, Item 1077, 'Benjamin Fletcher to Council of Trade and Plantation', 24 December 1698; CSPC 17, Item 26, 'T. Weaver to the Council of Trade and Plantations', 9 January 1699; CSPC 17, Item 167, 'Council of Trade and Plantations to the King', 9 March 1699.

52 CO 138/3/16, *Acts of Assembly Passed in the Island of Jamaica from 1681–1737 Inclusive* (London, 1738).

53 Peter Linebaugh and Marcus Rediker, *The Many-Headed Hydra: Sailors, Slaves, Commoners, and the Hidden History of the Revolutionary Atlantic* (Boston, MA, 2013), p. 158.

54 Gilje, *To Swear Like a Sailor*, p. 5.

55 Ibid., pp. 15–16.

56 Ibid., pp. 20, 22–3.

57 Tessa Watt, *Cheap Print and Popular Piety, 1550–1640* (Cambridge, 1991), p. 108.

58 'Ordinary of Newgate's Accounts', Old Bailey Online, www.oldbaileyonline.org, accessed 21 July 2022.

59 Robert B. Shoemaker, 'The Old Bailey Proceedings and the Represen-tation of Crime and Criminal Justice in Eighteenth-Century London', *Journal of British Studies*, XLVII/3 (July 2008), p. 563.

60 'Ordinary of Newgate's Accounts'.

61 Cordingly, *Under the Black Flag*, pp. 235–6.

62 'The Confession of Walter Kennedy, who was condemn'd at the Sessions of the Admiralty, for that he with other Pirates, had robb'd and plunder'd the Ship call'd the Loyal Rover, etc.', in *A Select and Impartial Account of the Lives, Behaviours and the Dying Words of the Most Remarkable Convicts from the Year 1700, to the Present Time* (London, 1760), vol. I, pp. 232–7.

63 'The Behaviour, Confession, and Dying Words of Capt. John Massey, who was Executed at Execution-Dock, on Friday the 26th of July 1723, for Piracy on the High-Seas, near St. James's Island on the Coast of North Africa', in *A Select and Impartial Account of the Lives, Behaviour and the Dying Words of the most Remarkable Convicts from the Year 1700, to the present Time*, vol. I, pp. 269–75.

64 'Philip Roche: Executed on 5th of August 1723, for many Murders on the High Seas and Piracy', Newgate Calendar, www.exclassics. com, accessed 10 November 2021.

65 'The Behaviour, Confession, and Last Dying Words of Philip Roche, who was executed at Execution-Dock at Wapping on Wednesday the 14th of August 1723, for Piracy on the High Seas', in *A Select and Impartial Account of the Lives, Behaviour and the Dying Words of the most Remarkable Convicts from the Year 1700, to the present Time*, vol. I, pp. 276–84.

66 Cotton Mather, *The Diary of Cotton Mather, 1681–1708* (Boston, MA, 1911), p. 122.

67 Cotton Mather, *Useful Remarks. An Essay upon remarkables in the way of wicked men. A sermon on the tragical end, unto which the way of twenty-six pirates brought them; at New Port on Rhode Island, July 19, 1723. With an Account of their speeches, letters, & actions before their execution* (Boston, MA, 1723), pp. 23–6.

68 Ibid., pp. 27–8.

69 Philip Ashton, *Ashton's Memorial; or, An Authentick Account of the Strange Adventures and Signal Deliverances of Mr Philip Ashton* (London, 1727), p. 21.

70 Ibid., p. 27.

71 Ibid., p. 28.

72 Little, *The Sea Rover's Practice*, pp. 92–3.

73 Captain Charles Johnson, *A General History of the Pyrates*, ed. Manuel Schonhorn (Mineola, NY, 1999), p. 48.

74 William Dampier, *Memoirs of a Buccaneer, Dampier's New Voyage Round the World* (London, 1697), 273.

75 Ibid., p. 367.

76 T. S. Rhodes, 'The Pirate Christmas', 23 December 2013, http://thepirateempire.blogspot.com.

77 Bartholomew Sharp, 'Captain Sharp's Journal of His Expedition', *A Collection of Original Voyages*, ed. William Hacke (London, 1699), pp. 44–5.

78 Basil Ringrose, *The Voyages and Adventures of Capt Barth Sharp and Others, in the South Seas* (London, 1684), p. 49.

79 Johnson, *A General History of the Pyrates*, pp. 133–4.

80 Richard Lazenby, a prisoner of John Taylor, from 'The Narrative of Richard Lazenby', in Fox, *Pirates in Their Own Words*, p. 284.

81 Marcus Rediker, *Between the Devil and the Deep Blue Sea: Merchant Seamen, Pirates and the Anglo-American Maritime World, 1700–1750* (Cambridge, 1989), p. 5.

82 Daniel Vickers, *Young Men and the Sea: Yankee Seafarers in the Age of Sail* (New Haven, CT, 2005), p. 147.

CONCLUSION: THE END OF THE GOLDEN AGE OF PIRACY

1 *The Tryals of Joseph Dawson [et al.] . . . for several Piracies and Robberies by them Committed, in the Company of Every the Grand Pirate, near the Coasts of the East Indies; and several other Places in the Seas. Giving an Account of their Villainous Robberies and Barbarities* (London, 1696), p. 28.

2 'London, June 11', *Daily Post*, 11 June 1725; David Cordingly, *Under the Black Flag: The Romance and Reality of Life among the Pirates* (New York, 1995), pp. 223–4.

3 *The Arraignment, Tryal, and Condemnation of Captain William Kidd, for Murther and Piracy, upon Six Several Indictments . . . As also, the Tryals of Nicholas Churchill [et al.] . . . To which are added Captain Kidd's Two Commissions: One under the Great Seal of England, and the Other under the Great Seal of the Court of Admiralty* (London, 1701), p. 184.

4 *News from Execution-Dock, or The last speeches and Confessions of the Two Notorious Pirates Captain George Cusack and Simon Harcourt, Executed at the place aforesaid, on Monday the 18th of Jan, 1674/5* (London, 1674). See also Robert C. Ritchie, *Captain Kidd and the War against the Pirates* (Cambridge, MA, 1986), p. 224.

5 J. A. Sharpe, '"Last Dying Speeches": Religion, Ideology and Public Executions in Seventeenth-Century England', *Past and Present*, CVII (1985), pp. 144–67. For further reading on the public execution ritual, see Simon Deveraux, 'Recasting the Theatre of Execution: The Abolition of the Tyburn Ritual', *Past and Present*, CCII (2009), pp. 127–74.

6 Peter Linebaugh, *The London Hanged: Crime and Civil Society in the Eighteenth Century* (London, 2003), p. xvii.
7 Michel Foucault, *Discipline and Punish: The Birth of the Prison*, trans. Alan Sheridan (New York, 1995), pp. 48–9; Margarette Lincoln, *British Pirates and Society, 1680–1730* (Woodbridge, 2015), p. 37.
8 These hangings were said to take place before the ordinary of Newgate took his position. The only descriptions found are in his footnotes in several cases: Old Bailey Online (www.oldbaileyonline.org, hereafter OBO), Ordinary of Newgate's Account, 15 December 1710 (OA17101215); 22 December 1711 (OA17111222); 31 October 1712 (OA17121031); 4 October 1713 (OA17131024); 2 November 1715 (OA17151102); 20 December 1717 (OA17171220); 31 October 1718 (OA17181031). 'The French pirates', *English Post Given and Authentick Account of the Transactions of the World Foreign and Domestick*, 11–13 November 1700 (London).
9 Evelyn Berckman, *Victims of Piracy: The Admiralty Court, 1575–1678* (London, 1979), pp. 4–5.
10 Ritchie, *Captain Kidd and the War against the Pirates*, p. 141; 28 Henry 8, c. 15, 'Offences Against the Sea Act, 1536', *Statutes of the Realm*, III, p. 671.
11 Ritchie, *Captain Kidd and the War against the Pirates*, p. 141; 28 Henry 8, c. 15, 'Offences Against the Sea Act, 1536', p. 671.
12 NMM, GOS/12, 25–7, 'Commission of Oyer and Terminer'.
13 Kris E. Lane, *Pillaging the Empire: Piracy in the Americas, 1500–1750* (New York, 1998), p. 125.
14 PC 1/1 f. 63, 'Copy of the Admiralty memorial for a proclamation concerning rewards to deserters from pirate ships', 27 November 1700.
15 Douglas R. Burgess, 'The Politics of Piracy: A Challenge to English Law and Policy in the Atlantic Colonies, 1650–1726', PhD thesis, Brown University, 2009, pp. 199–200.
16 *A Discourse of the Laws Relating to Pirates and Piracies, and the Marine Affairs of Great Britain* (London, 1726), p. 125; see also Janice E. Thompson, *Mercenaries, Pirates and Sovereigns: State-Building and Extraterritorial Violence in Early Modern Europe* (Princeton, NJ, 1996), p. 50.
17 BL Egerton, CH 7561, *British America and the United States: Warrants for Colonial Appointments, 1716–1725*.
18 CSPC 12, Item 59, 'Lords Proprietors to Governor Joseph West', 13 March 1685.

19 Douglas R. Burgess Jr, *The Pirates' Pact: The Secret Alliances between History's Most Notorious Buccaneers and Colonial America* (New York, 2009), p. 17.

20 CSPC 22, Item 975, 'Charge exhibited against the Proceedings of the Chartered Government of Rhode Island', 26 March 1705.

21 *Executed Journals of the Council of Virginia*, vol. II: *August 3, 1699–April 27, 1705* (Richmond, 1925), p. 69.

22 CSPC 18, Item 188, 'Col. Quary to Mr. Secretary Vernon', 6 March 1700.

23 CSPC 15, Item 1274, 'Council of Trade and Plantations to the Earl of Bellamont', 26 August 1697.

24 'At a Councill held at ye Main the 1st of June 1698', in *The Executive Journals of the Council of Virginia*, vol. I: *June 11, 1680–June 22, 1699* (Richmond, 1925), p. 384.

25 Lane, *Pillaging the Empire*, p. 168.

26 CSPC 18, Item 300, 'Col. Quary to the Council of Trade and Plantations', 10 April 1700.

27 CSPC 19, Item 100, 'Wm. Popple to Josiah Burchett', 28 January 1701.

28 CSPC 19, Item 180, 'Edward Randolph to the Council of Trade and Plantations', 19 February 1701.

29 Lane, *Pillaging the Empire*, p. 168.

30 Douglas R. Burgess Jr, *The Politics of Piracy: Crime and Civil Disobedience in Colonial America* (Chicago, IL, 2014), p. 3.

31 CSPC 15, Item 1178, 'Information of Thomas Robinson', 13 July 1697.

32 CSPC 34, Item 6, 'Richard Partridge, Agent for Rhode Island and Providence Plantations, to Sir Charles Wagner', 6 January 1724.

33 *Calendar of State Papers, Domestic* 243, 'By the king, a proclamation', 6 March 1701.

34 J. M. Beattie, *Crime and the Courts in England, 1660–1800* (Oxford, 1986), pp. 431–2.

35 SP 44/347 f. 474, 'Warrant to insert Robert Seely in the next general pardon for the poor convicts of Newgate for piracy, without condition for transportation, in compassion of his tender years' (1699).

36 Beattie, *Crime and the Courts in England*, p. 431.

37 CSPC 17, Item 15, 'Council of Trade and Plantations to Gov. the Earl of Bellomont', 5 January 1699. However, the English authorities never captured Avery. This was stated just in case he should eventually be captured.

38 CSPC 33, Item 411, 'Council of Trade and Plantations to the Lords Committee of the Privy Council, 10 January 1723.

39 *An Abridgement of the Laws*, p. 100.

40 Jonathan Dalby, *Crime and Punishment in Jamaica: A Quantitative Analysis of the Assize Court Records, 1756–1856* (Mona, 2000), p. 12.

41 Paul H. Blackman and Vance McLaughlin, 'Mass Legal Executions in America up to 1865', *Crime, histoire et sociétés/Crime, History and Societies*, VIII (2004), pp. 40–41.

42 Mark G. Hanna, *Pirate Nests and the Rise of the British Empire, 1570–1740* (Chapel Hill, NC, 2015), pp. 332–3.

43 CSPC 5, Item 950, 'Governor Sir Thomas Modyford to Sec. H. Bennet', 1 March 1665.

44 Captain Charles Johnson, *A General History of the Pyrates*, ed. Manuel Schonhorn (Mineola, NY, 1999), p. 264.

45 CSPC 29, Item 203, 'Governor Lord A. Hamilton to the Council of Trade and Plantations', 12 June 1716.

46 Lauren Benton, *A Search for Sovereignty: Law and Geography in the European Empires, 1400–1900* (Cambridge, 2009), p. 34.

47 Joseph Roach, *It* (Ann Arbor, MI, 2004), pp. 1–4.

48 Ibid., p. 211.

49 Geoffrey Cubitt, *History and Memory* (Manchester, 2007), pp. 10, 13. For more general theory about historical memory and oral culture during the early modern period, refer to Daniel Woolf, *The Social Circulation of the Past: English Historical Culture in Britain, 1500–1730* (Oxford, 2003); Adam Fox and Daniel Woolf, *The Spoken Word: Oral Culture in Britain, 1500–1850* (Manchester, 2002); Katharine Hodgkin and Susannah Radstone, *Memory Cultures: Memory, Subjectivity, Recognition* (Abingdon-on-Thames, 2009).

50 Samuel Sewall, *The Diary of Samuel Sewall*, ed. Mel Yazawa (Boston, MA, 1998), pp. 109–10.

51 NMM, PAD 1307, 'A Perspective View of the River Thames', March 1782.

52 *Boston Gazette*, 24 April–1 May 1732; *American Weekly Mercury*, 11–18 May 1732.

53 Cordingly, *Under the Black Flag*, p. 19.

BIBLIOGRAPHY

PRIMARY SOURCES

NEWSPAPERS

American Weekly Mercury
Boston Gazette
Boston News-Letter
British Journal Daily Post
Flying Post
London Gazette
London Journal
London Post with Intelligence Foreign and Domestick
The Metropolitan: A Monthly Journal of Literature, Science and the Fine Arts
New-Bedford Mercury
New York Gazette Monthly Chronicle
Post Boy
St. George's Chronicle and Granada Gazette
Weekly Journal or British Gazetteer

CALENDAR OF STATE PAPERS: COLONIAL SERIES AMERICA AND THE WEST INDIES

CSPC 5, Item 950 (1665)
CSPC 11, Item 1313 (1683)
CSPC 12, Item 59 (1685)
CSPC 15, Item 34 (1696)
CSPC 15, Item 324 (1696)
CSPC 15, Item 698 (1696)
CSPC 15, Item 1178 (1697)

CSPC 15, Item 1203 (1697)
CSPC 15, Item 1274 (1696)
CSPC 16, Item 1077 (1698)
CSPC 17, Item 15 (1699)
CSPC 17, Item 26 (1699)
CSPC 17, Item 167 (1699)
CSPC 17, Item 530.vi (1699)
CSPC 17, Item 621 (1699)
CSPC 17, Item 680 (1699)
CSPC 18, Item 14 (1700)
CSPC 18, Item 15 (1700)
CSPC 18, Item 188 (1700)
CSPC 18, Item 300 (1700)
CSPC 19, Item 4 (1701)
CSPC 19, Item 100 (1701)
CSPC 19, Item 180 (1701)
CSPC 19, Item 647.ii (1701)
CSPC 22, Item 975 (1705)
CSPC 29, Item 203 (1716)
CSPC 29, Item 331 (1716)
CSPC 31, Item 31i (1718)
CSPC 33, Item 411 (1723)
CSPC 33, Item 754.iv (1723)
CSPC 34, Item 6 (1724)

CALENDAR OF STATE PAPERS: DOMESTIC

CSP 243 (1701)

ARCHIVES

BODLEIAN LIBRARY

MS Rawlinson A 271, f 44b, 'Deposition of Joseph Man.', 11 June 1700

BRITISH LIBRARY

Add.MS.39946 f.28, 'Deposition against Benjamin Hornigold'
Add.MS.61620, 'Petitions of Pirate Wives', November 1707, 155b–156
Edgerton, CH 7561 British America and the United States: Warrants for
    Colonial Appointments (1716–25)
IOR/H/36, 'To Their Excellencies The Lords Justices of England
    The humble Petition of the Governour & Company of

Merchants of London trading into the East Indies',
21 September 1699

RP.8780, 'Autograph Letter Signed to Johnson Dickinson, discussing
trade matters including an account of the remnants of Captain
Kidd's crew and tales of buried treasure', Philadelphia, 9 July 1699

NATIONAL LIBRARY OF JAMAICA

MS 60, 'An Act against tippling, cursing and swearing', Jamaica Council
Minutes, vol. I, 8 November 1664

MS 60, 'An Act declaring the Laws of England in force in this Island
passed to the Council', Jamaica Council Minutes, vol. I,
10 November 1664

MS 60, 'At a Council Held at St Jago de la Vega', Jamaica Council
Minutes, vol. III, 14 March 1674

MS 60, 'Instructions for our Right Trust and Welbeloved John Lord
Vaughan', Jamaica Council Minutes, vol. III, 3 December 1674

MS 60, 'The Deposition of John Yardley Master to the Ketch John's
Adventure', Jamaica Council Minutes, vol. III, 5 July 1676

MS 1651/40, 'Petition of Merchants and Sugar Planters Against the
Navigation Acts', 1735

NATIONAL MARITIME MUSEUM

GOS/12, 'Commission of Oyer and Terminer'

PAD 1307, 'A Perspective View of the River Thames' (1782)

THE NATIONAL ARCHIVES

CO 1/43, fol. 59, 'Account of What Passengers, Servants and Slaves Have
Been Brought to This Island', 25 June 1671–March 1679

CO 137/11/45iii, *Deposition of Abijah Savage, Commander of the Sloop
Bonetta of Antigua before His Excellency Walter Hamilton*
(20 November 1716)

CO 137/14/9–30, *The Tryals of Captain John Rackham, and other Pirates.
Who were all Condemn'd for Piracy, at the Town of St. Jago de la Vega,
in the Island of Jamaica, on Wednesday and Thursday the Sixteenth and
Seventeenth Days of November 1720. As also, the Tryals of Mary Read
and Anne Bonny, alias Bonn* (Jamaica, 1721)

CO 138/3/16, *Acts of Assembly Passed in the Island of Jamaica from 1681–1737
Inclusive* (London, 1738)

EXT 1/261 ff. 197–9, 'The Petition of John Massey and George Lowther'

HCA 24/127, *Child vs. Clark* (1702)

HCA 24/132, *Gittus vs. Bowles* (1718)

HCA 1/55, fol. 22, 'Information of Richard Mandewell', 1722

HCA 1/55, ff. 23–4, 'The Information of Alexander Thompson', 2 March 1722

HCA 1/55 ff. 36–41, *The Examination of Philip Roche*, 11 April 1723

HCA 1/55 ff. 103–4, *The Examination of James Williams*, 27 March 1725

HCA 1/55 ff. 105–6, *The Examination of John Smith*, 2 April 1725

HCA 1/54 ff. 119–20, *The Information of Thomas Grant*, 28 April 1721

HCA 1/54 fol. 123, *The Information of Edward Green*, 29 April 1721

HCA 1/55 ff. 132–3, *The Examination of Robert Read*, 3 April 1725

HCA 1/99, *The Trials of Nicholas Simonds* et al., Rhode Island, 24 February 1724

HCA 1/99.3, 'Proceedings of the Court Held on the Coast of Africa'

HCA 1/99 f. 102, 'Proceedings of the Court held on the Coast of Africa upon Trying of 100 Pirates taken by his Majesties Ship Swallow' (1722)

PC 1/1 f. 63, 'Copy of the Admiralty memorial for a proclamation concerning rewards to deserters from pirate ships' (1700)

SP 44/347 f. 474, 'Warrant to insert Robert Seely in the next general pardon for the poor convicts of Newgate for piracy, without condition for transportation, in compassion of his tender years' (1699)

PRINTED SOURCES

28 Henry 8, c. 15, *Statutes of the Realm*, III

An Abridgement of the Laws in Force and Use in Her Majesty's Plantations (1704)

Abstract of the Laws Against Sabbath-Breaking, Swearing, and Drunkenness (Stockport, 1797)

The Arraignment, Tryal and Condemnation of Capt. John Quelch, and Others of his Company, &c. for Sundry Piracies, Robberies, and Murder, Committed upon the Subjects of the King of Portugal, Her Majesty's Allie, on the Coast of Brasil, &c. (London, 1704)

The Arraignment, Tryal, and Condemnation of Captain William Kidd, for Murther and Piracy, upon Six Several Indictments . . . As also, the Tryals of Nicholas Churchill [et al.] . . . To which are added Captain Kidd's Two Commissions: One under the Great Seal of England, and the Other under the Great Seal of the Court of Admiralty (London, 1701)

Ashton, Philip, *Ashton's Memorial; or, An Authentick Account of the Strange Adventures and Signal Deliverances of Mr Philip Ashton* (London, 1727)

Atkins, John, *The Navy Surgeon; or, Practical System of Surgery. With a Dissertation on Cold and Hot Mineral Springs; and Physical Observations on the Coast of Guiney* (London, 1742)

Aubrey, Thomas, *The Sea-Surgeon or the Guinea Man's Vadé Mecum* (1729)

Baer, Joel H., *British Piracy in the Golden Age: History and Interpretations, 1660–1730*, 4 vols (London, 2007)

Cockburn, William, *The Nature and Cure of Fluxes: To which is Added, the Method of Finding the Doses of Purging and Vomiting Medicines for Every Age* (London, 1724)

Crawford, Michael J. ed., *The Autobiography of a Yankee Mariner: Christopher Prince and the American Revolution* (Washington, DC, 2002)

Dampier, William, *Memoirs of a Buccaneer, Dampier's New Voyage Round the World* (London, 1697)

Dana, R.H. Jr, *The Seaman's Manual; Containing a Treatise on Practical Seamanship with plates; A Dictionary of Sea Terms; Customs and Usages of the Merchant Service; Laws Relating to the Practical Duties of Master and Mariners* (London, 1841)

Defoe, Daniel, *The Four Voyages of Capt. George Roberts* (London, 1726)

—, *The King of the Pirates: Being an Account of the Famous Enterprises of Captain Every, the Mock King of Madagascar. In Two Letters from Himself* (London, 1720)

A Discourse of the Laws Relating to Pirates and Piracies, and the Marine Affairs of Great Britain (London, 1726)

Downing, Clement, *A Compendious History of the Indian Wars* (London, 1737)

An English Sailor, *The State of the Navy Consider'd in Relation to Victualling* (London, 1699)

The Executive Journals of the Council of Virginia (Richmond, 1925), vols I–II

Exquemelin, Alexandre, *A History of the Buccaneers of America*, trans. Alexis Brown (Mineola, NY, 2000)

Farmer, John Stephen, *Slang and Its Analogues Past and Present: A Dictionary, Historical and Comparative, of the Heterodox Speech of All Classes of Society for More than Three Hundred Years; with Synonyms in English, French, German, Italian, etc.* (London, 1890)

Fox, Ed, *Pirates in Their Own Words: Eye-Witness Accounts of the 'Golden Age' of Piracy, 1690–1728* (self-published, 2014)

—, *Scattergoods and Swaggering Rascals: Documents Relating to English Piracy of the Tudor and Jacobean Period* (self-published, 2015)

A Full and Exact Account, of the Tryal of all the Pyrates, Lately taken by Captain Ogle, on Board the Swallow Man of War, on the Coast of Guinea (London, 1723)

A full and true Discovery of all the Robberies, Pyracies, and other Notorious Actions of that Famous English Pyrate, Capt. James Kelly . . . Written

with His own Hand, During His Confinement in Newgate; and
Delivered to His Wife, the Day of His Execution; Published by Her
Order and Desire (London, 1700)

Funnell, William, *A Voyage Round the World* (London, 1707)

Good, Byron J., *Medicine, Rationality and Experience: An Anthropological
Perspective* (Cambridge, 1993)

Gosse, Philip, *The Pirates' Who's Who: Giving Particulars of the Lives &
Deaths of the Pirates & Buccaneers* (New York, 1924)

*The Grand Pyrate; or, The Life and Death of Capt. George Cusack the Great
Sea-Robber With an Accompt of all His Notorious Robberies both at
Sea and Land. Together with His Tryal, Condemnation, and Execution*
(London, 1676)

Grose, Francis, *1811 Dictionary of the Vulgar Tongue* (1811)

Hacke, William, ed., *A Collection of Original Voyages* (London, 1699)

The History and Lives of all the most Notorious Pirates and Their Crews
(London, 1725)

Johnson, Captain Charles, *A General History of the Pyrates*, ed. Manuel
Schonhorn (Mineola, NY, 1999)

Jones, Hugh, *The Present State of Virginia, Giving a particular and short
Account of the Indian, English and Negroe Inhabitants of that Colony*
(London, 1724)

Klein, Lawrence, ed., *Anthony Ashley Cooper Third Earl of Shaftesbury:
Characteristics of Men, Manners, Opinions, Times* (Cambridge, 1999)

Letter from a Gentleman in New England (Boston, MA, 1742)

Ligon, Richard, *A True and Exact History of the Island of Barbados*
(London, 1673)

*The Lives, Apprehensions, Arraignments, and Executions of the 19 Late
Pyrates . . . As they were Severally Indited on St Margarets Hill in
Southwarke, on the 22d of December last, and Executed the Fryday
Following* (London, 1609)

MacDonald, John, *Travels in Various Parts of Europe, Asia, and Africa
During a Series of Thirty Years and Upward* (London, 1790)

Maggs Brothers, *Proclamations Against Piracy, 1603–1701* (London, n.d.)

Mather, Cotton, *The Diary of Cotton Mather, 1681–1708* (Boston, MA, 1911)

—, *Useful Remarks. An Essay upon remarkables in the way of wicked
men. A sermon on the tragical end, unto which the way of twenty-six
pirates brought them; at New Port on Rhode Island, July 19, 1723. With
an Account of their speeches, letters, & actions before their execution*
(Boston, 1723)

*The Metropolitan: A Monthly Journal of Literature, Science and the Fine
Arts*, vol. I: *May to August* (London, 1831)

News from Execution-Dock, or The last speeches and Confessions of the Two Notorious Pirates Captain George Cusack and Simon Harcourt, Executed at the place aforesaid, on Monday the 18th of Jan, 1674/5 (London, 1674)

The Ordinary of Newgate's Account of the Behaviour, Confession, and Dying Words of Capt. Joseph Halsey, Who was executed at Execution-Dock, on Wednesday the 14th of March, 1759, For the Murder of Daniel Davidson (London, 1759)

Paré, Ambroise, *The Workes of that Famous Chirugion Ambrose Parey*, trans. Thomas Johnson (London, 1649)

Piracy Destroy'd; or, A Short Discourse Shewing the Rise, Growth and Causes of Piracy of Late; with a Sure Method how to put a Speedy Stop to that Growing Evil (London, 1701)

Ringrose, Basil, *The Voyages and Adventures of Capt Barth Sharp and Others, in the South Seas* (London, 1684)

A Select and Impartial Account of the Lives, Behaviours and the Dying Words of the Most Remarkable Convicts from the Year 1700, to the Present Time (London, 1760), vol. I

Sewall, Samuel, *The Diary of Samuel Sewall*, ed. Mel Yazawa (Boston, MA, 1998)

Shelvocke, George, *A Voyage Around the World* (London, 1726)

Shurtleff, Nathaniel B., ed., *Records of the Governor and Company of the Massachusetts Bay in New England* (Boston, MA, 1853), vol. VI

The sixteen-year voyage in the Indies made by Jacob du Bucquoy, full of remarkable adventures, notably those which he experienced during his mission to the Delagoa River (Harlem, NY, 1745)

Stevenson, Robert Louis, *Treasure Island* (New York, 1994)

A Treaty for the Composing of Differences, Restraining of Depradations, and Establishing of Peace in America Between the Crowns of Great Britain and Spain (London, 1670)

The Trials of Eight Persons Indicted for Piracy (Boston, MA, 1718)

The Trials of Eight Persons Indited for Piracy &c. Of whom Two were acquitted, and the rest found Guilty. At a Judicial Court of Admiralty assembled and Held in Boston within his Majesty's Province of Massachusetts-Bay in New England, on the 18th of October 1717 and by several Adjustments continued to the 30th. Pursuant to His Majesty's Commission and Instructions, founded on the Act of Parliament – Made in the 11th and 12th of King William IIId. Intituled An Act for the more effectual Suppression of Piracy. With an Appendix, Containing the Substance of their Confessions given before Their Excellency the Governour, when they were first brought to Boston and committed to Gaol (Boston, MA, 1718)

The Trials of Five Persons for Piracy, Felony and Robbery (Boston, MA, 1726)

A TRUE RELATION OF *a most Horrid Conspiracy and Running away with the* SHIP ADVENTURE, *Having on Board Forty Thousand Pieces of Eight, and other Goods to a great Value. Together with the Cruel and Barbarous leaving and turning ashore upon the Island Naias, in the East-Indies, the Captain, and three Merchants which were Passengers, and Sixteen honest and able Seamen, Eight whereof miserably perished by Hunger and Hardship, and but Four of the Remainder yet come to England. Together with some short Account of what passed at the Trial and Condemnation of those who Committed that Fact* (London, 1700)

The Tryals of Joseph Dawson [et al.]. . . for several Piracies and Robberies by them Committed, in the Company of Every the Grand Pirate, near the Coasts of the East Indies; and several other Places in the Seas. Giving an Account of their Villainous Robberies and Barbarities (London, 1696)

The Tryals of Major Stede Bonnet, and other Pirates (London, 1719)

Tryals of Thirty-Six Persons for Piracy, Twenty-Eight of them upon Full Evidence were Found Guilty, and the rest Acquitted. At a Court of Admiralty for Tryal of Pirates, Held at Newport within His Majesties Colony of Rhode-Island and Providence-Plantations in America (Boston, MA, 1723)

The Voyages and Adventures of Capt. Barth. Sharp and others, in the South Sea: Being a Journal of the same. Also Capt. Van Horn with his Buccanieres surprizing of la Veracruz. To which is added The true Relation of Sir Henry Morgan his Expedition against the Spaniards in the West-Indies, and his taking Panama. Together with the President of Panama's Account of the same Expedition: Translated out of Spanish. And Col. Beeston's Adjustment of the Peace between the Spaniards and English in the West Indies (London, 1684)

Woodall, John, *The surgeons mate or Military & domestique surgery Discouering faithfully & plainly ye method and order of ye surgeons chest, ye uses of the instruments, the vertues and operations of ye medicines, with ye exact cures of wounds made by gunshott, and otherwise as namely: wounds, aposfumes, ulcers, fistula's, fractions, dislocations, with ye most easie & safest ways of amputation or dismembering. The cures of the scruuery, of ye fluxes of ye belly, of ye collicke and iliaca passio, of tenesmus and exitus ani, and of the calenture, with A treatise of ye cure of ye plague. Published for the service of his Ma. tie and of the com:wealth* (London, 1617)

Yonge, James, *The Journal of James Yonge Plymouth Surgeon, 1647–1732,* ed. F.N.L. Poynter (Hamden, CT, 1963)

SECONDARY SOURCES

Appleby, John, *Women and English Piracy 1540–1720: Partners and Victims of Crime* (Woodbridge, 2013)

Bacchilega, Christina, and Marie Alohalani Brown, eds, *The Penguin Book of Mermaids* (New York, 2019)

Barker, Francis, Peter Hulme and Margaret Iversen, eds, *Cannibalism and the Colonial World* (Cambridge, 1998)

Beattie, J. M., *Crime and the Courts in England, 1660–1800* (Oxford, 1986)

Benton, Lauren, *A Search for Sovereignty: Law and Geography in the European Empires, 1400–1900* (Cambridge, 2009)

Berckman, Evelyn, *Victims of Piracy: The Admiralty Court, 1575–1678* (London, 1979)

Blackman, Paul H., and Vance McLaughlin, 'Mass Legal Executions in America up to 1865', *Crime, histoire et sociétés/Crime, History and Societies*, 8 (2004)

Blakemore, Richard J., 'Pieces of Eight, Pieces of Eight: Seamen's Earnings and the Venture Economy of Early Modern Seamen', *Economic History Review*, LXX/4 (2017), pp. 1153–84

Bolster, Jeffrey W., *Black Jacks: African American Seamen in the Age of Sail* (Cambridge, 1997)

Brewer, John, *The Pleasures of the Imagination: English Culture in the Eighteenth Century* (London, 1997)

Bryson, Anna, *From Courtesy to Civility: Changing Codes of Conduct in Early Modern England* (Oxford, 1998)

Burg, B. R., *Sodomy and the Pirate Tradition: English Sea Rovers in the Seventeenth-Century Caribbean* (New York, 1995)

Burgess, Douglas R., *The Pirates' Pact: The Secret Alliances between History's Most Notorious Buccaneers and Colonial America* (New York, 2009)

—, 'The Politics of Piracy: A Challenge to English Law and Policy in the Atlantic Colonies, 1650–1725', PhD diss., Brown University, 2009

—, *The Politics of Piracy: Crime and Civil Disobedience in Colonial America* (Chicago, IL, 2014)

Butler, Lindley S., *Pirates, Privateers, and Rebel Raiders of the Carolina Coast* (Chapel Hill, NC, 2000)

Byrn, John D. Jr, *Crime and Punishment in the Royal Navy: Discipline on the Leeward Island Station, 1784–1812* (Aldershot, 1989)

Cabell, Craig, Graham A. Thomas and Allan Richards, *Captain Kidd: The Hunt for Truth* (Barnsley, 2010)

Caputo, Sara, 'Treating, Preventing, Feigning, Concealing: Sickness, Agency and the Medical Culture of the British Naval Seamen at the End of the Long Eighteenth Century', *Social History of Medicine*, XXXV/3 (2021)

Cordingly, David, ed., *Pirates: Terror on the High Seas, From the Caribbean to the South China Sea* (East Bridgewater, MA, 1999)

—, *Seafaring Women: Adventures of Pirate Queens, Female Stowaways, and Sailors' Wives* (New York, 2011)

—, *Under the Black Flag: The Romance and Reality of Life among the Pirates* (New York, 1995)

Cubit, Geoffrey, *History and Memory* (Manchester, 2007)

Curtis, Wayne, *And a Bottle of Rum: A History of the New World in Ten Cocktails* (New York, 2018)

Dalby, Jonathan, *Crime and Punishment in Jamaica: A Quantitative Analysis of the Assize Court Records, 1756–1856* (Mona, UT, 2000)

Devereaux, Simon, 'Resisting the Theatre of Execution: An Abolition of the Tyburn Ritual', *Past and Present*, 202 (2009), pp. 127–74

Dolin, Eric J., *Black Flags, Blue Waters: The Epic History of America's Most Notorious Pirates* (New York, 2018)

Druett, Joan, *She Captains: Heroines and Hellions of the Sea* (New York, 2000)

Duncan, Martha Grace, *Romantic Outlaws, Beloved Prisons: Unconscious Meanings of Crime and Punishment* (New York, 1996)

Foucault, Michel, *Discipline and Punish: The Birth of the Prison*, trans. Alan Sheridan (New York, 1995)

Fox, Adam, and Daniel Woolf, *The Spoken Word: Oral Culture in Britain, 1500–1850* (Manchester, 2002)

Fury, Cheryl A., ed., *The Social History of Seamen, 1650–1815* (Woodbridge, 2017)

Games, Alison, *Migrations and Origins of the English Atlantic World* (Cambridge, MA, 2001)

Gilje, Paul, *To Swear Like a Sailor: Maritime Culture in America, 1750–1850* (Cambridge, 2016)

Good, Byron J., *Medicine, Rationality and Experience: An Anthropological Perspective* (Cambridge, 1994)

Goodall, Jamie L. H., 'Tippling Houses, Rum Shops and Taverns: How Alcohol Fueled Informal Commercial Networks and Knowledge Exchange in the West Indies', *Journal for Maritime Research*, XVIII/2 (2016), pp. 97–121

Gowing, Laura, *Gender Relations in Early Modern England* (Harlow, 2012)

Greenberg, Douglas, 'Crime, Law Enforcement and Social Control in Colonial America', *American Journal of Legal History*, 26 (October 1982), pp. 293–325

Hancock, David Boyd, and Sally Archer, *Health and Medicine at Sea,*
    1700–1900 (Woodbridge, 2009)

Hanna, Mark G., *Pirate Nests and the Rise of the British Empire,*
    1570–1740 (Chapel Hill, NC, 2015)

Hanson, Neil, *The Custom of the Sea: The Shocking True Story of*
    Cannibalism and Survival (London, 1998)

Harris, Graham, *Treasure and Intrigue: The Legacy of Captain Kidd*
    (Toronto, 2002)

Head, David, ed., *The Golden Age of Piracy: The Rise, Fall, and*
    Enduring Popularity of Pirates (Athens, GA, 2018)

Hodgkin, Katharine, and Susannah Radstone, eds, *Memory*
    Cultures: Memory, Subjectivity, Recognition
    (Abingdon-on-Thames, 2009)

Hughes, B. P., *Firepower: Weapons Effectiveness on the Battlefield,*
    1630–1850 (New York, 1997)

Hugill, Stan, *Shanties from the Seven Seas: Shipboard Work-Songs*
    and Songs Used as Work-Songs from the Great Days of Sail (Mystic,
    CT, 1994)

Jameson, John Franklin, *Privateering and Piracy in the Colonial*
    Period (New York, 1923)

Jeans, Peter D., *Seafaring Lore and Legend: A Miscellany of*
    Maritime Myth, Superstition, Fable, and Fact (New York, 2004)

Keevil, John, *Medicine and the Navy* (London, 1957), vol. I

Klausmann, Ulrike, Marion Meinzerin and Gabriel Kuhn,
    Women Pirates and the Politics of the Jolly Roger (Montreal, 1997)

Klein, Lawrence E., 'Politeness and the Interpretation of the
    British Eighteenth Century', *Historical Journal*, XLV/4 (2002),
    pp. 869–98

Konstam, Angus, *Blackbeard: America's Most Notorious Pirate*
    (Hoboken, NJ, 2006)

Kritzler, Edward, *Jewish Pirates of the Caribbean: How a Generation*
    of Swashbuckling Jews Carved Out an Empire in the New World
    in Their Quest for Treasure, Religious Freedom, and Revenge
    (London, 2009)

Lane, Kris E., *Pillaging the Empire: Piracy in the Americas, 1500–1750*
    (New York, 1998)

Leeson, Peter T., *The Invisible Hook: The Hidden Economics of Pirates*
    (Princeton, NJ, 2009)

—, Peter J. Boettke and Jaymes S. Lemke, 'Wife Sales', *Review of*
    Behavioral Economics, I (2014), pp. 349–79

Lincoln, Margarette, *British Pirates and Society, 1680–1730* (Farnham, 2015)

Linebaugh, Peter, *The London Hanged: Crime and Civil Society in the Eighteenth Century* (London, 2003)

—, and Marcus Rediker, *The Many-Headed Hydra: Sailors, Slaves, Commoners, and the Hidden History of the Revolutionary Atlantic* (Boston, MA, 2013)

Little, Benerson, *The Sea Rover's Practice: Pirate Tactics and Techniques, 1630–1730* (Lincoln, NE, 2007)

Magra, Christopher P., 'Faith at Sea: Exploring Maritime Religiosity in the Eighteenth Century', *International Journal of Maritime History*, XIX/1 (June 2007), pp. 87–106

Marietta, Jack D., and G. S. Rowe, *Troubled Experience: Crime and Justice in Pennsylvania, 1682–1800* (Philadelphia, PA, 2006)

Moss, Jeremy R., *The Life and Tryals of the Gentleman Pirate, Major Stede Bonnet* (Virginia Beach, VA, 2020)

Nash, Gary B., *The Urban Crucible: The Northern Seaports and the Origins of the American Revolution* (Cambridge, 1986)

Nicholls, James, *The Politics of Alcohol: A History of the Drink Question in England* (Manchester, 2009)

Philbrick, Nathaniel, *In the Heart of the Sea: The Epic True Story that Inspired 'Moby Dick'* (London, 2005)

Price, Merrall Llewelyn, *Consuming Passions: The Uses of Cannibalism in Late Medieval and Early Modern Europe* (New York, 2003)

Rankine, James S., 'Pails, Pills, and Performances: Violence among Pirate Crews in the Golden Age', *The Problem of Piracy II: An Interdisciplinary Conference on Plunder across the Sea from the Ancient to the Modern* (4–6 August 2021)

Rediker, Marcus, *Between the Devil and the Deep Blue Sea: Merchant Seamen, Pirates and the Anglo-American Maritime World, 1700–1750* (Cambridge, 1989)

—, 'Life under the Jolly Roger', *Wilson Quarterly*, XII/3 (Summer 1988), pp. 154–66

—, *Outlaws of the Atlantic: Sailors, Pirates, and Motley Crews in the Age of Sail* (Boston, MA, 2014)

—, '"Under the Banner of King Death": The Social World of Anglo-American Pirates, 1716–1726', *William and Mary Quarterly*, XXXVIII/2 (April 1981), pp. 203–27

—, *Villains of All Nations: Atlantic Pirates in the Golden Age* (Boston, MA, 2004)

Rennie, Neil, *Treasure Neverland* (Oxford, 2013)

Ritchie, Robert C., *Captain Kidd and the War against the Pirates* (Cambridge, MA, 1986)

Roach, Joseph, *It* (Ann Arbor, MI, 2007)

Salinger, Sharon V., *Taverns and Drinking in Early America* (Baltimore, MD, 2002)

Schmid, Susanne, and Barbara Schmidt-Haberkamp, eds, *Drink in the Eighteenth and Nineteenth Centuries* (London, 2009)

Sharpe, J. A., '"Last Dying Speeches": Religion, Ideology and Public Executions in Seventeenth-Century England', *Past and Present*, 107 (1985), pp. 144–67

Shoemaker, Robert, 'The Old Bailey Proceedings and the Representation of Crime and Criminal Justice in Eighteenth-Century London', *Journal of British Studies*, XLVII/3 (July 2008), pp. 559–80

—, *Prosecution and Punishment: Petty Crime and the Law in London and Rural Middlesex, c. 1600–1725* (Cambridge, 1991)

Simon, Rebecca, 'Historical Film as a Learning Tool: Pirates of the Caribbean', Clio@Kings (2015)

—, *Why We Love Pirates: The Hunt for Captain Kidd and How He Changed Pirates Forever* (Coral Gables, FL, 2020)

Stanley, Jo, *Bold in Her Breeches: Women Pirates across the Ages* (London, 1995)

Stewart, David, *The Sea, Their Graves: An Archaeology of Death and Remembrance in Maritime Culture* (Gainesville, FL, 2011)

Thompson, Janice E., *Mercenaries, Pirates and Sovereigns: State-Building and Extraterritorial Violence in Early Modern Europe* (Princeton, NJ, 1996)

Vickers, Daniel, 'Maritime Labor in Colonial Massachusetts: A Case Study of the Essex County Cod Fishery and the Whaling Industry of Nantucket, 1630–1775', PhD diss., Princeton University, 1981

—, *Young Men and the Sea: Yankee Seafarers in the Age of Sail* (New Haven, CT, 2005)

Watt, Tessa, *Cheap Print and Popular Piety, 1550–1640* (Cambridge, 1991)

Williams, Daniel E., 'Puritans and Pirates: A Confrontation between Cotton Mather and William Fly in 1726', *Early American Literature*, XXII/3 (1987), pp. 233–51

Withey, Alun, *Concerning Beards: Facial Hair, Health and Practice in England, 1650–1900* (London, 2021)

Witte, John E. Jr, and Thomas C. Arthur, 'The Three Uses of the Law: A Protestant Source of the Purposes of Criminal Punishment?', *Journal of Law and Religion*, X/2 (1993–4), pp. 433–65

Woodard, Colin, *The Republic of Pirates: Being the True and Surprising Story of the Caribbean Pirates and the Man Who Brought Them Down* (San Diego, CA, 2007)

Woolf, Daniel, *The Social Circulation of the Past: English Historical Culture in Britain, 1500–1730* (Oxford, 2003)

WEBSITES

Bone, Katherine, 'Tortuga: Den of Pirates and Thieves', ed. Cindy Vallar, Pirates and Privateers: The History of Maritime Piracy (2015), www.cindyvallar.com/Tortuga.html
Brooks, Baylus C., www.baylusbrooks.com
Kehoe, Mark C., The Pirate Surgeon's Journals, www.piratesurgeon.com
Kennedy, Maev, 'Sailor's Rape Confession Uncovered in 17th-Century Journal', *The Guardian*, 18 September 2018, www.theguardian.com
London Lives, www.londonlives.org
Morris, Jonathan, 'Burgh Island Statue "Should Be Pilchards Not Pirates"', BBC News Online (16 February 2021), www.bbc.com/news
Newgate Calendar, www.exclassics.com/newgate
Norton, Rictor, Lesbian History, www.rictornorton.co.uk
Old Bailey Online, www.oldbaileyonline.org
Rhodes, T.S., The Pirate Empire, www.thepirateempire.blogspot.com

ACKNOWLEDGEMENTS

This book was written during the COVID-19 pandemic, which provided its own challenges and unique forms of help. There are many people I need to thank, and I apologize if I've missed someone.

First and foremost, I need to thank the people at Reaktion Books for their enthusiasm for this project. Dave Watkins got me started on the text and I thank Michael Leaman for his excitement and attention to detail to make this the right book for pirate academics and enthusiasts. I must also thank Amy Salter for her keen eye and notes to make this project stronger.

Speaking of pirate historians and enthusiasts, there are many shout-outs I need to make. First, to the historical community. Twitter and Facebook have both been great places to network and support each other. Thank you to Laura Sook Duncombe, Jamie Goodall, Jeremy Moss, Matt McLaine, Manushag Powell, Ed Fox and Mark Kehoe for your support, enthusiasm, resources and being there in spirit. In addition, I have some professional thanks to give to the writers and producers of the *Real Pirates* podcast, especially Mac Bexton, Luke Deckard and James Benmore.

Special thanks go, as always, to my friends, who have been the number one supporters of my pirate passions for the last ten-plus years. Huge shout-outs go to Dr Philip Abraham, Luke Burke, Alison Caffrey, Dr Thomas Colville, Rebekah Harding, Brid Hayden, Dr Philippa Hellawell, Gerry and David Hersey, Keli Kittinger, Dr Alice Marples, Megen O'Keefe, Sarah Pease-Kerr, Dr James Roffee, Rebecca Rollinson, Laura Smith, Dr Brandon Tachco and Libby Wright. Additional thanks go to Dr Evan Fisher and Dr Karen Kleeman.

Thank you to my professors along the way who always supported my pirate endeavours, enthusiastically and academically: Drs Richard Drayton, Eric Goldner, Laura Gowing, Richard Horowitz, Benjamin Klein, Christopher Magra and Frank Vatai.

I thank and give my love to my family for always being my cheerleaders as I continue my pirate work: Gayle and Mitch Plessner, Fred Simon, Sherwood and Ashton Egbert, Matt Egbert, Kat Plessner, Meghann Reiss, Ari Plessner, Grandma Renny and Pippin. I love you all!

And, finally, to Nate, my partner and champion, for your limitless support and company in Barnes & Noble. I love you.

PHOTO
ACKNOWLEDGEMENTS

The author and publishers wish to express their thanks to the below sources of illustrative material and/or permission to reproduce it. Some locations of artworks are also given below, in the interest of brevity:

From *The American Traveller* (London, 1741), photo John Carter Brown Library, Providence, RI: p. 133; Brockton Public Library, MA: p. 148 (*bottom*); from Theodor de Bry, *Decima tertia pars historiae Americanae* (Frankfurt, 1634), photo John Carter Brown Library, Providence, RI: p. 126; David Rumsey Map Collection, David Rumsey Map Center, Stanford Libraries, CA: pp. 150–51; Delaware Art Museum, Wilmington: pp. 76, 145 (*top*), 149; from Charles Ellms, *The Pirates Own Book* (Portland, ME, 1856), photos Library of Congress, Washington, DC: pp. 143, 212, 218; from A. O. Exquemelin, *De Americaensche zee-roovers* (Amsterdam, 1678), photos Library of Congress, Rare Book and Special Collections Division, Washington, DC: pp. 22, 142, 172; from *Harper's New Monthly Magazine*, LXXV/448 (November 1887), photos David O. McKay Library, BYU-Idaho, Rexburg: pp. 72, 75; Heritage Auctions, HA.com: p. 48; James Ford Bell Library, University of Minnesota Libraries, Minneapolis: p. 152 (*top*); from Captain Charles Johnson, *A General History of the Pyrates, from Their First Rise and Settlement in the Island of Providence, to the Present Time*, 2nd edn (London, 1724), photos Smithsonian Libraries, Washington, DC: pp. 6, 11; from Captain Charles Johnson, *A General History of the Robberies and Murders of the Most Notorious Pyrates* (London, 1724), photos Beinecke Rare Book and Manuscript Library, Yale University, New Haven, CT: pp. 17, 54, 111; from Captain Charles Johnson, *Historie der Zee-Roovers* (Amsterdam, 1725), photos John Carter Brown Library, Providence, RI: pp. 81, 113; from Captain Charles Johnson, *The History and Lives of All the Most Notorious Pirates, and Their Crews* (London, 1725), photos Library of Congress, Rare Book and Special Collections Division, Washington, DC: pp. 50, 57, 73, 84, 109, 117, 162, 171; from Captain Charles Johnson, *A General and True History of the Lives and Actions of the Most Famous Highwaymen, Murderers, Street-Robbers . . .* (Birmingham, 1742), photo Boston Public Library: p. 63; Library of Congress, Geography and Map Division, Washington, DC: pp. 26–7, 28, 29, 30–31; from Basil Lubbock, *The Blackwall Frigates* (Glasgow, 1922), photo University of California Libraries: p. 146; Museo Naval, Madrid: p. 152 (*bottom*); The National Archives, Richmond, London (ADM 101/7/8/53): p. 147 (*top*); National Gallery of Art, Washington, DC: p. 147 (*bottom*); New Britain Museum of American Art, CT: p. 141; from *Punch; or, The London Charivari*, CIII (10 December 1892), photo Robarts Library, University of Toronto: p. 203; from Laura Alexandrine Smith, *The Music of the Waters: A Collection of the Sailors' Chanties, or Working Songs of the Sea, of All Maritime Nations* (London, 1888), photo Faculty of Music, University of Toronto: p. 195; from Robert Louis Stevenson, *Treasure Island* (New York, 1919), photo Beinecke Rare Book and Manuscript Library, Yale University, New Haven, CT: p. 148 (*top*); from John Woodall, *The Surgions Mate; or, a Treatise Discouering Faithfully and Plainely the Due Contents of the Surgions Chest* (London, 1617), photo Francis A. Countway Library of Medicine, Boston, MA: p. 93; Yale Center for British Art, New Haven, CT: p. 145 (*bottom*).

INDEX

Page numbers in *italics* refer to illustrations

War of Spanish Succession 28
water 30, 36–8, 100, 123, 173–4, 211,
    217–18
  allocation of 12, 71, 157, 168,
    173, 188, 219
  as an ingredient 176
  in mythology 125, 199
  pilfered 67
Waugh, Frederick J, *The Buccaneers*
    148
weapons 8, 10, 12, 41, 42, 138–40,
    144, 153, 157
  broadsword 144
  bullets 97, 140, 157
  cannons 94–5, 97, 132, 138, 144,
    153
  cutlass 77, 95, 140–41, 144,
    155–6
  gun 71, 94, 97, 131–2, 134,
    137, 139, 144, 153, 158, 164,
    183–4
  gunpowder 71, 83, 137, 153, 157,
    166, 198

pistol 10, 12–13, 19, 71, 77, 110,
    139–43, 162, 195
shot 13–14, 42, 44, 71, 94, 140,
    144, 153
sword 13, 77, 111, 116, 139,
    143–4, 162–5, 195–6
Whydah 52, 132, 134, 156
William III, King 208, 226, 231
women 15, 40, 77, 82, 102–3, 105–6,
    126
  as bad luck 125
  as pirates 127–9
  in mythology 100, 125
  prostitutes 22, 32, 105
  violence toward 115, 117–18,
    123–4
  see also Bonny, Anne; Read,
    Mary
Woodall, John, *The Surgeon's Mate*
    93
Wyeth, N. C.
  'One more step . . . *141*
  Treasure Island cover *148*